a

HAUSA FOLK-LORE

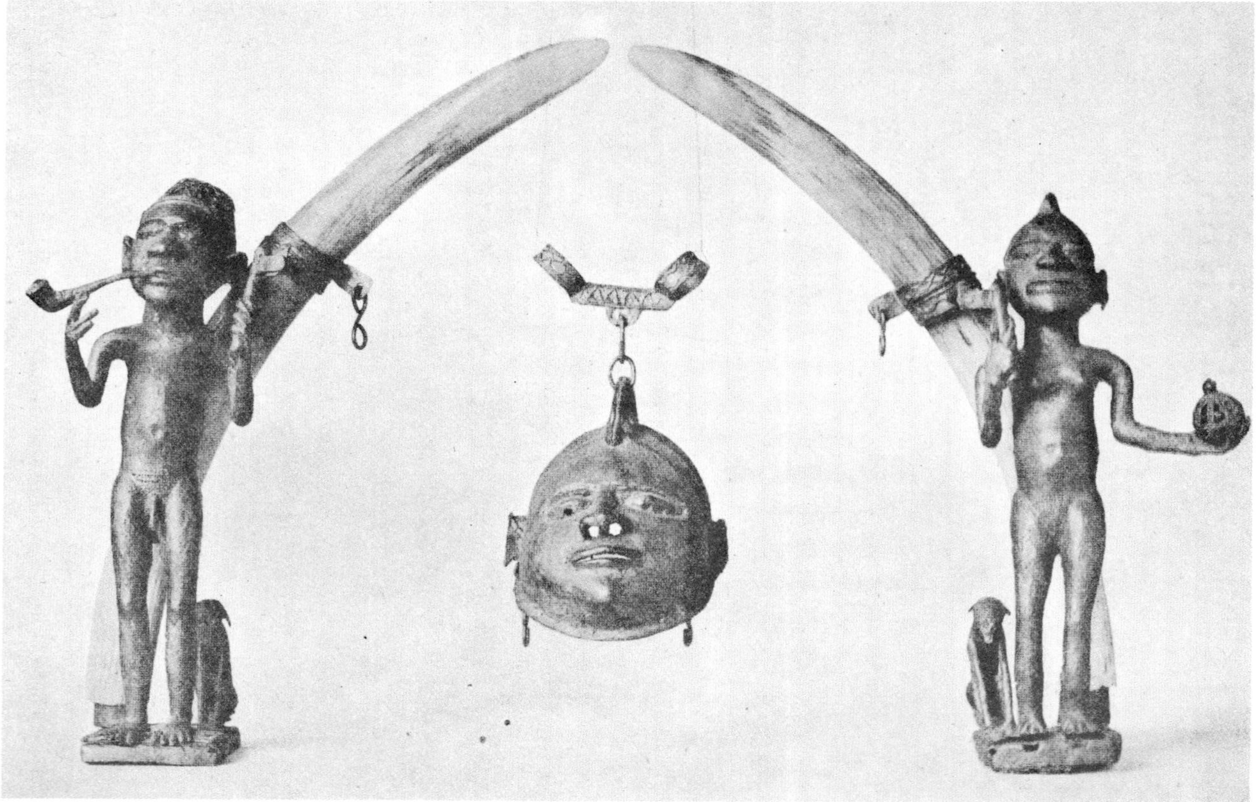

MODERN BRONZE CASTINGS, WEST AFRICA

[Fr

HAUSA FOLK-LORE
CUSTOMS, PROVERBS, ETC.

COLLECTED AND TRANSLITERATED WITH ENGLISH TRANSLATION AND NOTES

BY

R. SUTHERLAND RATTRAY

WITH A PREFACE BY

R. R. MARETT

IN TWO VOLUMES: VOL. I

OXFORD
AT THE CLARENDON PRESS

African customs and folklore

Oxford University Press, Ely House, London W. 1

GLASGOW NEW YORK TORONTO MELBOURNE WELLINGTON
CAPE TOWN SALISBURY IBADAN NAIROBI LUSAKA ADDIS ABABA
BOMBAY CALCUTTA MADRAS KARACHI LAHORE DACCA
KUALA LUMPUR SINGAPORE HONG KONG TOKYO

FIRST PUBLISHED 1913

REPRINTED LITHOGRAPHICALLY IN GREAT BRITAIN
AT THE UNIVERSITY PRESS, OXFORD
BY VIVIAN RIDLER
PRINTER TO THE UNIVERSITY
1969

PREFACE

It is our privilege at Oxford to be visited from time to time by officers of the Public Service, who modestly apply to us for instruction in Anthropology, more particularly as it bears on the history of the native races of the Empire. Not infrequently, however, they bring with them a previously acquired stock of anthropological information, such as almost takes away the breath of their duly constituted teachers. Thereupon the latter feel inclined to offer to change places; and, instead of teaching, to play the part of learners in regard to them.

Mr. Rattray furnishes a case in point. When he joined our School of Anthropology, he was already a past-master in all that relates to Chinyanja folk-lore, a subject on which he had actually published a useful book. Besides, though but recently transferred from British Central Africa to the West Coast, he was already at close grips with more than one of the languages current in that most polyglot of regions.

To claim, therefore, any share whatever in the origination of the present work would ill beseem one who merely offered sympathetic encouragement when Mr. Rattray proceeded to unfold his latest design. This design was to compass two ends at once—to obtain trustworthy linguistic material, and to explore the inner secrets of the Hausa mind—by giving a somewhat novel turn to an old and approved method.

As regards the collection of folk-lore, the approved method—in fact, the only method likely to satisfy the demands of science—is this: the observer must draft word-for-word reports of what he hears; and must further give the original words, when a foreign tongue is used, so that it may be possible independently to control the version.

Such a method, however, is more easily prescribed on paper than followed in the field. When the witness is illiterate—as commonly happens when there is genuine folk-lore to be gathered—its application proves exceedingly troublesome, for reasons that may readily be divined. A more or less formal dictation lesson has somehow to be given and received; and the several parties to it are only too apt to conspire each in his own way to render it a failure. Thus the story-teller, on the one hand, is probably shy and suspicious at the outset; is put out of his stride by the slightest interruption; and, becoming weary all too soon, tends to take short cuts, instead of following to the end the meandering path of the genuine tradition. The reporter, in his turn, is incessantly puzzled by the idiom, more especially since in such a context archaisms will be frequent; boggles over a pronunciation adapted to a monotonous sing-song delivery, or else, perhaps, to a dramatic mimicry carried on in several voices; and is likely to be steadily outpaced into the bargain.

Mr. Rattray's happy thought, then, was to remedy the practical shortcomings of the standard method by finding some one who, as it were, could dictate to himself; who, in other words, could successfully combine the characters of story-teller and reporter in his single person.

Moreover, as Mr. Rattray was not slow to perceive, the existing conditions of Hausa culture bring it about that the very type of helper needed is with due search to be procured. A *mālam* of the best class possesses all the literary skill which a knowledge of Arabic and of the Arabic script involves. None the less, he remains thoroughly in touch with his own people, a Hausa of the Hausas. In his hands, therefore, the traditional lore loses nothing of its authentic form and flavour. In short, the chance of literary manipulation may be ruled out.

Hence it would seem, if I may venture to say so, that the Government of the Gold Coast was no less wise than liberal in its policy when, by the grant of a subvention, it enabled *Mālam* Shaihu's work to be perpetuated in the fullest way, namely, not only by transliteration and translation, but likewise by actual reproduction in facsimile.

For, apart from its value as a masterpiece of artistic penmanship, this clear and, I understand, correct calligraphy must prove of great assistance to European students of Hausa to whose official lot it falls to wrestle with the productions of the native scribe. Then, conversely, if an educated Hausa aspire, as well he may, to learn the English language, together with the use of the English alphabet, he has here an invaluable means of comparing his own system of written symbols with ours. So much, then, for the more obvious advantages to be derived from a study of the *mālam*'s actual manuscript. Over and above this, it proves of assistance to the philologist, as Mr. Rattray shows, by making clear certain finer points of grammar in regard to which evidence was hitherto lacking. Also, I suppose, simply as exemplifying the characteristic differences between the African and the classical modes of writing Arabic, it would not be without a certain scientific interest of its own.

Concerning the worth of the collected matter to the student of language and to the folk-lorist, I am hardly called upon to speak here, even were I competent to do so. Suffice it to say that, in respect of its contents, the book does not, of course, claim to stand alone. Yet, though a considerable library of Hausa literature is already in existence, it can well bear to be enriched by another volume such as this, which manages to dispense with the middle man of another mental type, and brings us directly into contact with the native intelligence as it witnesses to itself.

For the rest, I take it that the study of Hausa folk-lore offers fascinating problems to the student, if only because it calls for a critical sifting and weighing of the most drastic kind. The culture of the Hausas is not, in any sense of that much abused term, primitive. They have undergone interpenetration on the part of the Fulani and other alien stocks. They have more or less universally embraced Mohammedanism. They engage in trading expeditions which bring them into touch with most of the peoples of West Africa. Altogether, then, they are far away from that state of aboriginal innocence in which a strictly homegrown tradition perpetuates itself by means of stories that almost amount to oral rites, so undeviating is their form, so solemn their import and associations.

On the contrary, the most characteristic feature of Hausa lore, when purged of its more obvious accretions from without, consists in the folk-tale; which some authorities go so far as to regard as typically reminiscent of some degenerated and desolemnized myth. Nor can it be denied that, for example, various survivals in this region of what may be termed in a broad sense totemism lend colour to the view that the animal story may have fallen from a far higher estate, if the criterion of value be the seriousness of the beliefs which it embodies. To the student of folk-lore origins, however, the material available here is at least as good as to be got nearer home; and, in so far as there still exist in Hausaland odd corners where customs lurk of a quite primaeval appearance, the chance of discovering the laws of change involved is relatively the better.

Besides, quite apart from the purely scientific interest in origins, the reader will come to understand the thoughts and ways of the Hausas as they are now. Their notions about right and wrong, for instance, are indicated pretty clearly by many of the animal stories; seeing that each animal tends to represent a type of character calling either for admiration or detestation, and, being more or less humanized into the bargain, affords a nucleus round which a nascent moral philosophy can be observed to gather.

Even more directly, too, may we obtain insight into the present conditions of Hausa culture by studying what the *mālam* has to say about their history, manners, and arts. If brief, his notices are always business-like and to the point; while he plainly has access to information—for instance, in regard to bronze-casting by the *cire perdue* process—for which the European investigator might for the most part snap his fingers in vain.

But, as the Hausas say, 'If you are not going to drink the pap, stop stirring it.' The pap, I am convinced, is excellent. So let us drink without more ado.

R. R. MARETT.

AUTHOR'S NOTE

ON first proceeding to West Africa (the Gold Coast), and on commencing a study of the Hausa language, the compiler of this work was struck by the comparatively high standard of education found among the Hausa MĀLAMAI or scribes. Arabic characters are used by them, as by the Swahili of East and Central Africa; but, whereas any natives met with there possessed but a very superficial knowledge of the Arabic language or writing, the Hausas could boast of a legal, historical, and religious literature, which was to be found preserved by manuscripts. The MĀLAMAI were everywhere the most respected and honoured members of the community. It was disappointing, however, at any rate for one who wished to study Hausa, to find that all their manuscripts were written not only in Arabic characters, but also in that language. This appears to be universally the case, even in Nigeria. The use of Arabic to-day among the educated Hausas corresponds to that of French and Latin in England in the middle ages.

The writer's intention was, as soon as he had acquired a sound colloquial knowledge of the Hausa language, to collect some of their folk-lore and traditions, taking down such information as was required verbatim, and translating afterwards into English. This plan he had adopted when collecting his *Chinyanja* folk-lore.

The advantage of such a system is that the original text will help the student of the language to appreciate its structure and idioms, in a way that the best grammars could hardly do. The translator will also be bound down thereby. There will thus be no room for embellishments or errors creeping in, as is liable to be the case when the investigator has had to rely on the vagaries of his cook, 'boy,' or other interpreter for his information. It follows that such a collection will be of more value from the anthropological standpoint. Indeed, of late years many collections of native folk-lore compiled according to this method have been called into being by the demand created by this new science of anthropology.

As is to be expected, there are not many persons who have the fortune—or misfortune—to spend four or five preliminary years in acquiring a knowledge of the language of the people whose traditions they hope to study; yet such a probation is very necessary, if the collection is to be of any real value to the anthropologist.

Stories and traditions collected through the medium of an interpreter are amusing, and might prove of interest in the nursery (though much would have to be omitted or toned down, as savage folk-lore is often coarse and vulgar according to our notions, and hardly fit *pour les jeunes filles*); but for the student of anthropology such collections cannot be considered to possess much value.

The anthropological theorist, who is probably some learned professor at one or other of our great Universities, where he made a life-study of primitive customs and beliefs, has, in most cases, to rely for his data on the field-worker. He needs to feel perfectly convinced that the information on which he is seeking to base some far-reaching generalization is absolutely correct; and this can hardly be the case, however skilled, conscientious, or well trained the field-worker may be, if the latter be wholly ignorant of the language of the people from whom he is collecting his information.

Now the literary skill of the Hausas, already referred to, led the writer to depart somewhat from the *modus operandi* employed in his *Chinyanja* folk-lore, the subject-matter of which was taken down from the lips of the raconteur.

For the present work the services of a learned MĀLAM, by name MĀLAM *Shaihu*, were secured. He himself wrote down, or translated from manuscripts in Arabic, such information as was required. Much of the work contained in the present volumes involved, first, a translation from Arabic into Hausa, secondly, a transliteration of the Hausa writing, and thirdly, a translation into English from the Hausa.

During the writer's 'tours' of service in West Africa, as also during his furloughs in England, this MĀLAM, who was entirely ignorant of English, made a collection of many hundreds of sheets of manuscripts (1907–11).

In the meantime the present writer was making a study of the Hausa language and script, by way of securing the key to their transliteration and translation. He was fortunate, in the course of his official duties, in being stationed for some time at YEGI on the VOLTA river. YEGI lies on the main caravan route between Nigeria and Ashanti. Each month thousands of Hausas from all parts of Nigeria cross the river here, going to and from Nigeria with kola or cattle. Such a position enables a student, even better perhaps than if he were resident in Hausaland, to get into touch with Hausas from all parts of Nigeria. It was thus possible to select such stories or traditions as seemed most generally and widely known, and therefore likely to be of historical value on account of their antiquity.

The Hausa given in the text is that of Kano or Sokoto, where by general consent the purest dialect is spoken.

The Hausa Manuscript. The writing is throughout clear, correct, and legible. It has been written with the *aya* (.˙.) between most of the words to facilitate easy reading. Some of the specimens of Hausa writing that have been reproduced from time to time are obviously the work of illiterate Hausas, or at best are very carelessly written manuscripts, and as such afford little criterion of the best work of these people. The hasty scrawls, which, it is true, form the larger part of the existing manuscripts, in which vowel-signs are missed out and words run together, often cannot be deciphered by the Hausas, and sometimes not even by the writers themselves, unless they know the context or subject by heart. Such manuscripts are therefore worthless for scientific purposes. They cannot, for instance, serve to disclose those nice points of grammatical construction which the perusal of a carefully written manuscript will reveal, though they can hardly be noted in the spoken language.

The Transliteration. This has been given, letter by letter, word for word, line by line. Thus it is easy for the student to follow the original on the page opposite.

The Translation. As literal a translation as is consistent with making the subject-matter at all readable has been given throughout. It is primarily as a text-book for students of the language that this work is intended, and for such a literal translation will be of most use. The author would crave the pardon of the general reader for the baldness and utter sacrifice of the English idiom which such a style of translation must necessarily involve. The latter may, however, find here and there a certain touch of 'local colour' in the phraseology, which may compensate for its other obvious defects.

The value of Hausa writings. Hitherto, perhaps, it has not usually been deemed essential to know much about Hausa writing. (A slight knowledge of it is necessary, it is true, for the higher standard Government examination.) This work attempts to go somewhat fully into the subject of the writing and the signs used, in order to assist the student who desires a knowledge of the writing that will enable him to decipher manuscripts as apart from the printed type. *The writer is convinced that a thorough knowledge of Hausa writing is essential for any advanced study of the language.* Thus he has so far been rewarded for the time spent in the minute perusal of the manuscripts comprising the Hausa portion of this book by the further elucidation or confirmation therein of grammatical structures not perhaps wholly accepted as proved, and by the discovery of some new idioms which, to the best of his knowledge, had apparently escaped the vigilance of previous writers on this subject, or else had taxed their powers of explanation.

The length of vowels, which is so distinctly shown in the written word, does not hitherto appear to have had that attention paid to it that it undoubtedly deserves. Yet the length of a vowel may alter the meaning of a word entirely, e.g. *gūda*, *gŭda ;* *sūna*, *sŭna;* *gādō*, *gădō*, and so on. Indeed, an educated MĀLAM would consider a word as wrongly spelt whenever a long vowel was written where it should have been short, or vice versa. In Hausa writing such an error would amount not merely to the dropping of an accent, as in English, but to the omission of a letter. Moreover such a slip may lead to serious confusion, since the tense of a verb, or even, as has been seen, the entire sense of a word, may depend on the length assigned to the vowel.

The author of *Hausa Notes*, perhaps the best treatise on the language yet written, remarks at some length on the apparent 'absurdity' of the want of any inflexion for the 1st, 2nd, and 3rd persons singular of the past tense, for the plural of which the well-known forms in *ka* exist, and thinks the forms for these persons are the same as those used for the aorist tense. Yet a perusal of almost any half-dozen pages of the present manuscript will reveal the hidden missing forms. Were the student to search for these by ear only, he might easily never discover them, as they are almost indistinguishable in the spoken word.

Again, the definite article,[1] for many years conspicuous by its

[1] First noted by Professor A. Mischlich.

absence, will be met with repeatedly in these pages in the final *nun*, or *ra*, or the *wasali* or *rufua bissa bīū*.

Enough has been said to show the value and importance of a close perusal of Hausa manuscripts; but emphasis must be laid on the fact that such writing must be the work of a learned MĀLAM, or probably these very details, which are of such importance to the scientific investigator, will be omitted, either through carelessness or ignorance.

Proverbs. So far as possible, the endeavour has been made to omit such proverbs as have already been collected and published.

The Notes. The student is expected to be familiar with the well-known works on the Hausa language by Canon Robinson, Dr. Miller, and others; hence only such phrases, words, or grammatical points as are not considered in these works are noticed here.

Acknowledgments. The debt is vast which the student of any language owes to those who have by their labours reduced that language to a definite form. This makes it possible in a comparatively short time for him to master what it has cost the pioneers many years of ceaseless labour to create out of nothing. Availing himself of the fruits of their labour, he can thus move forward to fresh fields of research. Such is the debt that the writer owes to Canon Robinson, Dr. Miller, and others. His thanks are also due to his friend Mr. Diamond Jenness, of Balliol College, Oxford, for revising the English translation; to Mr. Henry Balfour, Curator of the Pitt-Rivers Museum, Oxford, for having had the photographs taken that appear in this work, and for his valuable notes on the same which are again published through the courtesy of the Royal Anthropological Institute; to Professor Margoliouth for having translated the Arabic lines which occur in the Hausa script; to Mr. R. R. Marett, of Exeter College, Oxford, Reader in Social Anthropology, his tutor, who by his wonderful enthusiasm and ability may be said to have organized a school of working anthropologists, building upon the noble foundations laid by Sir E. B. Tylor and Dr. Frazer; to the authorities of the Clarendon Press, who, besides dealing most generously with a work not likely to prove remunerative, have likewise laid the author under deep obligation by their friendly interest and advice.

Finally, the publication of this work has only been made possible by the generous grant from the Government of the Gold Coast, to whom, as also to the Secretary of State for the Colonies, on whose recommendation the grant was made, the writer has the honour to tender his sincerest thanks.

R. SUTHERLAND RATTRAY.

EJURA, ASHANTI,
WEST AFRICA.
Sept. 8, 1911.

CONTENTS OF VOL. I

PART I

PART II

STORIES IN WHICH PEOPLE ARE THE HEROES AND HEROINES

ILLUSTRATION

ALPHABET AND WRITING SIGNS

The following are the letters employed in the Hausa Text :

Hausa Name of Letter.*	Letter.				Pronunciation in Hausa.	Remarks.
	Standing alone.	Connected with following.	Connected on both sides.	Connected with preceding.		
Alif	ا	ا	ا		—	The bearer of vowel-sounds only, as is also *ain*, really consonants.
Alif baki (black alif)				ـا		
Ba guje	ب				*b*	*Guje*, lit. *ba* with the twirl.
Ba		بـ	ـبـ	ـب		
Ta guje	ت				*t*	Lit. *ta* with the twirl.
Ta		تـ	ـتـ	ـت		
Tsha guje	ث				*tsch*	Lit. *tsch* with the twirl.
Tsha		ثـ	ـثـ	ـث		
Jim karami kōma bāya	ج				*j*	Lit. small *j* with a twirl behind.
Jim karami		جـ				Lit. small *j*.
Jim sābe			ـجـ			Lit. *j* with the part projecting.
Jim sābe kōma bāya				ـج		Lit. *j* with the part projecting and a twirl behind.
Ha karami kōma bāya	ح				*h*	Lit. little *h* pointing backwards.
Ha karami		حـ				Lit. little *h*.
Ha sābe			ـحـ	ـح		Lit. *h* with the part projecting.
Ha sābe kōma bāya						Lit. *h* with the part pointing backwards.

* These names are given by the *mālam* when teaching small children in the *masalachi* (schools) and are in no way classical, just as in English one might say big *A*, little *a*, &c.

Hausa Name of Letter.	Letter. Standing alone.	Connected with following.	Connected on both sides.	Connected with preceding.	Pronunciation in Hausa.	Remarks.
Ha mai-rua kōma bāya	خ				*h* (as in Scotch *loch*)	Lit. *h* with the water (i.e. drop, dot) and pointing backwards.
Ha mai-rua		خـ				*h* with the (drop of) water.
Ha sābe mai-rua			ـخـ			*h* with the projecting part and dot.
Ha sābe mai-rua kōma bāya				ـخ		*h* with the projecting part pointing backwards.
Dal	د	د	ـد	ـد	*d*	
Zal	ذ	ذ	ـذ	ـذ	*z*	
Ra	ر	ر	ـر	ـر	*r*	
Zaira	ز	ز	ـز	ـز	*z*	
Tsa mal hannu	ط	طـ	ـطـ	ـط	*ts*	
Zadi	ظ	ظـ	ـظـ	ـظ	*z*	
Kaf lāsan	ك	كـ	ـكـ	ـك	*k*	
Lam arat	ل				*l*	
Lam		لـ				
Lam jaye			ـلـ			
Lam arat				ـل		
Mim arat	م				*m*	
Mim		مـ				
Mim jaye			ـمـ			
Mim arat				ـم		

Hausa Name of Letter.	Letter. Standing alone.	Connected with following.	Connected on both sides.	Connected with preceding.	Pronunciation in Hausa.	Remarks.
Nun arat	ن				*n*	
Nun guda		نـ	ـنـ			
Nun arat				ـن		
Sodi arat	ص				*s*	
Sodi		صـ	ـصـ			
Sodi arat				ـص		
Lodi arat	ض				*l*	
Lodi		ضـ	ـضـ			
Lodi arat				ـض		
						Like *alif* bearer of vowel-sounds.
Ain baki wōfi kōma bāya	ع				—	Lit. *ain* with the open mouth and the twirl backwards.
Ain baki wōfi		عـ				*Ain* with the open mouth.
Ain likāfa			ـعـ			Stirrup *ain*.
Ain likāfa kōma bāya				ـع		Stirrup *ain* with the twirl back.
Angai baki wōfi kōma bāya	غ				*g*	*Angai* with the open mouth and the backward twirl.
Angai baki wōfi		غـ				*Angai* with the open mouth.
Angai likāfa			ـغـ			Stirrup *angai*.
Angai likāfa kōma bāya				ـغ		Stirrup *angai* with the backward twirl.
Fa guje	ڢ				*f*	*f* with the twirl.
Fa		ڢـ	ـڢـ			
Fa guje				ـڢ		

Hausa Name of Letter.	Letter. Standing alone.	Connected with following.	Connected on both sides.	Connected with preceding.	Pronunciation in Hausa.	Remarks.
Kaf wau	ف				*k* (guttural)	*Mai-rua*, lit. with the water, i.e. drop, dot.
Kaf mai-rua		فـ	ـفـ			
Kaf wau				ـف		
Sin arat	س				*s*	
Sin		سـ	ـسـ			
Sin arat				ـس		
Schin mai-rua arat	ش				*sch*	*Mai-rua*, *vide* above, *Kaf*
Schin mai-rua		شـ	ـشـ			
Schin mai-rua arat				ـش		
Ha kuri	ه				*h*	
Ha baba		هـ	ـهـ			
Ha kuri				ـه		
Wau	و	و	ـو	ـو	*w*	
Ya arat	ي				*y*	
Ya		يـ	ـيـ			
Ya arat				ـي		

VOWELS

The vowel-signs in Hausa are :

1. ـَـ (above the line) called *wasali bisa* = *a*.
2. ـِـ (below the line) ,, *wasali kasa* = *i*.
3. ـٜـ (below the line) ,, *guda casa* = *e*.
4. ـُـ (above the line) ,, *rufua* = *o* or *u*.

Long vowels are distinguished from short vowels in writing as in pronunciation, and the length of a vowel is of such importance that the meaning of a word is often entirely changed, or the tense of a verb altered according as a vowel is long or short.

Long vowels are distinguished from short in writing in the following manner:

1. A long *ā* sound by an *alif* following the *wasali bisa* (ـَـ).
2. A long *ī* sound by a *ya* following the *wasali kasa* (ـِـ).
3. A long *ē* sound by a *ya* following the *guda kasa* (ـٜـ).
4. A long *ō* or *ū* sound by a *wau* following the *rufua* (ـُـ).

EXAMPLES :

LONG VOWELS	SHORT VOWELS
1. بَا = *bā*	1. بَ = *bă*
2. بِي = *bī*	2. بِ = *bĭ*
3. بَٜي = *bē*	3. بٜ = *bĕ*
4. بُو = *bō* or *bū*	4. بُ = *bŏ* or *bŭ*

DIPHTHONGS

There are three diphthongs in Hausa ; they are written and pronounced as follows:

1. يَْ = *ai* (like *i* in nice).
2. وَْ = *au* (like *ow* in how).
3. يُْ = *oi* (like *oy* in boy).

READING SIGNS

1. (ّ) This is known as *karfī* (i.e. strength). It is placed over a consonant, which is then pronounced as if doubled.

2. (ء) Called *hamza*. It is put above an *alif* when the *wasali* is above, and below when the *wasali* is below. It has no effect on pronunciation. It is not used after a *wasali bisa* or *kasa biū*.

3. (ؤ) *Hamza da dauri* (*hamza* with a *dauri*) is placed over a consonant to indicate that a syllable is of medium length.

4. (°) *Dauri* indicates the end of a syllable or the omission of a vowel, and the vowel over which it is placed is doubled in pronunciation. This is most important as it alters the mood in certain pronominal forms of the verb.

5. (ً) *Wasali bisa biu*; (ٍ) *Wasali kasa biu*; (ٌ) *Rufua biu* — By the doubling of the vowel-signs the final vowel is pronounced nasally, that is, as if followed by an *n* (*nun*). Note the *alif* following a *wasali biu* has no *hamza*. The *wasali* or *rufua biū* is sometimes used instead of the final *n* to denote the definite article.

6. (آ, اِ) *Alif da tabi*, *bisa*, or *kasa* signifies that the *alif* and the following letter are not to be pronounced at all.

R. S. R.

PART I

HISTORICAL

[1] Bismi alahi alrahmani alrahimi wa sala alahu ala man la nabiu baadah
Wanan shi ne lābārin Hausa. Kōwa yā san shi garēsu tun zā-
-manin kākaninsu da uwāyensu, abin [2] karbōwa ne wurin mā-
-lamai(n)su da tsōfafinsu. Wanda ya zama wani, ba wanan ba,
bai zama [3] mai-chāu garēsu ba. Idan matanbaiyi ya tanbaye ka,
'Ana mafārin Hausāwa?' Ka che, 'Gaskīa mafārinsu [4] Barebari
da [5] Arewāwa.' Wada alāmari ya yi ya zama hakanan. Sarkin [6] Barno shi
da dōki da kafō na zīnāria. [7] Dōkin nan ba shi hanīnia banza banza,
sai rānan jumaa. Idan ya yi hanīnia, sai ka che hadari ne.
[8] Aka-bōye shi chikin gida. [9] Sarkin kūa, shi na da dansa, ya [10] di-
-nga baiwa mai-kiwō nasa kurdi da rīguna, dōmin shi fitō
da dōkinsa, su je, shi gama da gōdīa [11] tasa. Kulum hakanan.
[12] Ranan sai mai-kīwō dōki ya fitō da dōki, ya kāwō. Dan sarki
kuma ya fitō da gōdīa tasa. Su-ka-tafi dāji. Su-ka-yi [13] bāye.
[14] Sarki kūa yā [15] rigāyi, yā fadi. Kōwa [16] aka-gani dan dōkinga

---

In the name of Allah the Compassionate, the Merciful, and may t peace of Allah be upon him, after whom there is no prophet. This is t history of the Hausa (nation). It has been familiar to every one fro the time of their grandfathers and grandmothers, (and) is a thing whi has been handed down from the malamai (learned men) and the elder Any account other than this one is not authentic. If a questioner a of you (saying) 'Where did the Hausa people have their origin?' Say (him) 'Truly their origin was (from) the Barebari and Northerners'. A this is the account of how this came to pass. The king of Bornu h a horse with a golden horn. This horse did not neigh just at any tim but only on Fridays. If it neighed you would say it was a tornad It was hidden away in a house. Now the king had a son. He (the so continually gave him who looked after the horse money and rob in order that (he might persuade him) to bring his horse out, a they should come, and he should mate the horse with his mare. A it was always thus. (And) one day the man who was looking after t (king's) horse took (it) the horse out and brought it. The king's son t took his mare out. They went into the forest and the mare was covere Now the king has (had) previously said that whoever was seen (with) a fo from this horse

بسم الله الرحمن الرحيم وصلى الله على من لا نبي بعده

ومن شين لباو اقحوس كووابالسنش غمر مس قندا

مين كدا كتنس د عوابنس ابن كن بجوا ابني وقحا

لبيس د طو بقنس ارقم يكم ون بدا ارقنب =

بيكم مينشا او غمر مكسب ادر ققنبن متقبيك

اندا مقا ار نقو لسدوا كنا غلسكيا مقا ارقس بن كنبن

د ابن مواوا ود الامر بين يكم محكنن سن كين بين قو شنا

نم دوك د كجو دوكنن با شعنيق مند بنخ قع مناو بد

سن ار قمر بجو مع ادر بيو هنيق سن كبا ححد وبيق

اكبو بيش تكن غدا سن كين كو شنا د قسر بح

قعم بيو مينكو وقلس كمرد در بغمر د وقمر شعتو

م دوكنلس سبجي شقم د غمو د يا اقسر كلم حكنن

وقمر سن مينكيو وكروك بيقتو د دوك يكدا او د قلسكم

كنم بيقتو د غمو د يا اقسر سكتق داج سكم با بيس

سن كم كقو يا وغدس يدا قبح كوو اكقنم د قدوكنع

gidansa, shi-na-yanka shi. Yau ana-nan, [17] ranan gōdīa ta haifu. Har dā ya girma. Ranan dōkin sarki ya yi hanīnia. Sai dan dōki ya amsa. Sai sarki ya che, ' Kō gidan wa aka-gani, ayanka shi, kar [18] akāwō shi gabāna.' Sai fādāwa su-[19] ka-wātsu chikin gari. Su-na--neman dan dōki. Sai su-ka-je gidan dan sarki, kamar dōkin sarki da kafō nasa na zīnāria. Sai fādawa su-ka-che, ' Sarki yā che mu [20] tafō da kai.' Sai dan sarki ya dauki takōbi, ya sārē [21] mutun bīū, saura su-ka-[22] wātsē. Sai ya daura ma dan dōki sirdi, ya hau. Sarki ya che, [23] akāmō shi. Gari duka su-ka-hau dawāki, su-ka-bi shi. Ba su chika da shi ba. Yā [24] tafīa tasa. Sar--ki kūa yā che kar [25] ahawa dōki nasa. Idan bā dōkinsa ba bābu dōkin da ke chikāwa da shi. Dan sarki ya tafi, ya sabka kasar [26] Daura. Ya gani yar sarkin Daura, ita ke da [27] garin, shi na wurinta. Sai ranan ta che [28] ta-na-sonsa aure. Shi kūa ya che shi-na-so nata. Sai su-ka-yi aure. Yar sarki ta yi chiki, ta haifu dā, namiji, ta [29] yāyē. Ta yi chiki kuma, ta haifu mache, Mafārin [30] fitar Hausa

---

at his house, he would have his throat cut. Things remained at this, (an one day the mare gave birth, (and nothing happened) till the colt gr up, (when) one day the king's horse neighed, then the young hor answered. And the king said, ' At whose ever house they see it let (th person) be killed (lit. be cut), and do not let him be brought before m Then the councillors scattered (to make search) in the town. They we searching for the young horse. And they came to the house of the kin son, and behold as it were the king's horse with its golden horn. Th the councillors said, ' The king has said we must come with you.' Th the king's son lifted his sword. He cut down two men, the remaind were scattered. Then he saddled up the young horse. He mounte The king ordered he should be seized and brought (before him). T whole town mounted their horses (and) followed him. They did not co up with him. He has gone his way. The king, moreover, has giv orders that his own horse is not to be mounted, and if not his horse, th there was not the horse to overtake him. The king's son (rode) went and (eventually) dismounted in the country of Daura. He saw the daught of the king of Daura, she possessed the town. He stayed with her. A one day she said she wanted him in marriage and he too said he loved h So they married. The king's daughter became with child. She bo a child, a son. She weaned it. She was again with child (and) bore a gi And that was the origin of the Hausa nation.

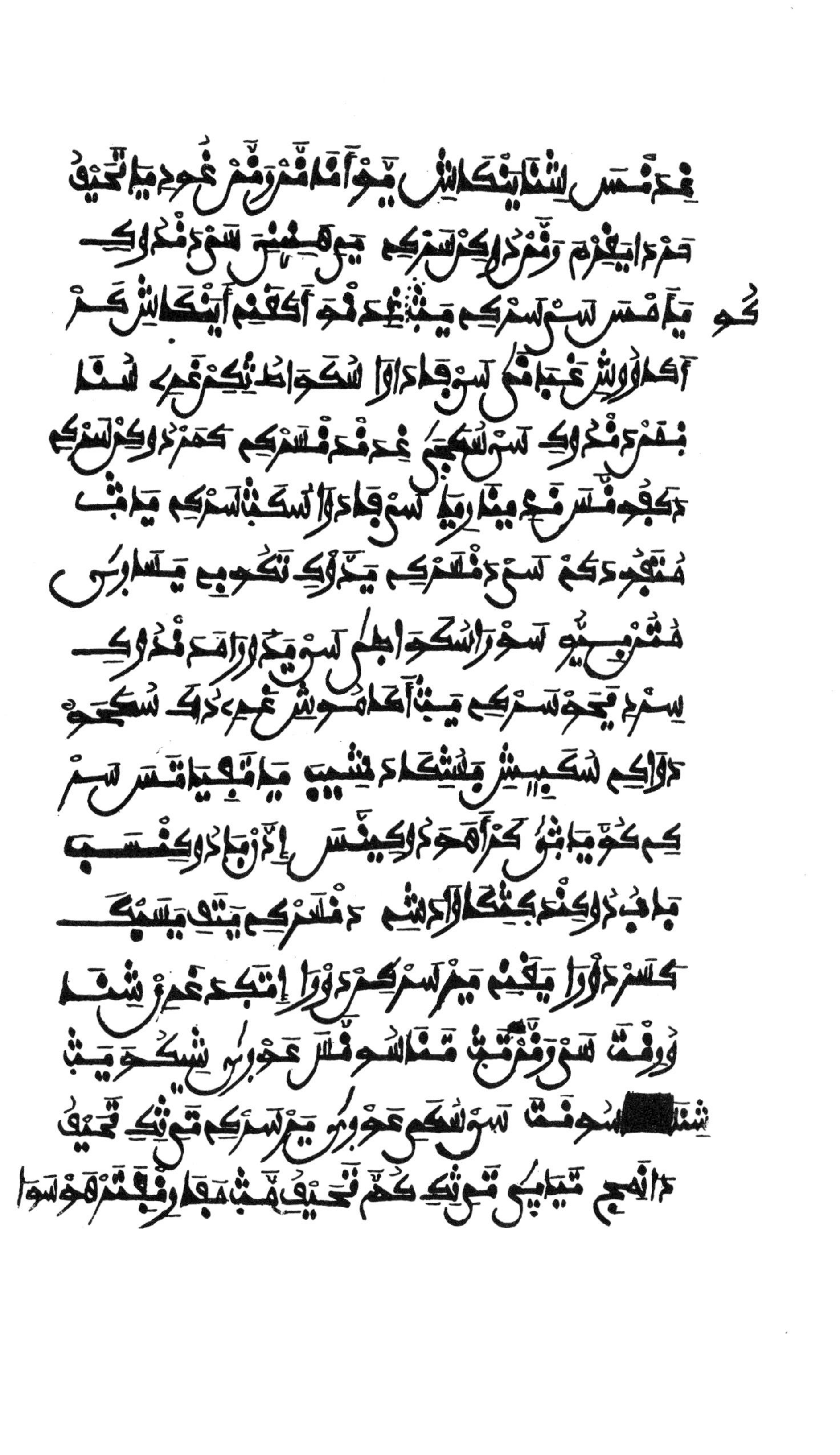

[illegible]
[illegible]
[illegible] [illegible]
[illegible]
[illegible]
[illegible]
[illegible]
[illegible]
[illegible]
[illegible]
[illegible]
[illegible]
[illegible]
[illegible]
[illegible]
[illegible] [redacted] [illegible]
[illegible]

ke nan. Barebari da Daurāwa su ne kākaninsu. Ama wajan Musulumch
daga [31] Barnō ya fitō. Hausawa, da Barebari, da kōwane iri, duka nan
yanma da wuri kāfurai ne. Saanan mālamai su-ka-che, wada alāmari ya
zama. Akw
wani mutun, chāna Barnō, daga yāyan sarākunansu, sūnansa Dalāma.
Da ya chi sarauta, ana-che masa Mainadināma. [32] Fasara tasa, wai sarki
[33] maabōchin [34] rinjāya. Saada sarauta tasa ta wuche, watani sai ya a-
-ika manzo, zūa-ga halīfa. Saanan kūa [35] Abūbakari-Sidīku, yarda(n) Ala
shi tabata garēshi, shi ne halīfa. Kā ga mafārin aikāwa tasa, chewa
[36] wanchānanka mutun yā kashe, shi-na-jin lābārin Musulumchi tun
bai chi sarauta ba. Kā ga sūnan manzo nasa, da ya aika, sū-
-nansa Gujālo. Sāilin da manzo ya zo, ya iskē halīfa, batun
yāki yā dauki hankalinsa, bai che ma manzo kōmi ba, sai ya che
da shi zamna nan, saanan bai kōma tuna magana tasa, dōmin
daukan hankalinsa da maganar yāki na [37] mazōwan tāwāye. Manzō ya za-
-mna chāna, har manzō ya mutu. Bāyan wata uku da kwānaki kadan
saanan Halīfa Abūbakari Sidīku shi kuma ya mutu. Bāyan watani
sāilinda aka-aje [38] Umaru Ibunuhutābi. Shi ne Halīfa bāyan Abūbakari

---

The Barebari and Daura people were their ancestors. But the Mohammeda
religion, as far as that is concerned, from Bornu it came. Hausas and Barebar
and whatever race (you can name) in the West were at first in early time
pagans. Then the malamai (scribes) said that this is what happened
There was a certain man away there at Bornu from among the childre
of their royal house, his name (was) Dalama. When he came to the thron
he was called Mainadinama, the meaning of that is, 'a chief more powerfu
than any other.' After he had reigned for some months then he sen
a messenger to the Caliph. Now at this time Abubakari-Sidiku, th
blessing of Allah be upon him, he was Caliph. You have seen th
beginning of his being sent, referring back to that man (Mainadinama)
was that he was hearing about Mohammedanism before he succeeded t
the kingdom. Behold the name of his envoy whom he sent, his name wa
Gujalo. At the time when the envoy came he found the Caliph's attentio
occupied with a war. He said nothing to the envoy. All he said was
'Remain here.' Then he did not again remember his words because his min
was so occupied with words of the war of the father of the twins. Th
messenger remained there till the messenger died. After three month
and a few days then the Caliph Abubakari Sidiku he too died. Afte
some months Umaru Ibunuhutabi was set up. He was the Caliph afte
Abubakari

بكنّ بر كبر دة ورا وا سو بى محمد كننسر أماوجر مسلمث
دغمبر فو ييجتوا هوسوا دبر مبر دكو وبى عم دكنمر
يمنم دو وعا فر ميبنو سكنن مالمم سكب و د الأمير يخما كو
ونفتن ثدرير فو دغ يا اير سر اكننس سو فنس دلمام
دميث سراوت أما بهلس هممر دفام بسر اتس و مسركم
ما أبو شر فجا لسكد سر وتاتس تو ب وقنم لسوما
يك منذ و دو وغليف سكنن كو أبو بكر صديق ميرد آل
شنتب غرمش شمبنو خليف كاغ مبا ونا بكدوا اتس ثوا
وفتا فنك منثر يا عبش شنا جرلاما رمسلمث مثن
مبث سروتاب كاغ سوفر منذ و فنس دمايك سو
منسر فجال ساهلنا منذ و ميذ و يا اسكى خليف بتمن
ميلك ميا دوك حنكلنس بيثمنذ وكوميب مهرينا
دشم كهلنا فمن سكنن بنكوم فر مفنا قلب دو ومر
دوكر فنكلنس دمفتر يا ك نمذ و وفتا وايم منذ ويم
مرفار مم منذ و يفتا باامير وت أك دكوانكم كدن
سكنن فليف أبو بكر صديق شيكم يمت باامير وقنم
ساهلنا أكا أبى عمر ابن خطاب شمبن خليف باامير أبو بكر

Asidīku. Sai ya tuna alāmarin manzō da mutūa tasa. Saanan su-ka-yi shāwara su sauran [39] sahabai. Su-ka-gama kai bisa aaika, zūa Barnō manzō. Aka-aiki Umaruasi, da takardū na Alkorani. Aka-che rubūtun Abdulāhi dan Umoru halīfa, da rawanī, da takōbī, da [40] kasausawa, da [41] garkūa, da [42] fūlar sarauta, da tarkache ma--suyawa, da akushī. Dukanta keauta ne, daga halīfa, zūa Maina--dināma. Sāilin da manzō ya kusa, sai ya aika garēsu, wanda [43] kāsanashe su lābārin zūansa. Sarkin Barnō, da mutāne(n)sa, su-ka-hau dawāki, su-ka-gamū da shī nīsa. Sāilin da ya shiga gari--nsa sai ya nada masa rawanī, ya [44] sābunta sarauta tasa, ya sa masa sūna, Sarkin Barno, ya ba shi dukan abinda aka-che shi ba shi, dōmin kyeauta wanan da aka-aiko da ita garēshi. Ya zamna garēsu. Shi-na-sanashe su adīnin Ala, da sunnō--ni manzō nasa, tsīra da aminchin Ala, shi tabala garēsu. Sun kashe, su-na-girmama shi, [45] matukan ban girma, su-na-neman albarka da sauran kalāchi nasa, da abinchinsa, da wurin aje.

Asidiku. Then he called to mind the report of the envoy and his deat Then they held a consultation, they his friends who remained. The joined their heads about the question of sending an envoy to Born Umaruasi was sent with manuscripts of the Koran. It was said th writing of Abdulahi the son of Umoru the Caliph, and turbans an a sword and spears and shields and the kingly fez and such things an plates; all these presents from the Caliph to Mainadinama. When th envoy drew near he sent to them one to acquaint them of the news of hi coming. The king of Bornu and his men mounted their horses and me him afar off. When he (the envoy) entered his town, then he bound the turba on him, he was established in his right to the kingdom, he was given the nam of the king of Bornu, he (the king) gave him everything he was told t give him, because of the presents which he (the envoy) had been sent wit for him. He lived among them. He was instructing them (the peopl of Bornu) in the creed of Allah and the names of His messengers, may th salvation and trust of Allah be assured to them. They continued to honou him, to the extreme that honour could be carried. They sought a blessin (by eating) the remains of his meals and his food and from the spot (he) se

الصديق سو قبّر الأمر فمنذر د مفتوا امس سعنّر سكي
قدور سو لسو ونحمبو وابجفوا سكقم كو بسو أيك
ذو بر فو منذو اك أيك عمر القاضي دفكم دو ما الفرءان
أكب ربوتر عبد الله ابن عمر فليق درو فم دتكوب
دكسو لسوا دغمر كو دفو لر سر وت دفر كب هد
لسيو د أكشي دكنت بجو فدفي دعم خليق ذو ميس
دقام سد لفد منذ وبكس سي ما ايك غمر كسر وفم
كد سنبش لابار فذ وفلس سر كر بر فو د متابس
سكحو دواكم سكفم دش فيمس لسد لفم يشغ فم
فمس سر وفد امس روف بسد ابنت سر وقد امس يسد
مس سو مى سر كر بر فو يبد لش د كر أبند أكب
لشبدلش د ومر بكوت ومر د أكد أيكو د إت غم مكش
يذ فر غم مس لشنا لسنبشس أد مير ال د اسنو
فم منذ و فلس حير اد أمنشر ال شتهت غم مس
سنكبش سنا غم محالش متكر بنغر مى سنا بمس
ألبرك دسو فكد اشيعسر د أبنشنسر دور فاجي

kafāfu nasa. Sāshensu su-na-neman albarka da fīātachen mājina tasa da mīawunsa. Su-na-hawan [46] shigifū, dōmin ganinsa. Su-na-neman alberka kuma da shāfan tufāfi nasa, da tākalminsa, da būlala tasa, har aka-che, su-na-neman albarka da daba tasa, da sauran harāwa tasa, da tōrōso nata. Ya rubūta masu takardū kuma, da rubū--tun hannu nasa, mai-alberka. Ya zamna bisa hakanan matukan zāmani, har aka-che garēshi, wadansu mazōwan kasa su-na bāyanka, su-na-sō Musulumchi indaa sun gane ka, daa sun bi ka. Bai gaskata ba, sai ya aiki mai-tōnō bōyē, ba asan sūnansa ba. Ya tafi, ya yi yāwō chikin kasan Hausa. Ya tōnē ya ji su-na-yabo Musulumchi, su-na-sō nasa. Ya kōmō, ya baiwa Umaru Ibunua--si lābāri. Umaru Ibunuasi ya gaia ma mutānensa, ya che su tafi. Su-ka-yarda. Saanan ya yi shiri. Ya aiki Abdulkarīmu--Mukaila zūa Kanō. Kwatamchin mutun dari uku, Lārabāwa, su-ka-bi shi. Sāilin da Abdulkarīmu ya kusa da su, sai ya aiki wanda ke-gaia masu. Ya zō, ya che, ‘Gaia masu manzō na manzō yā zō.’

---

his feet. Half of them were seeking blessing from the mucus from his nose and his spittle (by rubbing it on their persons). They were climbing the roofs in order to see him. They also sought blessing by touching his robes and his slippers and his whip, until it was even said they looked for a blessing from his beasts, and the remains of their fodder and their dung. Now he wrote manuscripts for them in the writing of his own hand, the blessed one. He lived amid such works up to the very end of (his) sojourn (and this went on) till he was informed that, ‘Other owners of (another) land are behind you (and) are wishing for the Mohammedan religion, should they see you they would follow you.’ He did not give (this report) credence until he had sent one to spy out (the land), his name is unknown. He (the spy) went and travelled over Hausa-land. He made secret inquiries, he heard they were praising the Mohammedan faith and that they wished for it. He returned and gave Umaru Ibunuasi the news. Umaru Ibunuasi told his people. He said they must go (and preach the Mohammedan religion). They agreed. Then he made preparations. He sent Abdulkarimu-Mukaila to Kano. About 300 men, Arabs, followed him. When Abdulkarimu was near to them (the people of Kano) then he sent one to inform them. He (the messenger) came and said, ‘Tell them the envoy of the envoy has come.’

كجا فجو قنس سد ابنفنس سنا بمر البرك دفيا فنجر ما جنا

قنس دميا وفنس سنا حون شغفو دوقر غفنس سنا بمر

البرك كحم دشا قنتجا فينس قنا كلينس دبو لال

قنس حر اكب سنا بمر البرك دد بتس دلسخو وحراوا

تنس د قحو ورطو فنت يربو قنا مس تكر دو كحم دوبو

قر هنسو فنس ميا البرك يغ مرو بار ككنر منكس

دامنم حر اكب غمر مكش ود مسر مذ او نكسو سنا

باينك سنا سو منلحش إرم السنفبك د السنبك

بنغسكتاب سن ماينك منسو فو بجمى بالسنسو قنلب

ينف يني يدا او شكر كسو هو لس ينو بنى ايج سنا يبو

منلفش سنا سو فنس يكو مو يبيو عمر ابن الفا

صم لابدش عمر ابن العاصم يقيا مختا ونس ميب

سنقم سكير د لسعنر مي وشم يا ايك عبد الكريم

المغيلي ذو كفو كتفشر منرد رى اك لاربداوا لسكيش

سد ولنغ عبد الكريم يكسر سو تبن ميا ايك ونم

بكفيا مس يي ذو يبشغيا مس منذو ونمنذ وياد و

Sāilin da ya zō masu ya gaia masu abinda aka-aiko shi da shi. Su-ka-gaskata shi, su-ka-karbi abinda ya zō da shi. Sāilin Kanō tā kashe alkaria che, ama bābu birni, sūnan [47] mutānen Kanō, Muhamadu-da-Jākara, sāilin da Abdulkarīmu ya sabka garēsu. Ya rubūta masu litāfi da rubūtun hannu nasa, mai-albarka, dōmin bai zō musu da litāfi ba, daga wajen Umaru Ibunu(l)asi. Dōmin hakanan alāmari yā kashe, dukan wanda ke sō shi iya rubūtu mai-chau, sai shi tafi zūa Barnō, shi zamna chāna, saanan shi kōmō. Ama Abdulkarīmu yā kashe shi-na-sanashe su sharaa Ala, da hukumchin sharaa, har su-ka-tanbaye shi abūbua da ba su kasan Lārabāwa. Bai san jawābin da zaa shi gaia masu ba. Sai ya che da su, su bari har shi kōmo. Akwai daga abinda su-ka-tanbaye shi, tunkū da yanyāwa, da gafia, da būdāri, da tsāra, da waninsa. Ya zamna garesu watani, kōwache rāna shi-na -sanache su Alkorani da Hadisai, masu-chau, har aka-che da shi, 'Akwai wata alkaria kusa da alkaria nan, ana-che mata Kāshina,

---

When he came to them he told them what (message) he had been sen with. They believed him, they received the thing which he had brough Now at this time Kano was an unenclosed town but not a walled town the name of the men (man) at Kano (was) Muhamadu Dajakara at the tim when Abdulkarimu alighted amongst them. He (Abdulkarimu) wrot them books in the writing of his own hand, the blessed one, because h had not come to them bringing books from Umaru Ibunu(l)asi. And thu it has come to be reported that every one who wished to be able to wri well let him set out towards Bornu and remain there (till he had learned t write) and then return (home). But Abdulkarimu continued to instruc them the laws of Allah and the commands of the law until they mad inquiries about things which were not (to be found) in Arabia. He di not know what answer to give them. Then he said to them to leave th matter open till he returned (to Arabia). Among the things they wer asking about were panthers, and civet-cats, and rats, and servals, and tige cats, and such like (whether clean or unclean). He lived with them (many months (and) every day instructed them well in the Koran and th Traditions, till at length he was informed, 'There is another town near thi town, it is called Katsina,

تسّ ؤلِنْغ ييغْ ؤُرقّس يِنْغيا مَسْ ئِيِنْغ أكّ ئِيكُو يْشْ دْ ئشّ
نْسكْغْسْكْتَلْشْ نْسكّكْرْ ئِيِنْغ ييغْ ؤرْ دْ ئشّ تسّ ؤلِنْ ركْنُو
تَلكْشْبُو ألْفْ ييرْثْ أمّا يابْ ييرْنِي سْوفْرْ فْتَايْمْرْ كْنُوا
مُحمّد دْ يابكْ تسّ ؤلِنْغ عبدْ الكْريمْ يِلّسْبكْ غْمْ ئِلّسْ
ييرْ مْجُو تَامَسْ يِتَاحُو دْ ؤُمْجُو مْرْ هْمْنُو فْسَرْ مِيَا أبْرْ ك
دْ ؤُقّمْ بييغْ ؤمْسْ دْ لِيَا فْكْمْبْ دْغْ ؤُجْمْ عْجْمْ ئِبْرْ عْ ئِصْمْ
دْ ؤُقّمْ مْكْنْ الأمْدِ يِتَاكْشْبُو دْكْمْ ؤُفْنْدْ بْكْمّلُو شْغْلُو
رْمْجُو فْتْ مْيِشُو تسّ شْتْنِ دْ ؤُمْبْرْ فْنُو شْغْ مْرْ ثْدَرْ تسْغْنْ
شْكُو مُو أمّا عبدْ الكْريمْ ياكْشْبُو شْنْدا سْنْبْشْسْ
• شْرْعْ ألّ دْ مْكْفْشْرْ شْرْعْ حْمْ سْكْتْنْبِيشْ أمْجُو مْبْجُو
دْ مْبَاسْ كْسّرْ لِّرْبَارا بْيِلّسْ جْجْوامْرْ دْ دَا أشْغْيا مَسَبْ
تسْ ميشْ لْسُو سْبْرْ حْمْ شْكُو مُو أكُو رْدْ غْ أبِنْغ =
سْكْتْنْبِيشْ تْنْكُوا دْ يِيّنْيارْ دْ غْمْجُو دْ مْجُو حْرُو دْ طَارا
دْ ؤُفْنْسْ يِيغْ مْرْ غْمْ مْكْسْ ؤُتْنْمْ كْوؤُثْ رَامْغْ يِشْغَا
سْنْبْشْسْ الفْرْ ئِرْحْدْ ميغْنْ مَا سْتَاوْ حْرْ أكْتْبْ
دْ ئشّ أكُو رْتْ الفْرْسُو كْسْرْ دْ الفْرْ يِتّمْ ئِفْرْ يِتْمْ كْدَا ئشّ

indaa sun gane ka, mutānen [48] garin, daa sun bāda gaskīa garēka da wanda ya aikō ka. Sāilin da ya ji hakanan, sai ya yi shiri, ya tafi da kansa, zūa garēta. Sāilin da su-ka-ji lābāri zūansa, sai su-ka-gamu da shi nīsa. Sāilin da ya sabka garēsu, ya sanashe su abinda ya sanashe su, ya fōri wanda ke rubūta musu litāfi. Aka-che, chewa shia, bai rubūta musu Alkorāni ba da hannu nasa, dōmin hakanan ne, mutānen Kanō sun sar Alkorāni, sun fi mutānen Kāshina har yau. Saanan bāyan kārēwa tasa daga alamarin Kāshina, sai ya kōma zūa Kanō, ya zamna kadan. Saanan, sāilin da ya yi nufi kōmāwa zūa Barnō, ya che da su, 'Da sannu naa kōmō garēku da jawābai abinda ku ka tanbaye ni garēta.' Saanan ya tāshi, ya tafi. Ama dayawa chikin mutānensa ba su bi shi ba sai kadan su-ka-bi shi chikinsu. Saura su ka zamna, su-na abin girmamāwa chikin Kanō. Danginsu sun kashe mabayana sananu chikin Kanō har yau, har mutāne su-ka-che masu sharifai, aa ba sharifai ba ne su dai Lārabāwa ne. Hakikan Abdulkarīmu yā sainya alkāli chikin Kanō, da shugaban sala, da mai-yanka, da wanda ke sanada yāra,

---

should the people of the town see you they would believe you and him who sent you.' When he heard (them speak) thus, then he made ready. He set out himself to go to it (the town). When they got news of his coming, then they met with him afar off. When he alighted among them he taught them about what (he had come) to instruct them in. He instructed one who was to write books for them. It was said, speaking of him, he did not write the Koran with his own hand, and because of this the Kano people surpass the Katsina in their knowledge of the Koran till to-day. Then, after the completion of his work at Katsina, he went back, going to Kano, (and) remained there a short time. Then when he thought of returning to go to Bornu he said to them, 'Shortly I shall return to you with the answer to what you were asking about.' Then he rose up and went away. But many among his people did not follow him, only a few among them followed him. The rest remained and continued to perform great deeds in Kano. Their descendants are found (and) known in Kano until to-day, till people called them seraphs, but surely they were not seraphs, they were just Arabs. Of a truth Abdulkarimu has set up a judge in Kano, and one to lead in prayers, and one to slaughter (live stock), and one who was to instruct the youths

ءار ءاسّغنبك ءمتاءبنّ غمر ءاسنّباء غنسكيا غمر نك ءاونّم
يا ءابنّكوك ءسا ءيلنّغ يج حكنّ ءسّنّ يمّ ءيشر يتاوّ ءككنس ءار
غمر ءمنّ ءسا ءيلنّغ ءسكم ءلا ءباون ءاونّس ءسّن ءسكّنّم ءديشم ءفيبس
ءسا ءيلنّغ ءيسّنبك غمر ءسّن ءيسّغنّبشس ءابنّغ ءيسّغنّبشس ءيجور
ءونّغ ءبكر ءبو ءتا ءمس ءيتاون ءاكت ءقواشم ءبيم ءمو ءقا
ءمس ءالفرء ءافيبّ ءدهنّنّو ءفس ءدو ءيمّ ءحكنّن ءيمّ ءسنّس
ءالفرء ءان ءسّنّف ءمتاءبنّ ءهاشر ءمرّيو ءسّغنّن ءبا ءيمّ ءكدا ءبرّمّوا
ءقس ءدّهم ءالامير ءنكاءشر ءسّن ءبكوم ءاوكو ءيدّ ءمرّ ءكدّن
ءسّغنّن ءسا ءيلّن ءديمّ ءنجر ءكّه ءمااوا ءذو ءبم ءفوا ءميجد ءسو ءح
ءدسّنّنو ءفنّه ءهو ءفو ءغمر ءنك ءدجواب ءابنّغ ءككنّنّم ءبيم
غمر ءمنّ ءسّغنّن ءمينا ءبنّ ءبيتاو ءامّا ءدمّيو ءفكر ءمتا ءبنّنس ءبسّبيشب
ءسّنّ ءكدّن ءهكيمش ءنكنّس ءسّو ءالسّكّدّ ءمرّ ءسّنّا ءابر ءغمر ءقّما ءار
ءنكر ءكنو ءدّ ءنغنّس ءسّنكشّو ءمبينّا ءسّنّو ءنكر ءكنّو ءا
ءحرّبيّو ءحر ءمتا ءبنّو ءسكنّبنّس ءسّر ءبّو ءعاء ءيماشر ءفيبو
ءسّو ءدّن ءالا ءوبا ءاوانّي ءحكيكر ءعبد الكريم ءيمّ ءسّنّي ءالفاضم
ءنكر ءكنّو ءدّ ءشو ءغبّ ءغحمل ءدّم ءمبيّنكي ءدّو ءفّغ ءكسّنّد ءيا ءار

Alkorāni, da mai-kiran salla. Ya halalta masu abinda Ala ya halalta, ya ha masu abinda Ala ya hana. Sāilin da ya kōma zūa ga Umaru Ibunula--si, ya ba shi lābāri da abinda su-ka-tanbaye shi. Sai Umaru Ibunula--si ya yi kurum, har ya kōma zūa ga halīfa, saanan ya aikō da jawā--binta, bāyan wata shida. Ya halalta masu sāshenta, ya hane su sāshe. Ama Abdulkarimu bai kōma zūa Barnō ba, bāyan kōmāwa tasa zūa garinsu, kō zūa Kanō. Hakanan Umaru Ibunulasi, ama yā yi sarautar Masar, bāyan kōmāwa tasa gida. Ama sauran garūrūa, su-na-zūa, sāshe zūa Kanō dōmin sanin adīni, sāshe kūa zūa Kāshina, har adīni ya chika kasan Hausa dukanta. Sai kasan [49] Kabi, chewa su, sun ki Musulumchi, su-ka-tabata bisa Kāfirchinsu. Su-ka-tabata chikinsa. Sarākunansu sun kashe, sūnansu, Barbarma, Argōji, Tabāriu, Zartai, Gōbari, Dadafāni, Katāmi, Bardo, Kudamdam Sharīa, Bādōji, Karfu, Darka, Gunba, Katatar, Tāmu. Wadanan dukansu sun ki Musulumchi bāyan shiga tasa kasan

---

in the Koran, and one to call (them) to prayer. He made lawful for th that which Allah had made lawful, and forbade that which Allah h forbidden. When he returned to go to Umaru Ibunulasi he gave him account of what they had asked him about. And Umaru Ibunulasi w silent (on the subject) till he returned to go to the Caliph and then he se an answer to it (the question) after six months had elapsed. He ma lawful for them half of it, half he made unlawful. But Abdulkarimu d not return to Bornu after his return to their (his, Abdulkarimu's) to or to Kano. Thus (also) Umaru Ibunulasi, but he ruled over Egypt af his return home. Now the remainder of the towns were coming in, h of them to Kano in order to know about the (new) religion, and half a to Katsina, until the creed filled all Hausa-land. Now the Kibi count speaking of them, they refused (to adopt) the Mohammedan religion, th continued in their paganism. They persisted in it. Their kings, (the were their names, Barbarma, Argoji, Tabariu, Zartai, Gobari, Dadafa Katami, Bardo, Kudamdam, Sharia, Badoji, Karfu, Darka, Gunba, Katat Tamu. All these refused the Mohammedan creed after his advent i the land

أَلْقُرْءَانِ دَ مَيْكِرَ فَضْلِ يَعَلَّنْتَ مَسُ أَبِنْدَ أَلَّيْ أَلْتَنَ يَهَنَّ
مَسُ أَبِنْدَ أَلَّيْ يَهَمَ لَسَامِلِنْدَ يَكُومَ دُوغُ عُمَرُ إِبْنُ الْعَا
صِمِ مِيَبَاشِ لَاجِبَدُو دَأَبِنْدَ سُكَتَنْبِيشِ سِنْ عُمَرُ إِبْنُ الْعَا
صِمِ يِيِي كُرُمْ حَزِيكُومَ دُوغُلِيفَ لَسَاعَنْرِيَ يِكُودُجُو
إِمِنْتَ مَايَمْرُوفْشِدَ يَعَلَّنْتَ مَسُ لَسَدِبِنْتَ يَهَنْبَسُ
سَابِثِ أَمَّا عَبْدُ الْكَرِيمِ بِيكُومَ دُوَبَرُ فُوبَ مَايَنْ
كُومَدُوَا أَمَسُ دُوغُمِ فَسُ كُودُوغُ حَنْوَا مَكَنْ عُمَرُ
إِبْنُ الْعَاصِمِ وَأَمَّا يَدَنْ لَسَرُ وَتَزْ مَصَمَرْ مَدَمَيِرْ كُومَدُوَا أَمَسُ
غِدَا أَمَّا لَسُورَزْ غَمُ وُرُ لَسَنَاظُو لَسَدَبِشُ دُوغُكْنُو دُوفِسْ
لَسِنْ أَدِمِيرِ لَسَدَبِشُ كُوَ دُوغُكَدَاشِرَ حَرَأَدِمِيرِ يِثِكْ كَسَمْ
هُوسُ دُكَمْتَ سَنْ كَسَمْ هُوسُ كَبْ مُثُوَالسُوَ سُنْفُ
فُسَلْمَفِ سُكَتَبَتْ مَسُ كَدِبِمْ فِنَنْسُ سُكَتَبَتْ فِكِفَسُ
لَسَدَاكُمْفُسُ سُنْكَبِشُ سُوفُلْسُ مَرِ مَرْمَ ۞ أَرْغُوجِ
قَمَبُرُو ۞ زُوقُ ۞ غُوجِمِ ۞ دَدُبَادُ ۞ سُكْتَامِ بَرْدُوَا كَدَمْدَمْ
تَثَرِيَا مَادُرِمِ كَرْفُجُو دُرُكَ غُفْنَ كَتَتَرْ تَدَمُوَا
وَمَقْنَ دَكَفْسُ سُنْوُ مَقَلْفِ مَايَرْشِفَا فَسَ كَسَمْ

Hausa. Saanan sāilin da Zaidu ya chi sarauta, sai ya musulumta da wadan ke tāre da shi, kasan Kabi ta musulumta, zūa wakatin Bata-Musa; wadan su ne sarākai Kabi chikin Musulumchi. Fārinsu, Zaidu, Muhamadu, Namakāta, Sulaimāna, Hisrikōma, Abdulāhi, Dunbāki, Alia, Usmānu, Chisgari, Barbarmanaba, Muwāshi, Muhamadu-Karfi, Bata--Musa. Bāyansu Fūmu ya yi sarauta. Ya juya Musulumchi da Kāfurchi Wadanan su ne wadanda su-ka-kāfurta. Fārinsu, Fūmu, Kautai, Gunba, Sakana-Murtāmu, Kanta, Rātaini, Gaiwa, Gado, Māsu, Chidagora, Gabangari, Maikebe, Marshākoki, Lazimu, Māshirāna, Makata. Wadanan su ne dukansu sun tabata chikin Kāfurchi. Sāilin da Kanta ya chi sarauta, ya sābunta Musulumchi, ya tanba mālamai abinda ke chikin litāfi. Ya tsaida adīni chikin zāmaninsa da wad-nda ke bie da shi, har kasan Kabi duka ta musulumta. Wanan shi ne sū-nansu. Kantāhu, Gōfe, Dauda, Hamidu, Sulaimāna, Mālu, Ishāka, Muhamadu-Nashāwi, Amuru, Muhamadu-Kābe, Kantanabaiwa, Muhomadu-Shīfāya, Hāmidu. Wadanan dukansu sun tabata chikin Musulumch

---

of the Hausas. Then at the time when Zaidu came to the throne [the he became a Mohammedan and those who were with him. The Ka country became Mohammedan up to the time of Bata-Musa. These we the kings of Kabi under the Mohammedan régime. The first of the was Zaidu, (then) Muhamadu, Namakata, Sulaimana, Hisrikoma, Abdulal Dunbaki, Alia, Usmanu, Chisgari, Barbarmanaba, Muwashi, Muhamad Karfi, Bata-Musa. After them Fumu ruled. He turned Mohammedanis into paganism. These were they who became pagans. The first of the (was) Fumu, (then) Kautai, Gunba, Sakana-Murtamu, Kanta, Ratair Gaiwa, Gado, Masu, Chi-da-gora, Gaban-gari, Maikebe, Marshakol Lazimu, Mashirana, Makata. These were they who all continued paganism. At the time when Kanta ruled he revived the Mohammeda religion (and) inquired of the learned men the contents of (their) book He established the faith in his time and in that of them who followe him, till the whole of the Kabi country became Mohammedan. The were their names, Kantahu, Gofe, Dauda, Hamidu, Sulaimana, Mal Ishaka, Muhamadu-Nashawi, Amuru, Muhamadu-Kabe, Kantanabaiw Muhamadu-Shifaya, Hamidu. All these continued in the Mohammeda faith.

تُوسِ سَعَنْ لَسَاهِلَنْ وُنِيمِ مِنْ سَرُوفْ لَسِ بَمُسْلِمَتْ دَرَدَمْ

بَكَنْدُ وَمَعَ بِشِ كَسَنْ كَبِ تَمُسْلِمَتْ دُرُ وَفَنْتَنْ مِتَا مُوسَو وُدَمْ

سُوبُكُ لَسَا اكُوكَبِ تِكِنْ مُسْلِمِنْ بَادُ وَفَلْسَنْ رَبِيمِ ۞ مُحَمَّدُ ۞

نَمَكَاتَ سُلَيْمَانْ حَسَنْ كُومَ عَبْدُ اللّٰهِ دُنْبَاكِم عَلِو

عُثْمَانْ فَسَعَنْ يَمْ بَدَمْ نَبِي مُوَاشِمِ مُحَمَّدْ. كَرُبِمِ بَتَا

مُوسَو بَا يَفَنْسَ فُوتُمْ يِبِي سَرُوفْ بِجُوبِ مُسْلِمِنْ دَكَابَرَتِ

نَبِي وُدَمْ سَوبُكُ وُدُمْطَ سُكَمَا بُرَمْفْ بَادُ وَفَسَنْ فُوتُمْ =

كُوتُو غُنْبُ سَكَنْ فَمْ فَدَامُوا كَنْتَا وَامِيرْ عَبْدُوا غَدَوا

فَدَاسُوا شِيعِ غُورْ غُمَبْرْ غُمَرْ مَمُوكَبِ فَرُشَاكُوكِ لَازِمْ

مَدِشَرَانَا مَحَمَاتَ وُدَمْ سُوبُكُ دُمَكَنْسَ سُنَّتِ بِكِنْ كَا

بُرُفِ لَسَاهِلَنْ كَمَنْتَا بِمِنْ سَرُوفْ بِلَسَابُمَتْ مُسْلِمِنْ بِتَبُو

مَدَالِمِ أَبْنَمْ بِكِنْكَنْ بِتَاوُبُو بِطَعِيمْ آدَمِيرْ فُكُنْ وَامِتَنْسَ دَرُمْ

نُدْبِيسُو دُبِشِمْ فَمْ كَلَسَنْ كَمِ دُكَ تَمُسْلِمَتْ وُفَمْ شِيبُو لَسَو

بِنْسَنْ كَمَنْتَاهُ غُوبُكُ دُرُمْ حَجِيمْ سُلَيْمَانْ مَالُو

إِلْتَمَاوْ مُحَمَّدْ فَشَاوْ آمُرْ مُحَمَّدْ كَدَابُ كَمَنْتَا نَبِيُو ۞

مُحَمَّدْ فَتِيمَادُ بَادُمْ وُدَمْ دُكَمَنْسَ سُنَّتِ بِكِنْ مُسْلِمِنْ

Sāilin da Barbarma ya yi sarauta, ya musāya Musulumchi, ya zama Kā-
-furchi. Kāfurchi ya tabata zūa wakatin Hūdu. Shi ne wananda Usmā
dan Fōdio ya yi yāki da shi. Ya kōre shi, har ya kashe shi
kusa da Kebi. Buhāri dan Abdu-Salāmi, shi ya kashe shi. Shi ne
sarkin Jega. Danginsu su ne sarākaita zūa yau. Yā kāre.
Ama chikin Kanō adīni ya tabata bāyan kōmāwa tasa, shi
Abdulkarimu, adīni ya dinga dadūa kulum, da girma da daukaka.
Ya tabata bisa hakanan shekaru dayawa, zūa wakatin [50] Mainamugabadi.
Shi ne wanda ya juya abinda Abdulkarimu ya aje. Ya walakanta
suna, ya daukaka sarauta, ya walakanta Musulumchi, ya girmama
gumākai, ya yi girman kai, ya yi shishigi. Māsu-waazu su-ka-
yi masa waazu, bai anpāne shi ba waazunsu sai ya dada gir-
-man kai. Shi-na-[51] alfahari. Ya tabata bisa hakanan har ya mutu. Dan u
-nsa Kunbāri ya zamna mazamninsa, ya bi tafarkinsa.
Ya tabata ga wanan har wakatin Runfa. Shi kuma ya dada Kāfurchi
da shishigi. Shi ne wanda ya aure būdrūa alif. Ya yi fōrō da
yin afi da turbīa gaba garēshi, saan gaisua. Ya che,

When Barbarma became king he changed the Mohammedan religion (a
became a pagan. Paganism lasted up to the time of Hudu. He was
one Usmanu the son of Fodio made war against. He drove him out (a
pursued him) till he slew him near to Kebi. Buhari the son of Ab
-Salimi, he it was who slew him. He was the king of Jega. His fam
are its kings till to-day. It is finished. But as for Kano in (it) the fa
continued after his, Abdulkarimu's, return (home). The faith continued
increase always with force and power. And it lasted on such footing
many years until the time of Mainamugabadi. It was he who chan
the order of things Abdulkarimu had set up. He set at naught the
(of Mahomed), he made the kingship all powerful, he disregarded
Mohammedan faith, he exalted fetish worship, and was arrogant.
surpassed (all his predecessors in evil). Instructors endeavoured to instr
him, but their admonitions were of no avail against him, but he increa
in pride. He was vainglorious. He continued thus till he died.
brother Kunbari reigned in his stead and followed in his ways. He
continued in this (evil) till the time of Kunfa. He also spread pagani
and evildoing. It was he who married 1,000 maidens. He instruc
(people) to prostrate themselves and put earth on their heads bef
saluting him. He said,

لسا بلخد بر مهرم يو سرات يفسار مسلفت يدم كا
فرث كافرث يتبث دور وفتر هود شينو وفر دعثمار
دفجود نى يو ياك دشى يكو رمش حر يكبشس
كسر يكح بحار دفجد السدام شى يكششس شينو
سر يكر يح دفغفنس سوبى سراكيت دويو ياكارو
آما ثكر كتو الدى مير يتبت بامير كوماد واتس شم
عبد الكريم الدى مير يدى فغ د دروا كلم دغم مادوروك
يتبت مسر ويكفر شكر ودميو دور وفتس مير مقحم
شين ورفد يجوس ايد عبد الكريم ياس يو لاكنث
سفر يدورك سرات يو لاكنث مسلفت يفم مم
غماكو يو غر مركى يو ششفم ماسوعظ سك
يمسر وعك يعا ايجد فشب وعظفس سر يحد د غم
منكى شنا الفحر يتبت مسر هكفر حر يفت د نحو
نسر كفبار يد مر مد مفنس يب قفم كنس
يتبت غومفر مر و فتررنق شيكم يد د كا فرث
دشتفى شينى وفد يعو وبد وا الف يو فورار ا
يتمر اف دفر بيا غب غمر مش سعر غيسوا يث

kar akirāyi wanda sūnansa yā katarta da sūnan uwāyensa sai da [52] alkunia. Ya bāta adīni dukansa, ya sai da yāya, ya ginan gidan sarauta, wanan da sarākai Kanō ke shiga har yau. Ya aikata abinda ya sō. Hakanan mutānen kasan Kanō dukansu, sai dai daia chewa su, su-na-rikō [53] suna, bābu girma garēsu, [54] fa che mutānen kasan Kanō ba su san dafūan gīa ba, sai kadan chikinsu, mutānen kauye. Hakanan ba su chin mushe. Su-na-[55] kāchia mātansu, su-na-rufe kānunsu da lulubi. Ba su wani aiki sai wanan. Su-ka-tabata bisa hakanan har aka-sāmu mālamai chikin Kanō, mai-gudu-ndūnia, mai-tsōrō Ala. Sūnansa Muhamadu-Zāri. Ya tsaya da waazu, Runfa bai ji ba kōwanin abinda ya ke yi masu waazu da shi. Sai su-ka-yi dabāra chikin kashinsa, har su-ka-kashe shi da dare, kashin [56] gīla, chikin tafarkin masalāchi, ya kwana [57] yankake, yā [58] sashe, har gari ya wāye. Aka-bisna shi wakatin luha. Kushewa tasa [59] sananīa che chikin Kanō. Ana-zīāra tata

---

let not him whose name happened to be the same as that of his paren[t] be called so, but (let him be called) by some sobriquet. He complete[ly] destroyed the creed, he sold free men, he built a palace, the one whi[ch] the kings of Kano enter to-day. He did what he wished. And it w[as] so with all the people of Kano except a very few, speaking of them, the[y] kept to the Mohammedan faith, they were not powerful, only the Kan[o] people did not know how to make beer, except a few among them, men [of] outlying villages. Thus they did not eat any animal that had died a natur[al] death. They removed the clitoris of their women, they covered the[ir] heads with a veil. They did nothing else but this. They continued [in] such (conduct) until learned men were found in Kano, who had renounce[d] the world, who feared Allah. (Of these learned men one) his name w[as] Muhamadu-Zari. He stood up and preached. Rumfa paid no heed [to] whatever admonitions he admonished them. But they planned to kill hi[m] till at last they did kill him in the night by slaying him from behin[d] in the road to the mosque, and he lay (there) murdered, cast aside, t[ill] dawn. He was buried about eight in the morning. His grave is known [in] Kano, it is visited

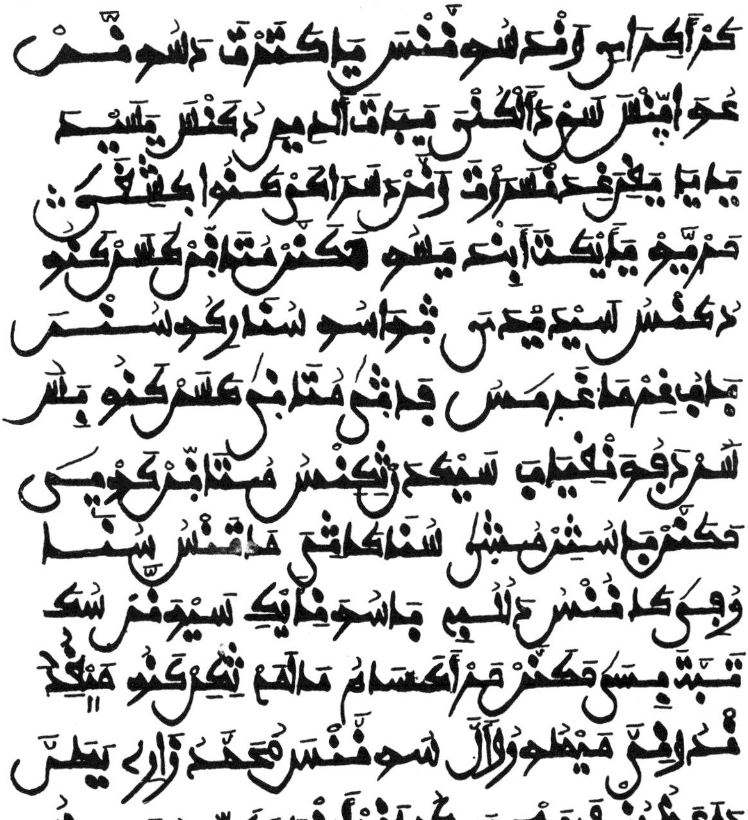

ana-tsarō nata, ana-che da shi [60] mai-kalgō, ana-neman albarka da ādua garēshi. Saanan Abdulāhi-Sako ya tsaya bāyansa. Shi-na-waazu, ba su ji ba garēshi, sai walākantatu, ama mainya mainya ba su ji ba. Sai su-ka-ba shi tsōrō, har ya fita, ya gudu, zūa kauye, dōmin shi yi ma mutānen kauye waazu. Saanda sarki ya aiki wanda ke kā--mō shi. Su-ka-kāmō shi, su-ka-dinga bugunsa, har su-ka-kāwō shi. Shi-na maras lāfia. Ya mutu bāyan kwānaki kadan. Kushewa tasa sananīa che bāyan [61] gwoboron dūtsi, ama ba azīāra tasa, ba atsarō nasa. Kāfurchi ya tabata hakanan har wakatin Muhamadu-Alwali Shi ne wanan [62] Usmānu dan Fōdio ya yi yāki da shi, bāyan zamansa chikin sarauta shekara gōma sha bakwoi. Ya fita shi da mutānensa, ya gudu, zūa [63] sāsan dāma. Wani bai san wurin da ya zamna b
har yau, aka-che Barnabarna, aka-che ba nan ba. Mālami su-ka-che tun zua Abdulkarīmu, har zūa zāmani Usmānu dan Fōdio, saraki sabain da shida. Kushewansu dukansu tā tabata chikin birnin Kanō, bīu, Bāwa da Muhamadu-Alwali, ama chikin Kāshina. Adīni ya tabata bāya

---

and watched over, he was called 'the Kalgo man', blessings are sough by prayers being made for him. Then Abdulahi-Sako stood up (t proclaim the creed) after him. He was admonishing them but they pai no heed to him, except some people of no importance, but those i authority did not hear. And they frightened him so that he fled to th outlying towns in order to instruct the people of the lesser towns. The the king sent one to seize him. They seized him, and continually flogge him till he was brought before (the king). He was (by this time) ill an died after a few days. His grave is known, (it lies) behind the roc (known as) 'the single rock', but it is not visited or watched over. An so it came to pass that paganism existed till the time of Muhamadu-Alwal It was he Usmanu, the son of Fodio, made war on, after he had rule in the kingdom for seventeen years. He (Usmanu-dan-Fodio) drove hi out and his men, he fled in the direction of the country on the right an none know where he settled till this day, (some) say Barnabarna (some say it was not there. The learned men said that from the coming c Abdulkarimu till the coming of Usmanu, the son of Fodio, there wer seventy-six kings. All their graves have remained in the town of Kanc but two of them, that of Bawa and Muhamadu-Alwali, are in Katsin The creed continued after

أَمَا طَرُوقَتَّ أَمَا قْعَرِشْم مَيْكَلْقُو أَمَا بَقْمْ أَلْبَرْكَ دَعَادُعْ
غَمْ مُشْ سَعْقْمْ عَبْدَ اللَّهِ سَكُوبَطُو مَا قَيْنَسْ شِنَا وَعَظْ
بْلِلْجَبْ غَمْ مُشْ سَرْوَه لَاكْنْتَتُو أَمَا مَقْنُو مَقْنُو مَلَاسُجَبْ
سَوْسَكَبَاشْ طُورُرْ حَمْ بِجَتَّ يُقْدَ دُرَكَخْيِي دُوقَّسْ
شِيمَمْتَا بَمْ كَخْبِي وَعَظْ سَعْقْمْ سَرْكِي يَأْيْكِ وَقْدَ بَكَا
مُوشِرْ سَكَكَا مُوشِ سُكَدَ نْعَ يَقْنْسْ هَرْسَكَكَادُرُ
شِّ شْنَا مَرْسَاقِي يَمُتْ بَامَيْرْكُوَانِكِم كَحْرْ كُبْشُوَ
قَسْ سَنْيَاقْ بَامَيْرْ غُبْرْ دُوطِ أَمَا جَا أَزْبَاوَ أَقْسَرْ بَا
أَطْرُوقَّسْ كَاقِرْقِ يَتْبَتْ تَكَشَّ مَزْوَقْتِرْ مُحَمَّدْ أَلْحُوَلْ
شِينِي وَقْمْ دَعْثْمَارْ دَقْبُودِنِ بِيمَاكِيمْ شِ بَايَّسْ
دَمَقْسَ نْكُرْ سَرْوَتْ بَشْكَمْ غَوَمْ شَبَكُوشْ يَعْتُ شِم
دُمْتَا قَنْسَ يَقْدَ ذُرَ أَسَسْرَدَامْ وَقْبَيْلَسْرُ وُقْدْ يَقْمْ قْنَابْ
حَرْيُو أَكَبْ بَرْ زَبْرُو أَكَبْ بَا قَنَابْ مَالَقَمْ سُكَبْ قْرَدُرْ
عَبْدَ الْكَرِيم جُمْ حَرْدُو ذَامَنْرَعُثْمَارْ دَقْبُودِنُو سَرْكَ
سَبْقِرْدِ شْدَ كَبْشُو قُسَرْ دَكْنْسَرْ تَامْتَبْتْ نْكَرْمَ قْرْكُو
بِيُو بَاوَرْ مُحَمَّدْ أَلْحُوَلْ أَمَا نْكُرْ كَاشَرْ أَلْحِ مِيرِ يَتْبَتْ بَايَّسْ

kōmāwan Abdulkarīmu. Adīni ya dinga dadawa kulum, ya tabata
da girma. Mutānin [64] Gōbir su-ka-dinga zūa Kāshina, su-na-
-karban adīni garēsu, da gaskīa, da kōkari. Su-ka-shiga
chikinsa bāki dai. Adīni ya tabata garēsu kuma,
tamkar da ya tabata chikin Kāshina. Ama Musulumchi ya tabata
chikin Kāshina; hakanan zūa wakatin Agarga. Shi ne farkō
wanda ya juya abinda Abdulkarīmu ya aje chikin Kāshina.
Māsu-waazu su-ka-yi masa waazu. Bai ji ba. Ya tabata ga Kā-
-furchinsa har ya mutu. Kaura ya yi sarauta, da dansa,
ya bi hainyar ubansa. Kāfurchi ya tabata har zāmanin
Wāri-mai-kworia. Shi ne wanda ya yi shishigi, ya yi gir-
-man kai, girman kai baba. Ya auri budrūa alif. Ya [65] kinkumu
chikin barna, bai bari ba. Shi-na-neman māgani dōmin
shi [66] dawama chikin dūnia, kar shi mutu, har wani [67] bōka ya rū-
-de shi, wai ba shi mutua harabadi. Wanchananka mai-
-māgani ya aikata masa abinda ya aikata daga māgani.

---

the return of Abdulkarimu. The faith continued to grow always and took firm hold. Men from Gobir continued to come to Katsina and were adopting the Mohammedan faith with (in all) truth and earnestness, they embraced it, all together. The faith took hold among them also as it had taken hold in Katsina. And so it was until the time of Agarga. He was the first who changed the state of things that Abdulkarimu had established in Katsina. Instructors (strove) to admonish him. He heard not. He remained in his heathenism till he died. Kaura ruled the kingdom, and (then) his son; he followed the path his father had taken. Paganism continued till the time of Wari-mai-kworia. It was he who did evil and was most arrogant. He married 1,000 maidens. He embraced evil (and) did not cease. He sought for (a) medicine in order that he might go on living in the world and not die, till (at last) a certain wizard deceived him, saying he would never die. That doctor did for him what he did from (his knowledge of) medicines.

كوقداو فعبد الكريم أدمير قدم فع ددروا كلم يتبه
د غمرما متا فمر عجو بم سكدم مع ذو كدا شر سنه
كمر بمر الديمر غمر مسر د غشكيا د كوكمر سكشع
ثكمنس بها كيدمر الدمير ميتبت غمر مسر كمر يه
تكمر د ميتبت ثكمر كدا شر أمة مسلمة يها متبمنة
ثكمر كدا شر حكمر لا ور وفيس أعمر غ شيبن فمر كمو
وفد بحو مر أبد عبد الكريم ميا جي ثكمر كدا نشم
ما سر و عجد سكيمسر و عجد بيجب بيتبن عمكا
فر فمنس حمر يمد كمو وبو سر وفد د د فمس
يب حمنمر أبمنس كدا فرث ميتبت حمر زامنر
وار فيكوريا شيبن وفد ميو شسشع بين غمر
مركمي غمر مر كمي بمب ميكو وبمر زوا [redacted] يكمكم
ثكمر بمر فمي بمبمر ميب شنا قمرعا غمنم درقمر
شدومر ثكمر دوبمي كمر شمت حمرو نبو كمو بمرو
د مكش و نبا شمتو حمر أيج ونها منك مي
ما غمنو ما أيكما مسر أنبد يا أيكنا د غدا غمنم

Sarkin nan ya ba shi dūkīa dayawa, aka-che bāwa dari, kuyenga dari, da dōki dari, da kōre dari, da sānia dari, mache da bajinin sānīa dari, da rāgō alif, da akwia alif. Ya ba shi tufāfi wadanda ba su [68]kidāyuw dōmin yawa, da wanin wanan, Ala shi ne masani. Chikin zāmaninsa ne aka-sām mālami bīu chikin Kāshina, māsu-gudu dūnia, māsu-tsōrō Ala. Sū-nan guda Muhamadu-Ibnumusina, sūnan guda kūa, Muhamadu-Dunmurn Kōwane daia chikinsu ya yi waazu, waazu mai-shiga chikin zuchīa, bai [bai] ji ba. Sai su-ka ba shi tsōrō dōmin su bar waazu. Ba su bari ba. Sarākai kūa, ba su ji ba, har mālamai nan su-ka-mutu. Chikin Kāshina kushew tasa sananīa che har yau, wurin yārō da baba ana-zīyāri tasa, ana-kīwo, ana-neman albarka da adua garēsu. Ama Wari-mai-kworia, chew shia, ya zamna shekara tokwas bāyan an-yi masa māganin, kar shi mutu. Ya mutu chikin shekara ta tara. Sāilin da ya mutu gardaman sarauta ta a-bko tsakānin yan sarākai. Sāshe su-ka-kashe sāshe, har aka-kashe kamar mutun alif chikin birnin Kāshina, tsakānin dā da bāwa. Saanan kanin Wāri ya chi sarauta, bāyan ya kashe dan Wāri.

This king gave him much wealth, it was said one hundred slaves, on hundred female slaves, a hundred horses, a hundred black tobes, an a hundred cattle, cows and bulls a hundred, and a thousand rams, an a thousand goats. He gave him robes which could not be counted b reason of their number, and things of this description, Allah he kno (what all). In his reign two learned men made their appearance i Katsina, men who renounced the world (and) who feared Allah. Th name of one was Muhamadu Ibnumusina, the name of the other also wa Muhamadu Dunmurna. Each one among them gave instruction, (such instruction as enters into the heart. He did not hear them. Then the made them afraid in order to dissuade them from preaching. They di not desist. The kings also did not pay any attention till these learne men died. In Katsina their graves are known till to-day, where young an old visit and guard, and at which blessings are sought by prayers for then Now Wari-mai-kworia, speaking of him, he lived eight years after he ha had the medicine made for him to prevent his dying. He died the nint year after (taking) it. When he died a quarrel about the kingdom aros among the king's sons. Half were slaying the other half until about 1,00 men were killed in the town of Katsina among both free men and slave Then the younger brother of Wari ruled after slaying the son of Wari.

سِرِكِنْشِ مِبَاشِ دُوكِيَا دَمْبَجُ اَكَبْ بَاوَدِ رِكِبَنْغُ
دِرِ دِدُوكِ دِرِ دَكُوبَمُدِرِ دَقَايِيَا دِرِ مَبْ دَبِجِنِ قَدَ فِيَا
دِرِ دَرَاغُو اَلِفْ دَاَكُمِ اَلِفْ مِبَاشِ قُدَاكِ وَدَ مُدَمِ بَا اَسْكَدَ اِيُوَا
دُوقَمْ بِجَوَا دَوَقِمْ وَقِمْ اَوْلَشِبِنُ مَسِنِ ثِكِرْ زَامِثْنِسِبِنِ اَكَسَامَ
قَدَ اَلِمِ بِيُو ثِكِرْ كَدَاشِرِ مَدَاسِغُدَ وَدَوِشِ مَدَاسِطُو رَوَالْ سُو
قَمْ غُدَ اَمُحَمَّدَ اِبْنِ مَسِنِ سُوقَمْ غُدَاكُو مُحَمَّدَ دَقَمْ رَا
كُوَافِي دَمْنِكِ مُسِ مِيُو وَعَظُ وَعَظُ مِيشِقِ ثِكِرْ دُثِيَا بَمْ
مَبِجَبَ سِي اَلِيمِ سِكِبَا اِشِرِطُو وُدُو مِرِ سِنِمِ اُوَعَظُ بِسْمِ نِبِيبِ
سِرَ اَكُمِ كُو مِسِجَبَ حَمْ مَدَ اَلِفْ مِرَ سُكُمْتُ ثِكِرْ كَدَاشِرِ كِشُوَا
قَسِ سِغُنِيَا قِثِ حَدَمِيُو وُدُمِيَا رَادَ مَبِ اَفَدَ زِيَا وَاقَسِرِ اَمَدَ
كِيُو اَمَدَ فِقَمْ اَلِيمْ كُو دَعَدَ غُمِ مُحَسِ اَمَدَ وَاوَمِبِكُمْ بِرِ ثِيُوَا
شِ مِغُ مُرِ شِكُمِ ثِكُوسِ بَامِيرِ اَنِمُسِ رَادَ غَنِمِ كُمْ اَثِمُتْ
بِغُثِ ثِكِرْ شِكُمِ قَثِرِ سَابِلِقُدَ بِغُثِ غُمْ دَمْرِ سِرِ وُقَمْ قَا
نِكِ حَكَ اَقْرِ بِنِرِ سِرَاكُمِ سَاشِي سِكِكِشِ سَاشِي حَمْ
اَحَكِشِ عَمْرِ مُتِرِ اَلِفْ ثِكِرْ بِمِ قَمْ كَدَاشِرِ مُكَدَ مُنْدَا
دَبَاوَ سِغُمْرِ فِنْدِ وَاوِثِ سِرِ اُفْ بَامِيرِ بِيَا حَكِشِ دَمُوَارِ =

Shi kuma ya tabata bisa Kāfurchinsa. Kāfurchi ya tabata chikin Kāshina har wakatin Bāwa-Dungaimāwa. Shi ne wanda Usmānu dan Fōdio ya fita daga Kāshina, shīa da mutāninsa su ka nufi [69] Marādi, su-ka-zamna chāna har yau. Danginsa sun kashe, su-na-yāki da dangin Usmānu dan Fōdio har yau. Ama Gōbir su-ka-tāru, su-ka-tabata bisa adīni, su-ka-tabata chikinsa har wakatin Bābari. Shi ne fārin wanda ya musāya suna, ta zama [70] bida, ya daukaka ginin Kāfurchi, ya yi girman kai. Māsu-waazu su-ka-yi masa waazu, bai karba ba, sai ya tabata bisa Kāfurchinsa har ya mutu. Bāchira ya chi sarauta, ya aikata kaman aikinsa, sai ya dada barna da batarwa, kunfan Kāfurchi ya daukaka chikin kasar Gōbir, sarā--kanta su-ka-yi girman kai, su-ka-sai da dīa, su-ka-aikata abinda su-ka-sō, har alāmari ya zama, kōwane sarki ya chi sarauta, sai shi auri budrūa dari. Sai su dai ba su san dafuan gīa ba, sai kadan chikinsu. Ba su chin musai, ama sāilin da zaa gaisua su-na-zuba kasa ga kainsu, su-na-bauta ma tūru, māsu-rikō

He again continued in heathenism. (And) heathenism continued in Katsina till the reign of Bawa-Dungaimawa. It was he Usmanu, the son of Fodio drove out of Katsina, he and his men, they went to Maradi, they settled there until to-day. His descendants continue to make war on the descendants of Usmanu, the son of Fodio, till to-day. But the (men of) Gobir assembled together and continued in the faith and dwelt in it till the reign of Babari. He was the first who changed the true faith, it became lax, he exalted (and) set up paganism (and) was arrogant. The preachers (of the faith) preached to him but he would not receive (their instructions), but persisted in his heathenism till he died. Bachira ruled over the kingdom, he did what his predecessor had done, he added to the evil he had done, and the harm, the foam from the wave of heathenism rose in the land of Gobir, its kings were proud. They sold free men, they acted as they wished until report had it that every king that ruled married one hundred maidens. But (the only redeeming point was) they did not know how to make beer, except a few among them, (and) they did not eat animals that had died a natural death, but when they greeted (their kings) they poured earth over their heads, they served idols. (Some) who cleaved to the faith

شيكم يتبت بسركد افر ثنس كد افرث يتبت ثكم
كدشر حمر وفتر بجا ار در غيدا وا شيبو ونْدم عثمان
دم فجوم بن ميجت دغم كداشر يشي دم قتا فنس سكنف مرادا
سكدم مر ثار حمر ميو دم فنس سنكبش سنا يا ك دم فق
عثما ودم فجوم بن حمر ميجو أما غوبر سكتا و سكنبت
بسر الدي مير سكنبف ثكفس حمر وفتر با مري شيبى
قدرز ونْدم يفسابن سثمر تغم بدم يدر ككى غفر
كد افرف ميي غمر مكم ما سوعدا سكيمس وعطا
بن كم باب سن يتبت بسر كد افم فنس حمر يمت
با ثمر ميث لسر وف يا أنكت بجهر أنكنس لسن يم دبمر ملى
دبتر ا كنقر كد افرث يدر ككى ثكم كسر غوبر لسرا
عنت لسكي غمر مكم سكليم دي سكد أنكت أبكم
سكسو حمر الأمري يغم كوفل سركم يث لسروت
لسن شعوو بدر ولادري لسن سوم بن بسسم دفو ففاب
سنكع ونكمس با اسثر مسن أما اسا ملنع دا اغيلثوا
سثان مب كسو غكنس سنا بجم قام قتور ما اسركو

su-na chikinsu, sāilin kadan ne, walākantatu, bābu girma garēsu. Su-ka-tabata bisa hakanan har wakatin [71] Bāwa-jan-gwarzō. Ya dada Kāfurchi, ya yi girman kai, har aka-sāmu mālami chikin zāmaninsa, mai-gudun dūnia, mai-bautar Ala, ana-che masa Alhaji Jibrīlu Aka-che, chewa shīa, ya tafi tun Gōbir, ya je Maka, ya yi haji, ya zamna chana kama shekara ishirin. Aka-che ya zamna Masar shekara gōma sha takwas. Ya zamna chikin Maka shekara bīu, saanan ya kōmō zūa Gōbir. Ya waazche su sābunta dare da rāna, bōye da bayene. Su-ka-ki abinda ya fadi, sai su-ka-nufi kashinsa. Sarākunan Hausa duka su-ka-gama kai bisa su-kashe shi. Ba su iya ba. Mālamai sun kashe Kālāwa, sāilin ama ba su iya fadin wani abu chikin sani, sai bōye, dōmin tsōrō sarākai. Sai Alhaji-Jibrīlu, chewa shia, yā tsaya da waazu, ya yi kōkari bayane, ba su iya sun kashe shi ba. Shi kūa bai iya yā hane su ba ga abinda su ke chiki. Sai su-ka-dada shishigi da Kāfurchi-chikin wakatin nan.

---

were (still) among them, at that time only a few (and) without power influence among them. And they continued thus till the time of Baw jan-gwarzo. He went on (living) in heathenism. He was arrogant a learned man was found in his reign, one who had fled from the wor one who served Allah. He was called Alhaji-Jibrilu. It was said, speaki of him, he went from Gobir, he came to Mecca and performed the pilgrima and resided (away) there twenty years. It was said he lived in Egy eighteen years. He stayed in Mecca two years, and then returned Gobir. He instructed them each new day and night, in secret and open They refused the thing (message) he brought and thought to kill hi All the kings of Hausa(land) plotted to slay him. They could not. T malamai were in Kalawa at that time, but they could not speak from th (store) of knowledge for fear of the chiefs. Only Alhaji-Jibrilu, speaki of him, he stood (fast) in (his) preaching and strove openly (and) they w not able to kill him. He could not, however, prevent them (doing) the e they dwelt in. And they continued in evildoing and heathenism in t reign.

سنر نكنس تبا ملين كد فنبو ولا كنتو بدا ماب غمر مى
غم مكس سكنبت بمسر مكنش مر وفتن با ارجبن غمر زو
يدم كدافبرث ميو غمر مر كحى حمر اكسادم مدالم ثكر
زامنش ميكد زدوفر ميبوفمر ال امدا بثمس الحج جبريل
الكث بثوا انشي يب تك ثمر غوبم بجي مك بيو جج يج
مر ثر كمر بشكر عشر اكث مد مر محمر بشكر
غوم شا تكوس يغ مر ثكر مك بشكر بيو سعنر
يكو مو دو غوبم يو عغنبس تسا منت دوري رامى
بوبى دبنبى سكك ابند يبقع تسر سكنى كنش نس
تسر اكنر موسر دك سكلغم كتي مسر سكيشنر ح
بسعياب مدالم سنكشو فدا ضار اسا ملن اما
با اسعي وقح فوفاب ثكر تسر اسن وريي دومر
طوو تسر اكي تسى الحج جبريل ثوا انشى يا
طى وعلا يمر كوكرى مبنر بسعى سنكبشب
نيكو بنكى با هنسب غم بنر سبكنكم
تسر سكم دشنغ دعا فرث ثكرو فتنس

Aka-haifi Usmānu dan Fōdio, sāilin da Alhaji Jibrilu ya mutu. Usmānu dan Fōdio ya fāra waazu kadan kadan, har Bāwa-jan-gwarzō ya mutu. Dan uwansa, Yaakubu, ya zamna mazamninsa. Sāilin Usmānu ya bayana waazu sarari, har ya aikata abinda ya aikata, yā kāre.

Mun[72] takaita zanche nan. Ala
shi ne mai-katari. Yā kāre.
Tsīra da aminchin Ala
shi tabata ga anabi.
Amin.

(Then) Usmanu, the son of Fodio, was born at the time when Alhaji Jibrilu died. Usmanu, the son of Fodio, began to preach little by little ti (the time when) Bawa-jan-gwarzo died. His brother Yaakubu reigned in hi stead. Then Usmanu proclaimed (his) preaching openly till he did wha (all the world knows) he did (and) finished. We have drawn the histor to a close.

Allah, he is the one who knows all. It is finished.

The salvation and blessing of Allah be upon the prophet. Amen.

أَكَعَيِّ عُثْمَانُ دَنْ فُودِيُ لَسَامِلْنْدَ أَلْحَجْ جِبْرِيلْ

يَمُتْ عُثْمَانُ دَنْ فُودِيُ يَقَارَ وَعَظْ كَدَرْكَدْ نْ

تَرْمَبَا وَجَنْ غَمْزُ وَيَمُتْ دَنْ فُودِيُ مَسَرْ بَفُوبْ =

يَمْ مَرْ مَدْ مُتَنْفُسْ سَامِلْنْ عُثْمَانُ يَبِيَّرْ وَعَظْ

سَرُورَى تَمْ مَيَأَنْكَتَنْ أَبِنْ مَيَأَنْكَتَنَا يَأَكَاوُسْ

مُنْتَكِنْتَ دَمْنْشِ فَمْ ال

شَيْنِ هِكْتِنَى مَاكَارِي

طَمَّتْ ادامنتشرال

شَتْبِتْ غَمْزُبْ

آمِينْ

PART II

'STORIES ABOUT PEOPLE'

No. 1.

[1] Bismi alāhi alrahmami alrahimi, wa sala alāhu ala mam la nabiu baadahu

Wanan [2] bābi ne na gātanar mutāne.

[3] Gātanan, gātanan, ta je, ta kōmō. Bāwan sarki shi ke da [4] maatansa, aka-che ta-na-neman maza. Ya che karīa, maata ta ba ta neman maza. Sai ranan wata tsōfūa ta che masa, 'Kulum idan ka tafi fādanchi, sai ta je wurin maza'; sai tsōfūa ta che, 'Yau ka hau dōkinka, ka che zaa ka kauyē, ka kwāna.' Sai bāwa sarki ya damra sirdi, ya hau, ya kāma hainya, ya tafi. Da marenche ya yi, [5] bai zaka ba, shi kūa ya che,

---

In the name of Allah, the Compassionate, the Merciful, and may the peace of Allah be upon him, after whom there is no prophet. This is the beginning of a story about people. A story, a story. Let it go, let it come. A slave of a chief had a wife, and it was said of her she was of a loose character. He (the husband) said it was a lie, (and) that his wife did not go after men. At last, one day, a certain old woman said to him, 'Always when you go to the council then she (your wife) is after the men'; and the old woman said, 'To-day mount your horse (and) say you are going to an outlying village (and) you are going to sleep there.' Then the chief's slave saddled up, mounted, took the road and went off. When evening came he had not come, for he had said,

بسم الله الرحمن الرحيم وصلى الله على من لا نبي بعده

ؤمن يعدل منكن ∴ فغالقنت ∴

متابكي

نعدا فنن نعدا فنن ∴ قجي ∴ نكو موش ∴ بداو

تسركم ∴ نشبكد ما فنفش أكش ∴ نفنا فجمن ∴

مذا ∴ يتب فكريا ∴ ما ألتاف ∴ نبلف ∴ نمر مذا ∴

سن ومر ∴ اقطوفوا ∴ نمتب ∴ مس ∴ كلم ∴ إدن ∴

كتب فاد فشم ∴ السن تجمي ∴ ور فمذا ∴ السن طوفوا

تتب ∴ ييجو ∴ نمحو ∴ دو كنك ∴ نكب ∴ دا أك

فوبن ∴ عكوار ∴ السن ماو ∴ السركم ∴

يمر ∴ السرد ∴ يعجو ∴ يكلام ∴ تغمن ∴ متو

دمجم مبت ∴ ميتي ∴ مينم كب ∴ تشيكو ∴ يابد

'Ina je, baa ni kōmōwa,' [6] Maatar kūa, ashe [7] galādīman gari, da wāzīri, da wani bāwa(n) sarki, sūnansa Dūnīa, [8] baubāwa ne, da fitar mai-gida, sai maata ta aika gun farkonanta, ta che 'Mai-gidana yaa tafi kauyē, ama baa shi kōmōwa yau, sai gōbe.' Sai [9] galādīman ya sai nāman arba da shinkāfar alfin, wāzīrin gari ya sai nāman arba da shinkāfar alfin. Bāwan sarki Dūnīa ya sai nāman arba da shinkā-far alfin, aka-kai mata. Dare ya yi, sai galādīma ya zo, aka-sainya masa shinkāfa da nāma, shi-na-chi. Sai ya ji mōtsin tākalmin wāzīri. Sai ya fāda karkashin [10] gadō, aka-dauki shinkāfa, aka-rūfe.

'I am going and shall not return.' Now the wife (possessed some lovers), the galadima and the vizier, and a certain of the chief's slaves, a foreigner, by name 'The World', and on the master of the house going out, then the wife sent to (these) her lovers, she said, 'My master will go to an outlying village, and he will not return to-day but to-morrow.' Then the galadima brought four thousand cowries worth of meat and two thousand cowries worth of rice to bring to the woman. When night came the galadima arrived, the meat and rice was set out, and he ate. Then he heard the sound of the slippers of the vizier, and down he fell under the bed, and the rice was lifted and covered up.

ازقابى ∴ بما انكو موو ا ∴ هدقتر كو ∴ أشى ∴ غما ديما

غم ∴ دوازيم ∴ دوقبا او ∴ سركم ∴ سو ففس ∴

دوقس ∴ بجوبدا وقبى ∴ دجتر ميغدا ∴ سن قدامى ∴ م

تمايك ∴ غنعم كننتن ∴ تبا لا ميغدا اقى ∴ يبدأقه

كحوبى ∴ أما ∴ بدأشكو موو ا ∴ يجو ∴ سن غو بس ∴

سن غدا ديما ∴ يلسن ∴ قدا مرن ∴ أورب ∴ م شنكا بقر ∴ البقر

وازيم فغر ∴ يلسن قدا مرن ∴ أورب ∴ م شنكا بقر ∴ البقر ∴

بدا او ∴ سركم ∴ دوقس ∴ يلسن ∴ قدا مرن ∴ أورب ∴ د شنكا

بقر ∴ البقر ∴ أككيمت ∴ دومبيتن سن غدا ديمد

يخو ∴ أكسبا مسن ∴ شنكا بقى ∴ دقام ∴ شنلف ∴

سن ∴ يجى ∴ موجمر ∴ قدا كلمر ∴ وزيم ∴ لسن يقادر ∴

فمر كشر ∴ غدو ∴ أكدم وك ∴ شنكا بقى ∴ أكروم

Ashe wāzīri ne. Sai ya zamna; shi kuma
aka-ba shi shinkāfa da nāma, shi-na-chi. Sai ya ji
mōtsin tākalmin Dūnīa, shi-na-che
mai-gida ne. Sai ya fāda karkashin-gadō.
Sai ya iskē [11] galādīman [12] zamnē. Sai ya-che,
'aa galādīma ne?' Ya che, 'I,' ya che, 'mu rufa ma kaimu
asīri,' ya che, 'Bābu laifi.' Su-na-nan, zamnē.
Sai aka ba Dūnīa nasa rabō; shi kuma
shi-na-chi. Sai su-ka-ji mōstin kōfatō
dōkin mai-gida, [13] yā zō. Sai Dūnīa ya yaada
akoshin tūō; ya fāda karkashin gadō.

Sure enough it was the vizier. Then he sat down, (and) he also was given rice and meat. He ate. Then he heard the noise made by the slippers of him called 'The World'. He thinks it is the master of the house. So he fell under the bed, when he discovered the galadima sitting (there). Then he said, 'Oh, it's the galadima, is it?' And he said, 'Yes,' (and) said, 'Let us keep this secret.' And he said, 'There is no harm in that.' They were sitting there then, (and the one called) 'The World' was given his share, and he also was eating. Then they heard the hoofs of the horse of the master of the house; he has come. Then 'The World' threw away the plate of food (and) fell under the bed.

أبشن ؞ كوارزميم فلن ؞ لسن يدخ ممن ؞ شيكم ؞ =

أكبداشن ؞ شنكافن ؞ دنقدام ؞ شناف ؞ لسن يج

موطن ؞ قداكلمن ؞ دورفيد ؞ شناف ؞

مينفدا بلن ؞ لسن ؞ يقدام ؞ فنكشن ؞ غمدو ؞

لسن ؞ يداسبكن ؞ غملادي يمد ؞ دمنبن ؞ لسن يب

أأ ؞ غملادي يمنبن ديبن ؞ دإء ؞ ميب ؞ مرقمكيم

أسيمر ؞ ميثا ؞ يماب ؞ اليفي ؞ لسنافن ؞ دمنبن

لسن ؞ أكبدو رفيا ؞ فداسن بوا ؞ شيكم ؞

شناف ؞ لسن ؞ لسكج ؞ موطن ؞ كوقبو

دوكن ؞ مينلدا ؞ يادو ؞ لسن دونيد ؞ مييادم

أكيشن قدورو ؞ يقاد ؞ فنكشن ؞ غمدو ؞

Sai Dūnīa ya gani mutum. Sai ya che, [14]'Ke wācheche anan?' Sai galādīma da wazīri su-ka-che, 'Mu ne.' Sai Dūnīa ya che, 'Galādīma me ta kāwō [15] ki nania?' Sai su-ka-che, 'Dōmin Alla, Dūnīa ka bari mu rufa makanmu asīri.' Sai Dūnīa ya che, 'Tō, ku yi kulum.' Sai su-ka-yi shirū; mai-gida kūa shi-na wurin dōkinsa, [16] shi-na--kunche sirdi; bai sani ba. Sai ya che maata ta ba shi rūa, shi yi wanka. Ta ba shi rūa, ya yi wanka. Sai ya shiga dāki, ya zamna bisa gadō. Sai maata ta che, 'Sannu da zūa.' Sai ya [17] gaza amsāwa, shi-na--mamāki, shi-na-che, 'Dūnīa, Dūnīa.' (Dōmin da aka-yi masa karīa, aka-che [18] mātasa ta-na-neman maza, ga shi ya zō bai ga kōwa ba), shi-na--fadi, 'Dūnīa, Dūnīa.' Maata tasa ta-na-che,

---

Then 'The World' saw a man (there). He said, 'Who are you?' Then the galadima and the vizier said, 'It is we.' Then 'The World' said, 'You, galadima, what brings you here?' And they said, 'For the sake of Allah, World, let us keep this secret among us.' And 'The World' said, 'All right, keep silent.' Then they kept still. The master of the house meanwhile was at his house taking off the saddle, he did not know. Then he told his wife to give him water to wash. She gave him water and he washed. Then he entered the house and sat on the bed, and his wife said, 'Greetings to you on your coming.' He did not reply, he was wondering and saying, 'The World, the World' (because he had been lied to and told his wife went after the men, and behold, he had come and saw no one). And he kept saying, 'The World, the World.' His wife said,

لسن دو فيبا ؛ يخنم ؛ متن ؛ لسن يحب ؛ بحو ابب ؛ أقمن ؛

لسمن ؛ غمدا ديم ؛ دو او بيم ؛ سكحب ؛ مو فمن لسن

دو فيبا ؛ يحب ؛ غدا ديم ؛ متكدا وك ؛ مثمن ؛ لسن

سكحب ؛ دو مين ؛ آن ؛ دو فيبا ؛ كمبر ؛ مر فمكنم ؛ أسير

لسن دو فيبا ؛ يحب ؛ مو ؛ كحن ؛ كلمم ؛ لمن ؛ لسكن ؛

شمر و ؛ مبكدا ؛ كحو ؛ شندا و فدو كمس ؛ شد ؛

كمب ؛ لسرد ؛ مسيب ؛ لسن يحب ؛ مامن ؛ قبداش

روا ؛ شيحو مكن ؛ قبداش ؛ روا ؛ بيحو نكن ؛ لمن ؛

يشغ ؛ داك ؛ يحم من ؛ مسقدو ؛ لسن ؛ مامس

مب ؛ لسنو ؛ دو آن ؛ لسن يحد ؛ امسدا وا ؛ شدا

مامدك ؛ مشداب ؛ دو فيبا ؛ دو فيبا ؛ دو قمن

داك يقمس ؛ كمر ؛ آن كحب ؛ مدا قلس ؛ مقدا بقمن ؛

مدا ؛ غداش ؛ يدو ا ؛ مبحع ؛ كحوا ؛ ب ؛ لشد

قحي ؛ دو فيبا ؛ دو بيا ؛ مامدا اقمس ؛ منداب ؛

'Me ya fāru mai-gida?' Sai Dūnīa baubāwa shi-na-che da shi ake yi. Ashe ya yi fushi. Sai ya che, [19] 'Ke ya dulin wa--nan Dūnīa ki ka lena, Dūnīa kadai ki ka gani, ba ki gani galādīma da wāzīri ba, sai Dūnīa, dōmin kin lena Dūnīa?' Sai kōkūa ta kable chikin dāki. Sai galādīma da wāzīri su-ka-fita da gudu, su-ka-bar Dūnīa da mijin maata, su-na-kōkūa. Tsōfūa ta-na-kuwa, ta-na-che, gudunmawa, har aka-zō, aka-raba su. Gari ya wāye, aka-kai sharaa wurin sarki. Sai mai-maata ya [20] maida magana. Sai fādanshi ya pashe da dārīa. Sai sarki ya che, 'Ina galādīma da wāzīri?' Aka-che ba su zō ba. Sar--ki ya che 'Atafi, agani lāfia'. Aka-je

---

'What is the matter, master?' Now he (by name) 'The World', the foreigner, thought it was to him he was speaking. Truly he waxed angry, and spoke, saying, 'You ——, is it (him called) "The World" only you have to find fault with? Look, do you not see the galadima and the vizier, but only "The World", seeing that it is "The World" you are finding fault with (only)?' On that all was confusion in the room, and the galadima and the vizier ran out, and left him called 'The World' and the woman's husband fighting. The old woman was shouting and calling for help. They (people) came and separated them. Next morning the matter was brought before the chief, when the woman's husband stated the case, but the councillors split themselves with laughing, and the chief said, 'Where are the galadima and the vizier?' and he was told they had not come. And the chief said, 'Let some one go and see if all is well with them.' (And) they went

بيقارُ ∴ مبغدا ∴ تَسِنْ دُوفِيا ∴ بَمُوبادُو ∴ اِشْدَافْ
دَشِيَا اَبِحِنّ ∴ اَشِيَا أُبِّيفَشِمْ ∴ تَسِنْ مِيفْ ∴ بِكِيّدُو اِشْكُو
فَمّ ∴ دُوفِيَا ∴ يِكَحَلِنْ ∴ دُونِيَا كَدَمّ ∴ يِكَكَفَمْ
بِكَفَمِ ∴ غَمَدَا دِيمْ ∴ دَوَازِبِرِقْ ∴ تَسِنْ دُونِيَا ∴ دُوقَمْ
كَنْلِنّ ∴ دُوفِيَا ∴ تَسِنْ كُوكُونْ تَكَبَلِنْ ∴ تَكَسْ
دَاكِ ∴ تَسِنْ ∴ غَمَدَا دِبِيمْ ∴ دَوَازِبِمِ ∴ تَسْكَفَة ∴ دَغُمْ
تَسَكَبِمْ ∴ دُونِيَا ∴ دَمِجْنَمَا أُقَنْ ∴ تَسَنَا كُوكُوّ ∴
كُوفُوا ∴ تَقَنَاكُوّ ∴ قَنَافْ ∴ كَمُدْ نَفُوا ∴ تَمْ
اَكَخُو ∴ اَكَمْ بَدَاسِنْ ∴ غَمِيتُوايِنْ ∴ اَكَكِنْ ∴ شَمْ عَ
وُفُسِنْ كَمْ ∴ تَسِنْ فِيمَا أُقَنْ ∴ يَجِيكَ ∴ اِمْكَفَنْ ∴ تَسَنْفُ
قَادَنْشِمْ ∴ بِيكَشِنْ ∴ دَدَّاوِيَا ∴ تَسِنْ تَسِنْكَمْ ∴ مِيفْ
إِقْمَا غَمَدَا دِبِيمْ ∴ دَوَازِمِيمِ ∴ أَكِفْ ∴ جَلَدُوفِ ∴ تَسِمْ
كَمْ ∴ مِيفْ ∴ اَنْقِفْ ∴ اَغَمِّمْ ∴ لَابِقِعِنْ ∴ اَكِجِكِي ∴

aka ishe galādīma da waziri, baa su gida. Ashē sun shiga dāji, har wayau ba agansu ba, dōmin kumia. Dōmin hakanan mutum mai-girma bai kamāta shi yi aikin da bai kamāta ba. Shi ke nan.

[21] Kungurus kan kūsu.

---

and found that the galadima and the vizier were not at their house. Of a truth they had gone to the bush; and until now they have not been seen, for very shame. And the moral of this (is that) it does not behove a man of position to act improperly. That is all. Off with the rat's head.

أَكَدا اِشْبُر ⁘ غَلا دِ ميحُم ⁘ دَوارِ بِيم ⁘ بَدأُسُن غَدا ⁘ أَمْبَشِن

سُنْشِقَم ⁘ دَاإِم ⁘ حَمْرَ وَبَجُو ⁘ بَاأَغْبَلُسُبَ ⁘ دُرِقَّمْ

كُفَّمَّ ⁘ دُرِقَّم قَحَكَقَّم ⁘ مُشْتَرْ ⁘ مَيْقِحْ مَسَ ⁘ بِمَ

بَنْكَحَدا قَ ⁘ يِشَّسَ ⁘ أَيْكَرْ ⁘ دَبَيْنْكَحَا قَتِبَا ⁘ شِيبَكَمَّ

قُنْقُمْ سْنَ ⁘ كَحَمْ ⁘ كُوسَنْ ⁘

No. 2.

[1] Gātanan, gātanan. Wanan tāsūnīar
yārinya che. Wani mutun ke da yāyansa uku,
bīū maza, daia mache. [2] Machen ita ake sō.
Sai [3] baban wansu ya tafi da su dāji. Ya che
su je itāche. Da su-ka-je dāji, sai ya kāma ta.
Ya hau itāche da ita; ya-damre bissa itāche;
ya zō, ya-che, 'Yārinya [4] tā batche dāji, (ba su)
ba su gane ta ba. Sai su-ka-kōmō gida.' Su-na-
-kūka. Sai ubansu ya tanbaye su me ya fāru.
Su-ka-che, 'Kanwamu che ta batche chikin dāji, (ba mu)
ba mu gane ta ba, munyi nema mun gaji, ba mu gane ta ba.'

A story, a story. This tale is about a maiden. A certain man had three children, two boys and a girl, (and) it was the girl he loved. Then (one day) their big brother went with them to the forest (bush), telling them to come for sticks. And when they had reached the forest, he seized her (the girl), climbed a tree with her, (and) tied her on to the tree, (and) came (and) said, 'The maiden has been lost in the forest,' (and said) they did not see her, so they came home. They were weeping. Then their father asked them what had happened, (and) they said, 'Our young sister she was lost in the forest (and) we did not see her. We searched until we were tired, but we did not see her.'

غَمَا اتَقَنْ ∴ غَمَا اتَقَنْ ∴ اَقَمْ قَا طُوفِيَمْ ∴

يَدُ و فِيَتْبْ ∴ وَقَشْنْ ∴ بَكَدَ مِيَا بِيَقْسَنْ ∴ غُكَ

اَبَكْسُو ∴ اِمَّتْ ∴ مَبْقُمْ ∴ مَقْبْ ∴ دَمَّنْ ∴ دَا ∴ مَخَا ∴ مِيُّو ∴

بَتْ ∴ دَاجِ ∴ سُوَاُ ∴ يَنَجِدْ ∴ اَفْسَنْ ∴ مَبَيَّنْ ∴ لَسْمْ ∴

اَمَاقْ يَكَا لَسْنْ ∴ دَاجِ ∴ دُسْكَجَيْ ∴ اِقَامَتْبَنْ ∴ سُجَكَيْ

اِقَامَتْ ∴ مِسَنْ ∴ مُجَرَ ∴ بَكَّ مُجْ ∴ دَاقِّ ∴ اِتَاقْبْ ∴ يَحَوْ ∴

بُسْكَ ∴ دَاجِ ∴ قَتَا بَتْ ∴ رَفْمَنْ ∴ بِيدْ ∴ مِيقْ ∴ يَدُوا

سُنَا ∴ غِدَا ∴ مُوا ∴ كُكُو ∴ لَسْمْ ∴ بَسْقَجَنَبْ

اَرْ ∴ مَبْقَدْ ∴ مَيْشْجِبَسُ ∴ اَمْنْسَنْ ∴ لَسْمْ ∴ كُوكَيْ

مَقْغَ ∴ دَاجِ ∴ تُكْمْ ∴ تُتَجِبْ ∴ كُنُومْ ∴ سُكَجْ

بُجَنَبَتْ ∴ بِقُلْقَ ∴ مُنْقَجْ ∴ بَمَنْ ∴ مُنَّسْ ∴ بَمَلْقَبْتَبْ ∴

Sai ubansu ya che, 'bābu laifi.' Ana-nan wata rāna sai fatāke su-ka-zō, su-na-wuchewa chikin dāji. Ta ji maganansu. Sai ta-che, 'Kū, kū, kū, ma- -su gōrina, idan kun je [5] unguan tudu, ku gaida wana Hallabau, ku gaida wana Tanka-baka, ku-gaida wana Shadusa?' Sai fatāke su-ka-ji hakanan. Sai su-ka-che, tsuntsūa ke yin wanan abu. Sai kuma, ta kāra. Sai mādugun ayari ya-che, [6] shii-je shi-gani, kō menene ke yin hakanan. Sai ya tafi; ya je; ya iske yārinya bisa itāche, [7] daure. Sai ya-che, 'Masūrai kō masū-mutūa?' Yārinya ta che, 'Masū-

---

Then their father said, 'It cannot be helped.' Then one day traders came and were passing in the forest. She (the girl) heard their voices and she (sang) said, 'You, you, you, who are carrying kola nuts, if you have come to the village on the hill, greet my big brother Hallabau, greet my big brother Tanka-baka, (and) greet my big brother Shadusa.' When the traders heard this they said that birds were the cause of this (singing). Then again she repeated (the song). Then the leader of the caravan said he would go (and) see what it was that was doing (singing) thus. So he went off (and) came across the maiden fastened to the tree. And he said, '(Are you) alive or dead?' The maiden said, 'Alive,

سَنْ أُبَنْسَنْ مَجْ بَادُبْ ؞ لَيْجِمْ ؞ أَمَّا ڢُمْ ؞ وُقَرَانْ ؞

سَنْ قَتَدَ بَكِنْ ؞ سُكَذُرْ ؞ سُنَدَاوُ بُحَوَا ؞ ثِكِمْ دَامْ

ثَقِيجْ ؞ مَغَنْشَنْ ؞ لَسَمْ تَبَثْ كُوكُوكُو ؞ هَا

سُڢُورُوثْ ؞ إِادَّزْ ؞ كُڢْجِي ؞ مُنْغُوقَتُنْ ؞ كُغِيجِ

وُقَامْ ؞ حَلَّلْجُو ؞ كُغِيجِ ؞ وُقَامْ ؞ قَنْكَ ؞ بَكَنْ

كُغِيجِ ؞ وُقَامْ ؞ شَدُلَسْ ؞ لَسَنْ قَتَدَ بَكِنْ ؞ لُسْكِجِ

قَكَنْثَنْ ؞ لَسَنْ لَسَكَبْ ؞ طُمْ طَوَا ؞ بَكِيِّنْ ؞ أَلْقَمْ

أَبْ ؞ لَسَنْ كُحَمْ ؞ تَحَكَارْ ؞ لَسَنْ مَادُغُمْ ؞ أَيِمْ ؞

بَبَثْ ؞ لِشْحَجِنْ ؞ لِثِغَخِمْ ؞ كُومُبَنَبْ ؞ بَكِيِّمْ

تَكَنْثَنْ ؞ لَسَنْ بَتَڢْ ؞ بِجَنْ ؞ بِيَدَا لَسْكَنْ ؞ بِيَادُڢَنْ

بِسَّنْ ؞ إِقَدَاقْ ؞ دُورُنْ ؞ لَسَنْ مَبَثْ ؞ مَسُوارُسْ

كُومَسُو ؞ مُثُّو ؞ بَيَدُوڢَمْ ؞ مَتَبْ ؞ مَسُلُوا

rai (masurai).' Sai shi mādugu, dakainsa ya hau bissa itāche, ya kunche ta. Da wuri kūa, shi, [8] mādugun ya nemi haifua, bai sāmu ba. Sai ya che 'Wanan yārinya daka ina (daga enna)?' Sai yārinya ta che, 'Ubamu ya haife mu, mu uku, bīū maza, uwarsu guda. Ni kūa, ni kadaiche, gun uwata. Ubamu kūa da uwamu su-na-sō na, ba su sō yan uwana, dōmin hakanan baban wamu ya tafō da ni nan, ya rūde ni ya che mu tafi itāche, ya zō da ni nan, ya daure ni bisa itāche, ya tafi, ya bar ni. Ubanmu atājiri ne, dōmin hakanan, ya yi mani hakanan.' Sai mādugū

---

alive.' So the leader of the caravan himself climbed up the tree and untied her. Now long ago the caravan leader had wished for offspring, but he was childless. Then he said, 'Where is the maiden from?' And the maiden said, 'Our father begat us, we were three, two boys by one mother, I also alone, by my mother. Our father and mother loved (me), (but) did not love my brothers. And because of that our big brother brought me here, deceiving me by saying we were going for sticks. He came with me here, tied me to a tree (and) left me. Our father is a wealthy man, and because of that, he (my brother) did this to me.' Then the leader of the caravan

وَرِنْ اَسَتِ ⁘ شَيْبَا دُعُمْرِ ⁘ كَيْسَنْ يَحَوْ ⁘ مِسَنْ

اِقَدَفْ ⁘ يَكُنْبَتْ ⁘ دُوُرُ ⁘ كُوَّ ⁘ شَيْبَا دُعُمْرِ

يَا فِمِ ⁘ تَيْقُوَا ⁘ فَيْسَدُ مُقَ ⁘ اَسَرْيَتْ ⁘ كُوَقْسْ

85

يَا رِتَّ ⁘ دُكَاِمُرْ ⁘ اَسَنْ مَدُرِقْ ⁘ قَبْتْ ⁘ اُمَّمْ

يَحَنْجِمْ ⁘ مُوَاكَ ⁘ فِيُّوْمَدَا ⁘ اِمُوُلْسَنْ

غُدَا ⁘ فِيكُوَّ ⁘ يَكَدُ فِتْ ⁘ غُمْلُكُوَا اَمْسِنْ

اُمَّجُمْ ⁘ كُوَّ ⁘ دُغُوَّمْ ⁘ سَنَاسُومُنْ ⁘ مِدُ اَسَنْ

سُو ⁘ يَنْغُوَ اَلمُرْ ⁘ دُوقَمْ ⁘ تَكَنَّرْ ⁘ يَبَّرْ ⁘ تَرْمْ

يَنْقُودُ فِيتَّرْ ⁘ يَادُو دِمُرِنْ ⁘ يَتْ ⁘ مَنْجِمْ

اِقَدَفْ ⁘ يَدُودُ رُفِمْ ⁘ قُنَّرْ ⁘ يَدَّوْرُ مُرِنْ ⁘ مِسَنْ

اِقَدَفْ ⁘ يَنْقَفْ ⁘ يَبَّرُو ⁘ اُمَنْمُ ⁘ اَقَدْ جِرْ مُنْ

دُوقِمْ ⁘ هَكَنَّرْ ⁘ يَبَّمْرْ ⁘ تَكَنَّرْ ⁘ اَسَمْ هَدَا دُغُمُو

sai ya che, 'Ni kūa, kin zama dīāna.'
Sai mādugū ya kai ta gida; ya yi jinya,
har ta warke. Ta-na nan gunsa har ta issa
aure. Ta zama budrūa, bābu irinta kō-
-ina. Da kōwane [9] bigire ana-jin lābāri-
-nta, ana-zua garin kalō(n)ta, har ranan
shi baban wansu, ya balaga, bai sāmu
maata ba. Sai ya ji lābāri, aka-che wani a-
-tājiri shi-na da dīansa, gari kaza,
sararin nan, bābu kamanta. Sai shi kuma ya je gun
ubansu, ya che ya ji lābārin dīar wani atājiri,
ita shi ke sō. Sai ubansa ya gama masa

---

said, 'As for me, you have become my daughter.' So the leader of the caravan took her home (and) nursed her till she recovered. She remained with him until she reached a marriageable age, and grew into a maid whose like was nowhere. And whenever she was heard of, people came to look on her, until a day (when) her elder brother reached manhood. He had not found a wife. Then he heard the report which said that a certain wealthy man had a daughter in such and such a village; in all the country there was not her like. Then he went to their (his) father (and) said he had heard about the daughter of a certain wealthy man (and) it was her he wished (to marry). So his father gave him

قَسْ يَيَبْ ∴ فِيكُوَ ∴ كَخْمَ تَمَ ∴ دِيتَاقِي ∴

لَسْ مَادُ غُوَا ∴ يَكَبْتَ يَمِدَا ∴ يَيِيِّجِنْ ∴

تَرْ قَمُوُ بُجَّر ∴ قَمَاقَّنْ ∴ غُنْسَلَ تَحْرَقَا بِسْ

أَوُبُكُن ∴ قَتَحَم ∴ يُمُدُوُر ∴ يَدَابُ ∴ إِرْقَتَ ∴ كُو

إِقَا ∴ ءكُوَرْقَّابُن ∴ بِيخِرُسَ ∴ آقَّا بِيرْ ∴ لَأُبْدُر

قَتَ ∴ أَقَادُرَّ ∴ غَمِرْ فَكَلُوق ∴ تَحْرْ ∴ وَقَّمْ

قِيبِيم ∴ تَبَّنْ ∴ وُقْسُنْ ∴ يَدَابْلَخْ ∴ يَيْسَامُ ∴

مَأْقَبَ ∴ لَهْنَ يِجِ لَأُبْدُر ∴ أَكَبْ ∴ وَقِيَا

تَادِجِرَ ∴ شِنَادَ ∴ دِيَّنْلَس ∴ غَمِرَكَدَا

لَسَرْ مِنْقَّن ∴ يَدَابْ ∴ كَحَقَّتَ ∴ لَهْنِشَبُكَّمَ ∴ يَجَنْ ∴ ءُ

أُبْقَسْ يَبَّ ∴ يَدَابِج ∴ لَأُبْدَارِ دِيَّمْ ∴ وَقِيَا تَادِجِر

∴ إِقَ ∴ يِشُبَكْسُوَا ∴ لَسَنْ أُمَقْلَس ∴ يَخَحَاقَلَس

kāyā; ya je wurin neman aure. Da ya tafi Ala ya yi masa katar, ya sāmu. Aka-ba shi yārinya. Su-ka-yi aure. Su-ka-zō gida, zaa shi [10] sa yārinya zane, yārinya ta kia. Kulum kakanan, sai idan su-ka-tafi gōna, sai ta daukō turmi, da tabarīa na zīnārīa, da ubanta ya ba ta. Ta daukō hatsin, da uwar miji ta ba ta, wai ta yi fura. Sai ta zuba-chikin turmi(n) zīnārīa, ta-na-daka, ta-na-fadi, 'Daka, daka, turmīna, [11] uba yā kōmō uban miji, waiō kaitōnia, uwa tā kō- -mo uwar miji, waiō turmīna.' Hakanan har ta kāre daka. Ta-na-kūka, ta-na-wāka

---

gifts, (and) he came to seek a wife in marriage. And Allah blessed his quest and he found what he sought, and the maid was wedded to him. They came home, but when he would consummate their union, she would not give herself to him; (and) it was always thus. Only, when they (all) went off to the farms she would lift her mortar and golden pestle which her father had given her, saying she was going to make 'fura' cakes. And she poured the grain into the mortar of gold and pounded and (sung) said, 'Pound, pound, mortar, father has become the father of my husband, alas for me! Mother has become the mother of my husband, alas, my mortar!' And so on till she had finished pounding. She was weeping (and) singing.

يبهلّس ؞ أرّ ؞ دمتّق ؞ أورس ؞ أورنقّمن ؞ يجلى ؞ كدايد
أرّس ؞ لسكمّ ؞ يمدارفمن ؞ أكبداشن ؞ يمسلام ؞ كتّرن
يمدارفن دفمن ؞ سيبداورنّ ؞ دأشن ؞ غدا ؞ سكذوا ؞
نمومن ؞ لسكتقين ؞ إدّن لسن ؞ حكفنّ ؞ كلّمن ؞ تفنّ ؞
نفدين نداويا ؞ دتبربدا ؞ قمرمم ؞ أكوا تمدّ لسن
؞ نعورن دحطمر ؞ أكو تمدّ ؞ يبدات ؞ دأبنتّ
تكمن ؞ تخدق لسن ؞ فرّ ويتمّ ؞ تنبات ؞ مجّ
قدي تمندا ؞ تسنادك ؞ يمنداويا ؞ دي ؞ تنرمم
؞ مو أبدايدكر ؞ تنرميبنا ؞ دكّو ؞ دكّو
قادكو ؞ أوا ؞ فيمّ ؞ كيتّو ؞ ويمّوا ؞ أبنرمجّ
تكتّنر ؞ أتنرميتن وبّوا ؞ نعورّ مجّ ؞ مو
؞ تتناواك ؞ تتناكوكي ؞ دك ؞ تنرنكار

Ashe wata tsōfūa na nan ta-na-ji abinda,
ta ke fadi. Kulum hakanan, sai ranan ta kwarmata
ma uwāyan miji. Sai ta che, 'Idan zaa ku gōna,
ke uwar miji ki fita, ki ba ta hatsi, ki che,
ta daka fura, zaa ki gona, idan kin fita,
ki labe, ki kōmō, ki shige daki, ki yi
kurum, ki ji abinda ita ke fadi.' Yau uwar miji
ta fita, ubansu ya fita, yāra da māta duka
su-ka-fita, su-ka-che, zaa su gōna. Aka-jima,
sai uwar miji ta kōmō, ta shiga dāki,
12 ta-na-kunche. Sai yārinya ta dauko turminta
na zīnārīa, da tabarīanta na zīnārīa, ta-na-

Now a certain old woman of the place heard what she was (saying). It was always so, until one day she told the mother of (the girl's) husband, and she said, 'When you are all about to go to the farm, do you, mother of the husband, come out, give her grain, (and) bid her pound "fura", as you are going to the farm. When you get outside steal away (and) come back, enter the house, (and) remain silent (and) hear what she says.' So the mother of the man came out, their father came out, the boys and the woman all came out, and said they were off to the farm. A little while after the man's mother came back (and) entered the hut (and) crouched down. Then the maiden lifted her mortar and golden pestle. She was

أَبْشُنْ ؞ وَرَقَ طُوفُوَا ؞ مَا فَقَّنْ ؞ قَمَنَاجِ ؞ أَمِنْدَ ؞

تَبَكُنْ ؞ قَدِ ؞ كُلُّمْ ؞ تَكَنَّنْ ؞ آسْ وَقَّنْ ؞ قَكُرْ مَتَا

مَغُوَايِنْ ؞ مِجِ ؞ لَسْ قَبْ ؞ إِدَّنْ ؞ دَاكُ ؞ غُوفَنْ

بِغُوزْمِجِ ؞ كِفِنْتَ ؞ كِبَادَتْ ؞ تَطِمْ ؞ كِبُ ؞

تَدَّكَ ؞ فُرَا ؞ دَأْكِ غُوفُمْ ؞ إِدَّنْ ؞ كِنْفِنْتَ ؞

كِلَبَنْ ؞ كِكُوفُو ؞ كِشِبْغَنْ ؞ دَاكِ ؞ كِسَّنْ ؞

كُرُمْ ؞ هِجِ ؞ أَمِنْدَ ؞ تَبَكُفِجِ ؞ مِيُو غُوزْمِجِ

تَفِنَّ ؞ أُمِنْسُنْ مِيفِتَنْ ؞ مِيدَوَا ؞ دَمَاقَحُنْ ؞ دُكُ

لُسَكَفِنْتَ ؞ سُكَبْ ؞ دَأْسُ ؞ فُوقَنْ ؞ أَكِجَحْ ؞

لَسْ غُوزْمِجِ ؞ تَكُومُوا ؞ تَشِغْ ؞ دَاكِ ؞

تَنَا كُنْبْ ؞ لَسْ مِيدَارِ فُنْ ؞ قَدَّ رُكُوا ؞ قُمْ مِنْتَ

؞ قَدِ مِيفَارُ تَنَّ ؞ دَقَيْرِ مِنْتَ ؞ قَدِ مِيفَارُ تُوْ ؞ قَنَا

wāka, ta-na-fadi, 'Daka, daka, turmīna, uba
ya kōmō uban miji, wayō turmīna uwa
ta kōmō uwar miji, wayō kaitōnia.'
Ta-na-yin wāka hakanan, ta-na-kūka da hawāye.
Uwa kūa ta-na dāki, ta-na-ganinta, har ta gama
abinda ta ke yi duka. Mutānen gida, da su-ka-tafi
gōna, su-ka-kōmō. Uwa ba ta che kō-
-mī ba. Da dare ya yi, sai ta gaya ma mai-gida, ta che
'Kā ji, kā ji, abinda yārinya nan ke yi.' Uba,
ya che, 'Kō yārinya da ta bache, kō ita che?'
Sai su-ka-che, 'Ama idan ita che, akwai wani tambō
ga bāyanta, tun ta-na [13] jārīriya, aka-bar ta
dāki wurin wuta, ya kōne ta?' Aka-kirāwō ta.

---

singing and saying, 'Pound, pound, my mortar, father has become (my) husband's father, alas, my mortar! Mother has become (my) husband's mother, alas for me!' She was singing thus (and) shedding tears, the mother also was in the room and was watching her until she had done all she had to do. When the people of the house who had gone to the farms came back, the mother did not say anything. When night came, then she told her husband; she said, 'Such and such the maid did.' The father said, 'Could it possibly be the maid who was lost?' Then they said, 'But if it is she there is a certain mark on her back ever since she was an infant, she had been left in a house with a fire (and) it had burned her.' She was summoned.

أبر ∴ قرمينا ∴ ككه ∴ دك ∴ قنا فج ∴ كواك

= عوار ∴ قرمينا ∴ وبيو ∴ مجر أبر ∴ اومو كدي

قمن ∴ أكبنو ∴ اجبو ∴ مجر عو ∴ اومو كدق

قوايص ∴ د كمو كو ∴ قنا كو ∴ قنكمت ∴ كواك ∴ قنا

قمح ∴ تنت ∴ عم قنا ∴ كداقن ∴ كوا عم

بنكسد ∴ ادع ∴ مكبا ∴ قنا ∴ كد ∴ قمكبت ∴ فنأ

كوه ∴ بنبت ∴ عوا ∴ اومو كوكس ∴ قمو عم

قبت ∴ ادكبمهم ∴ قمقن ∴ لسن ∴ ميبيم ∴ دكد ∴ ميب

أبر ∴ كمن ∴ قنبيو ∴ ميد ∴ أفند ∴ كمدكن ∴ كاد

∴ قبت ∴ أوكو ∴ قبت د ∴ قمنو ∴ بوأك ∴ قبت

وقنسو ∴ فوكأ ∴ قبت ∴ أكد ∴ أمدأ ∴ قبت كسلس

∴ قركبأ ∴ قريجبد ∴ قنتقت ∴ قنيب ∴ لبقع

∴ قنودا ∴ أككا ∴ قبوكي ∴ قوقرو ∴ كاد

Aka-gama ta da Ala da anabi aka-che, 'Mutume nan,
da ya yi maki aure nan, ubanki ne, kō kūa
anba shi rikō ne?' Sai yārinua ta kīa
ta fadi. Aka yi, aka yi, ba ta fadi ba. Sai [14] uban
ya che, 'Kāwō bāyanki en gani.' Ta juya
bāyanta. Su-ka-ga tanbo, wanda wuta
ta kōne ta tun tana jārīria. Sai
su-ka-che, 'Ashe hakana ne, tunda fārin
da ki-ka-zō dōmin me ki (ki) gaia mani?'
Sai su-ka-sani diarsu che. Sai
su-ka-aike gun ubanta, wanda
ya tsinche ta, aka-gaia masa kaman da aka-yi.

They adjured her by Allah and the Prophet (and) said, 'This man who gave you in marriage, is he your father or were you given to him to be brought up only?' But the maiden refused to answer. Try as they could they could not get an answer. Then the father said, 'Present your back that I may see.' She turned her back, (and) they saw the scar where the fire had burned her when she was an infant. Then they said, 'Truly it is so. From the first when you came why did you (refuse) to tell me (us)?' And they knew it was their daughter. And they sent to her (foster) father, the one who had found her, and he was told what had happened.

أكلمداف ∴ دأل ∴ دأقب ∴ أكب ∴ منبمر ∴

دميتهك ∴ أفرومتر ∴ أمنكبثر ∴ كوكو ∴

أبدلثر رفوبي ∴ لسني مطرفمر ∴ قفر

تبجر ∴ أكمر ∴ أكمر ∴ بتقديبب ∴ لسع أبمر

يمثب ∴ كداور ∴ مدابنك ∴ إنكفنم ∴ تبجوس

بدابنتة ∴ لسكغ ∴ مسبو ∴ ومدو مرش

تكوفنة ∴ مفنتنابدار بيمر ∴ السر

لسكث ∴ أبشر مكنرمار ∴ مفندقاورش

دعكذوا ∴ دوقمرجبكر ∴ كغيامرش

لسمر لسكسر ∴ حميمر لسث ∴ لسمر [redacted]

لسك أيكمر ∴ عمر ∴ أمنتة ∴ ومد [redacted]

يمطنبنة ∴ أكغيامسر ∴ كحمر ∴ دأكي

Sai shi kūa ya che, ' Bābu laifi ina rōkō
ku ba ni yārinya, idan nā ga wani, in ba shi.
Sai su kuma su-ka-ki yarda.' Miji kūa, da ya ji
hakanan, sai ya dauki kwari, da [15] bakā tasa,
ya shiga dāji, ya rataye kainsa, ya mutu. Mafārin
kiyaya [16] yan uba ke nan. Shi ke nan, [17] kungurus
kan kūsu.

And he said, 'There is no harm done. I beg you give me the maiden. If I have found another I shall give her to him (the husband).' But they (the girl's real father and mother) refused to consent to this. As for the husband, when he heard this he took his quiver and bow. He went into the forest (and) hanged himself. He died. And this was the beginning of hatred among the children of one father by different mothers. That is all. Off with the rat's head.

اَسَنْ شِيكُوَ ؞ يَبثْ مَلُبُ ؞ اَيْبِجِمْ ؞ اِقَدَرْ وُكُوَ

كبَدَرْ ؞ يدَا وُنْمَ ؞ اِدَّنْ ؞ قَاعمُوَنْ ؞ اِنْبَداشِ ؞

اَسَعْ لِسُو كُحَّمْ ؞ لِسكِيَرْدَ ؞ مِجْ كُحَّوَ ؞ دَ بِجِ

مَكَنَّرْ ؞ اَسَنْ يَحَرْ وُكِ ؞ كُخُوْرِ ؞ دَ رَبكا اِقَسَرْ ؞

يَلْتُعَ دَاِمْ ؞ يَمَا اِقَبَّيُ ؞ كَيْسَرْ ؞ مَهُشْ ؞ مَقَارِنْ ؞

فِيَّرْ ؞ يَنْلُبُ ؞ كَبَسْتَّرْ ؞ شِيبكيَّنْرْ ؞ فُنْكُرْسْ ؞

كُرْقُوسْ ؞

No. 3.

Wanan tātsūnīar kōnan dāji che.

[1] Gātanan, gātanan, ta je, ta dāwō. Sarki
ya bari aka-sa ma dāji wuta. Aka-gewaye,
ba asāmu kōmi ba, har dāji ya kōnē
duka. Sai wani mugun yārō ya gani wani rāmē.
Ya gina, bai ga kōmi ba, sai wata tsōfūa
ta fitō achiki. Da fitowa, sai ta pasa kūwa,
ta che, 'Sarki [2] yā sa ma dāji wuta, kōwa
yā gani rāmenga yā wuche, sai kai ka gina,
yau [3] kaa gani. Sai ta fāfari yārō. [4] Sai
yārō ya buge ta da gatari. Ta tuma bisa,
ta zama shāfō, zaa ta fauche shi, sai ya halbe ta;

This tale is about a bush-burning. A story, a story. Let it go, let it come. A chief gave permission for the grass to be burned. They went all round but did not see anything (game) until all the grass was burned. Then a certain bad boy saw a hole and dug (there); he did not see anything. But an old woman came out, and on her emerging she screamed (with rage) and said, 'The chief has set fire to the bush; (hitherto) whosoever has seen this hole has passed on, and now you must dig it up. To-day you will see.' Then she sprang on the boy, but the boy struck her with his axe. Up she leaped and turned into a hawk, and when she was about to swoop down on him he shot at her;

وَفَمْ قَا طُو فِيَمْ كُو فَمْ دَا بِثْ ؞

نَمَا مَنْثَنْ ؞ نَمَا مَنْثَنْ تَبِجَمْ ؞ مَدَ اُوْ ؞ لَسَرْكِمْ ؞

يَبِيعَ ؞ أَكَسَلَامَ ؞ دَاجِ ؞ وُقَمْ ؞ أَكَغُوَيِي ؞

بَاْلسَامُ ؞ كُوجِمْبَ ؞ حَمْرَدَاجِ ؞ يَكُوفِي ؞

دُكْ ؞ لَسَرْوَفِمُو غُمْ ؞ يَبَاوُرْ ؞ يَغَنِيمْ ؞ وَفِرَابِرْ ؞

يَفِغْمْ ؞ مَيِغْ كُوجِيبِ ؞ لَسَرْوَنَطُوفُوا ؞ =

تَبِفُنُوا ؞ أَنَكِمْ ؞ دَبِفَنُوا ؞ لَسَرْ تَقَسَكُورْ ؞

قَبِثْ ؞ لَسَرْكِمْ ؞ يَبَا لَسَحَدَاجِ ؞ وُنَمْ ؞ كُوَرَا ؞

يَاغَنِيمْ ؞ وَابَنْغُ ؞ يَبَاوُثْ ؞ لَسِيكَمْ ؞ مَكَخِمْ ؞

يَبِقْ ؞ كَدَاغَنِمْ ؞ لَسَرْ تَبَلَقَمْ ؞ يَبَاوُرْ ؞ لَسَرْ

يَبَاوُرْ ؞ مَبُجُمَتْ ؞ دَغَا فَمْرِ ؞ مَنْثَمْ ؞ بِلَسَرْ ؞

قَدَهَمْ ؞ شَافُوَا ؞ دَأَنَبِقُو بِشَرْ لَسَرْ يَعَلِبَثْ

hakanan har ta rinjāye shi. Ya gudu. Shi-na-gudu, ya je,
ya iske zanzarō, shi-na-sāka. Sai zanzarō
ya che, 'Ina zaa ka.' Ya che, 'Wata tsōfūa ta korō ni.' Sai
zanzarō ya che, 'Zamna nan ta tafō.' Sai yārō ya za-
-mna. Shi-na nan, sai tsōfūa ta zō, bābu shāwara,
sai ta zābura, zaa ta kāma yārō. Sai zanzarō ya hade ta.
Sai zanzarō ya dauki sīlīli guda daia, ya ba
yārō, ya che, shi damre tsakar bāyansa. Sai
yārō ya damre shi, har bāyansa zaa shi tsumke.
Mafārin ka gani chikin zanzarō da girma
ke nan, tsōfūa ke chiki. Bāyansa kua,
da ya zama sīlīli, yārō ya damre shi

---

and so (they fought on) until she got the better of him. He ran away. (As) he ran he came across a wasp, he was weaving cloth. Then the wasp said, 'Where are you going?' He said, 'An old woman chased me.' Then the wasp said, 'Sit here (till) she comes.' So the boy sat down. He was there when the old woman came sure enough, and she sprang to catch the boy; but the wasp swallowed her. He lifted a single thread and gave it to the boy (and) said he must tie it round his middle. So the boy tied him up, until his back was almost cut in two. That is the origin of what you see; the wasp's belly is big, the old woman is inside. His back, which has become a thread, the boy bound it

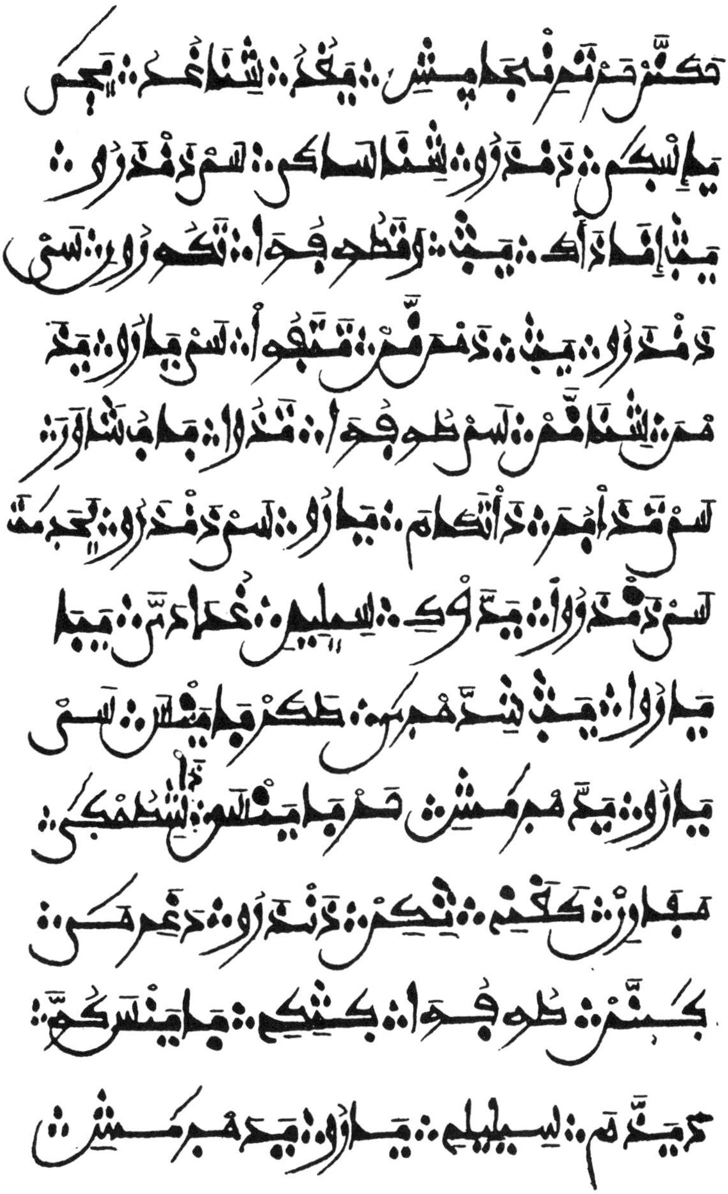

ga [5] tsara bāya. Shi ke nan, [6] kungurus
kan kūsū. Kūsu ba ya chi
kaina ba, sai in chi
kain dan banza.

---

at the middle, behind. That is all. Off with the rat's head. The rat will not eat my head, rather will I eat (its) head, son of a worthless fellow.

غَطَرَبِيَ ؞ شِيبِكَنْ ؞ فُنْفُرُسْ ؞

كَرْفُوسُ ؞ فُوسُنْ ؞ بِيَاثِ

كَيْنَا بَ ؞ لَسِبِلْ أَمْثِ ؞

كَرْ مُفَنْغَا ؞

No. 4.

Wanan tātsūnīar [1] gayā che.

[2] Gātanan, gātanan, ta je, ta kōmō. Sarki ya haifi
dīansa mai-keau, bābu kamanta achikin gari.
Sai ya che, 'Wanda ya yi nōma raana-gaya, gōnansa
ya wuche-kōwa, [3] shi ka aure dīa sarki. Yau,
ranan sarki ya yi gaya, atafō ayi masa nōma,
ama wanda ya yi nōma, ya wuche kōwa, shi ke da [4] maatā.'
Yau ashe hawainya ya ji tundadewa,
ya je, shi-na-chin māganin nōma. Yau da raanar gaya
ta zō, hawainya shi-na gida, bai fitō ba, har mā-
-sunōma su-ka-yi nōma, su-ka-yi nīsa. Kāna
hawainya ta zō. Da ya sāra hauya kasa sō daia,

This is a story about an alliance. A story, a story. Let it go, let it come. A chief begat a beautiful daughter; she had no equal in the town. And he said, 'He who hoes on the day the people come together and whose area hoed surpasses every one else's he marries the chief's daughter. So on the day the chief calls his neighbours to hoe (*gayā*), let them come (the suitors) and hoe for him. But he who hoes and surpasses every one else, to him a wife.' Now of a truth the chameleon had heard (about this) for a long time past, (and) he came along. He was eating hoeing medicine. Now when the day of the hoeing came round the chameleon was at home. He did not come out until those hoeing were at work and were far away; then the chameleon came. When he struck one blow on the ground with the hoe,

وقَمْ قَدْ اطُو فِيَّمْ عَيَابْ ::

غَدَ اقَنَّ نِي دَ اقَنَّ تَجِي تَكُو مُوا :: سَدْ كِي :: يَحَيْبِ ::

دِينَسَ :: مِيكُو :: بَدَبُ :: كَفَنْدَ :: اِثْكِيرْ غَمِي ::

لَسْ يَبَّثْ :: وَفَدْ يَبِّنُو مَو :: رَاقْ اَفْغَيَا :: غُمُو مَنْ لَسَّ ::

يَوُبْ :: كُوَا :: شِيكَكُو وُمَوْ :: دِمَّسَرْكِي :: يَوْ ::

وَقَّمْ :: لَسَرْكِي :: يَبِّي غَمَيْدَ :: اَقَجُوا :: اَيِمَسَ فُو مَى ::

اَمَّا وَقْدَ :: يَبِّ فُو مَيْ :: يَوُبْ كُوَا :: لِيَيكِدَ مَا قَرْ

يَوْ :: اَشَوْ :: قَو يِيمِنِّ :: يَدَجِ :: قَنْدَ دِمَوَا ::

يَجِي شِنَا قَرْ :: قَدَ غَيْنُ فُو مَى :: مَّيَوْ :: دَرَا قَرْ غَمِينَ ::

تَدُو :: قَو يِيمِنِّ :: لِشَنَا غَدَا :: يَبِيقُو بُ :: قَدْ مَا

لِسُو مَي :: لِسَكِّي :: فُو مَو :: لِسَكَّ مِيسَّ :: كَدَلِ

قَو يِيمِنْ :: تَجُوا :: دَيَّسْدَ :: قَو مَو :: كَلَّسْ :: سُوتَرْ

sai ya hau bisa hauya ya zamna. Sai hauya
ta kāma nōma, ta-na-tafia tar! har ta chika
da manōma, ta wuche, ta kai bākin [5] kunya.
Hawainya ya sabka, ya zamna, ya füta, kāna
manōma sun-ka-kāwō. Saanan sarki,
shi bai yarda ba, sai wanda ya yi gudu, ya tsēre
kōwa duka, shi ke aure dīarsa.
Sai [6] gumki ya che shi ya fi kōwa
gudu. Sai su-ka-yi gudu, sai hawainya ta zama
[7] tanpasua, ta tuma, ta mane ga wutsīar
gumki. Sai gumki shi-na-gudu, har ya wuche
kōwa, har ya kāwō kōfar gidan

---

then he climbed on the hoe and sat down, and the hoe started to hoe, and fairly flew until it had done as much as the hoers. It passed them, and reached the boundary of the furrow. The chameleon got off, sat down, and rested, and later on the (other) hoers got to where he was. Then the chief would not consent, but now (said) he who ran and passed every one, he should marry his daughter. Then the hartebeest said he surpassed every one in running. So they had a race. But the chameleon turned into a needle; he leaped (and) stuck fast to the tail of the hartebeest, and the hartebeest ran until he passed every one, until he came to the entrance of the house

لسن يعجوش ، ميسن قحوش ، ميحّمن ، لسن محوش ،

تكام فوموس ، قمنا تبجس ، قمن ، ممن مثنك

دمنومو ، تحوش ، تكس ماحكمن ، كمنيا

محويبس ، يلسبك ، ميحمن ، يمجوق ، يكاق

منومو ، لسكنكاور ، لسعقس ، لسن كم ،

شيبيبين دب ، لسن وقدبين غدن ، يجمبري

كووا ، دك ، شيبكس اوين ح ميس لسن

لسن غحكم ، ميش ، تشن ماق ، كووا ،

غمد ، لسن لسكس غدن ، لسن حوميس ، قمدّم ،

تنبوسوا ، تيشم ، قيمبس ، غحطيس ،

غمكم ، لسن غمكم ، شنا غمد ، قمن بحوش

كووا ، قمن يكاور ، كووقمن ، غمد

(gidan) sarki. Ya wuche. Sai hawainya ya saki wutsīar gumki. Ashe hawainya ya gani yārinya. Sai ya rungume ta. Kāmin gumki shi kōmō, sai ya tarda hawainya shi-na--rungume da yārinya. Sai gumki ya rika kūka da hawāye. Mafārin abinda ka ke gani ga idānunsa, kaman hawāye ke nan, tun ranan ya ke kūka, bai share hawāye ba.

[8] Kungurus kan kūsu.

---

of the chief. He passed it. Then the chameleon let go the hartebeest's tail; of a truth the chameleon had seen the maiden. So he embraced her, and when the hartebeest came along he met the chameleon embracing the girl. Thereupon the hartebeest began to shed tears, and that was the origin of what you see like tears in a hartebeest's eyes. From that day he has wept and not dried his tears. Off with the rat's head.

غد ملسركم ⁖ يجوش ⁖ لسى حويشّ ⁖ يلسك ⁖

وطيمّ ⁖ غمكم ⁖ أبش حويشّ ⁖ يدا عنم ⁖

يدوفم ⁖ لسى يمر نعجت ⁖ كدامر ⁖ غمكم ⁖

لشكو مجد ⁖ لسى يمترد ⁖ حويشّ ⁖ لشنا ،

ومغجو ⁖ ديدوفم ⁖ لسى غمكم ⁖ ميرك ⁖

كوكى ⁖ دحواير ⁖ مقاور ⁖ أمند كبكنم

غمدا مثلس ⁖ كمر ⁖ حواير ⁖ بكنر ⁖ مثمر قمر

⁖ يبكوكى ⁖ ويشا وحواييب ⁖

كنكر سن ⁖ كمر قحو سن

No. 5.

Wanan tātsūnīar
[1] shasharbō mani che.

Wani mutum ke da [2] mātansa bīū, guda tā haifu yāya bīū, guda kūa ba ta haifu ba, sai dan wani ke wurinta. Shi kua ba shi sō wanda ta haifu, sai wanda ba ta haifu shi ke so. Yau ananan ranan yunwa ta zō garinsu, sai shi tafi dāji, shi sāmu abinchi. Shi hana mai-yāya, shi bai maras dīa. Su chi, su bīū. Hakanan kulum, ranan ya tafi dāji, ya sāmu kwain zābō gūda ishirin. Sai ya kirāye ta, ya che, 'Ki zābi guda daia, wanda ya fi girmā.' [3] Sai ta dauki

---

This story is (called) 'Whack me'. A certain man had two wives; one bore two children and the other had not any children, except the child of another who lived with her. Now he (the husband) did not like the one who had borne, but the one who had not borne. Now it came about that a day of famine came on them. Then he (the husband) went to the bush (and) found food, and refused the one with children and gave to the one without children, (and) they two ate; and it was so always. And one day he went to the bush and found guinea-fowl's eggs, twenty in number. Then he called her (the one he did not love) and told her to choose the largest of them. So she took

وَ

فَرْقَلْطُوفِيَرْ ؞

شَشَرْبُومَنِشْ

وَفِمْتُنْ ؞ بِكَلَمْ مَاتَنْفُسْنْ ؞ مِيُوأْ ؞ غُدَا ؞ قَاتَيْفْ

بِيَابِيَنْ وِيُوا ؞ غُدَا لُحُوَ ؞ بِتَحَيْفُبْ ؞ لَسَرْدْ فُوَقْ

بِكَسُووُفْتَ ؞ لِشِيكُوَ ؞ بِدَاشِسُوَ ؞ وَفُمْ تَحَيْفْ

لَسْ وَفُدَ ؞ مَتَحَيْفُ ؞ لِشِكَسُوا ؞ مِيُوا أَفَافَمْ ؞

وَقَّمْ ؞ بِيُفْوَ ؞ قَدُو ؞ غَمْ فُسُنْ سَبِيشَتَي ؞ دَاجِ

شِسَلَامُوَا ؞ أَمِنْتِ ؞ لِلشَّمَ ؞ فِيُنْ ؞ بِيَابِيَنْ شِبَرْ

مَرْسَدِ بِيَنْ ؞ لُسِثْ سُوبِيُو ؞ حَكَنْ كُلُمْ ؞ رَقَّمْ

بِتَي ؞ دَاجِ ؞ بِسَلَامُوَا ؞ كُوَيْدَامُو ؞ غُدَا ؞

عِشَمْرِشْ لَسَنْ بِكَرَامِثْ ؞ بِيشْ ؞ كُدَابِ ؞ =

غُدَادَمُوَ ؞ وَفْدَبِيفِ ؞ غِمْ مَنْ ؞ لَسَنْ فَدَوْكِ ؞ =

guda, ta je, ta dafa, ta ba yāra. [4] Su-ka-chi.
Ranan ita kuma [5] ta je dāji, ta sāmu
hatsinta, ta [6] talga kunū, ta kirāye shi,
ta che, 'Dūba chikin yan [7] farutanka,
ka tsōma guda daia wanda ya fi girma ka lā-
-she, ka tāshi, ka bar ma yāra saura.' Sai
ya rika dūba yan yātsa, shi-na-jujuyāwa,
shi-na-fadi, 'Wani [8] zaa ni tsōmāwa chiki?' Shi-na-
-fadi, 'Wanga kō wanga?' Ashe hannunsa
guda shi-na wurin gūtsunsa, shi-na-kunta walki.
Sai ya kunche [9] walki maza maza, ya tūra chikin
kunū. Idānun maata shi-na-dūban wani wuri,

---

one, she went and boiled it, and gave it to the children to eat. And on that day she too went to the bush, she found corn, and stirred (it into) gruel. And she called him (her husband) and said, 'Look among your nails and dip (into the pot) one, the largest one of all, then lick (it), rise up, and leave the rest to the children.' Then he began to examine his nails, he turned them about, saying, 'What one must I dip in?' (and) he kept saying, 'Is it this one or that one?' But all the time his one hand was between his legs loosening his skin waist covering. Then he swiftly unfastened it, and plunged it into the pap, (in the pot) (when) the woman's eyes were looking the other way;

نُدَا، قِجِن .. مَدَق .. مَبَايدَارَا .. لسكن ..

رَقَّمْ .. إِنَكُم .. قِجُودَاج .. قَسَامُوا .. =

حَطِنْت .. قَتَاْغ .. كُنُوا .. تَكَرَايِشْ

قَشْ .. دُوبَن .. قُكَن .. يَنْجَم تَنْكَ .. =

كَطُوم .. نُدَادْتَن .. وَقْدِيق .. نُغْرَمُن .. كَلَا

شْنُ .. كَنَاشْ .. كَنْبَرْمَيَارَا .. لَسُوْرَا .. لَسَن

يَمْرَكَ .. دُوبَ .. بَنْيَاط .. بِشَنَا جُوجُويَاوْ ..

شِنَاقِدِ .. وَبْدَاوُ .. طُومَدَارَا .. ثِكْ .. شِنَا

قِدِ .. وَقْغ .. يُكُوقْغ .. أَبْسُ .. تَنْغَس ..

نُدَا .. شَنَاوُ وَنْكُوطَنْس .. شَنَاكُنْت وَلْكَم

.. لَسْ يَكْنَب .. وَلْكُم .. مَغَمَخ .. يَمُّوْ .. ثُكَن

كُنُوا .. إِدَامْرَمَاكْنِ .. شَنَادُو بِنْوَنُورِي ..

ba ta gani ba. Sai ya tāshi ya che, '[10] Nā tsōma dai.' Sai ta che, '[11] Kai ka ji da abin fadi.' Sai ta [12] kyale. Wata raana ta tafi dāji, ta ganō [13] māra. Sai ta wuche. Sai māra ta che, 'Kāka ki ke wuche ni ba ki gaishe ni?' Sai ta che, '[14] Sannū.' Sai māra ta che, '[15] in gwiya.' Sai [16] maatar nan ta kyale, ta wuche. Sai māra ta che, 'Ba ki tanbaya na sūnana?' Sai maatar nan ta che, 'Kāka sūnanki?' Sai māra ta che, 'Sūnana, [17] Shibshibtō mani,' Sai maatar nan ta kyale, zaa ta wuchewa. Sai māra ta che, 'Ba ki tanbaya sūnana?' Sai maatar nan ta che, 'Kāka sūnanki?' Sai

---

she did not see. Then he stood up and said, 'I have put one in.' And she said, 'You will get put to shame over this,' and she refrained from saying any more. Another day she went to the bush, and saw a spoon and she passed on. But the spoon said, 'How is it you would pass on and not salute me?' So she said, 'Greetings to you.' And the spoon said, 'Greetings.' Then the woman would have let it go at that, and passed on, but the spoon said, 'Will not you ask my name?' So the woman said, 'What is your name?' And the spoon answered, 'My name is Help me.' And the woman did not speak again, and was about to pass on, but the spoon said, 'Will not you ask me my name?' So the woman said, 'What is your name?' And

بتقفيب ؞ ءاسن يتنا ءيشن ؞ ميخ ما طو مو ءيزن ؞

ءسن تخب ؞ ءيكيج ؞ دا ءيمر قد ؞ ءاسن تجلبو ؞

وتمرارن ؞ تتبججاج ؞ تمقفنوا ؞ ما را ؞ ءاسن

تموف ؞ ءاسن ما ورا تب ؞ يكاك ؞ يكجكو يم

تماك يغيبشن ؞ ءاسن تخب ؞ ءاسنو ءا ؞ ءاسن ما را ؞

تخب ءافغن ؞ ءاسن ما ءتمرن ؞ تكبلي ءا تموب

ءاسن ما را ؞ تخب ؞ تمايكتشبيا ون ؞ ءاسو ما ون ؞

ءاسن ما ءتمر قمرن ؞ تخب يكاك ؞ ءاسو تنكي

ءاسن ما ورا ؞ تخب ءاسو ما رن ؞ يشتشبتو مر

؞ ءاسن ما ءتمر قمرن تكبي ؞ دا ءاتمو ثبوا ؞

ءاسهن ما را ؞ تخب باكتشتبي ءاسو ما ون ؞ ءاسن

ما ءتمر قمرن ؞ تخب يكاك ؞ ءاسو تنكي ؞ ماسن

māra ta che, 'Sūnana Shibshibtō mani.' Sai māra ta che, 'Ke kūa che, Shibshibtō mani in jia.' Sai ita kūa ta che, 'Shibshibtō mani in jia.' Sai māra ta che, 'Kāwō kworianki.' Ta kāwō kworianta, sai māra ta rika zuba mata tūō, ta zuba mata har kworianta ya chika. Ta tafō gida, ta dī-ba, ta bai mijinta. Saura kūa ita da yāra su-ka-chi. Gari ya wāye, sai mijinta ya zō. Sai ya che, 'Dōmin Ala ina ki-ka-sāmū abinchi nan?' Sai ta che, 'Na sāmu kudi ne, na gani hatsi, na saye, na daka, na [18] tūka tūō.' Sai ya che, 'Bābu laifi.' Sai ya tāshi, ya fita, ya bar ta.

---

the spoon said, 'My name is Help me'; and the spoon said, 'You too say, Help me that I may taste.' So she also said, 'Help me that I may taste.' Thereupon the spoon said, 'Bring your calabash.' She brought her calabash. Then the spoon kept filling it with food, he poured it out for her till her calabash was full. She went home, took it out, and gave her husband, and the remainder she and her children ate. Next day her husband came and said, 'For the sake of Allah where did you get that food?' Then she said, 'I got money, I saw grain, I bought it, I pounded it, and made food.' And he said, 'That is all right,' and stood up, and went out, and left her.

مارا ؞ قبث لسوما ر ؞ شبشبتو امن ؞ لسم مارا ؞
تبث ؞ بكبكو ؞ قبلشبشبتو من ؞ إفجن ؞ لسن
إتكو ؞ قبث لشبشبتو من ؞ إفجن ؞ لسم مارا ؞
تبث كاوو ؞ كم ينك ؞ تكاوو كم يمنت ؞ لسن
مارا ؞ تم كذ بامت ؞ شوو ؞ تذ بامت
تم كم يمشت ؞ ينك ؞ قشتبو اغدا ؞ تحي
يب ؞ قبن محنت ؞ لسوراكو ؞ إقد قيداوا ؞
لسكث ؞ غم ؞ يجوايكن ؞ لسن محنت ميذو ؞ لسن
يبثذ و مم ؞ ال ؞ إقد اكسامو ؞ إمنثمر ؞
لسم قبث ؞ قد لسام ؞ كح يمبن ؞ قغنغ قطم
قسبين ؞ قدك ؞ قشوك ؞ قشوو ؞ لسم يمبث
بلو لبيم ؞ لسم يمتاشن بيجنا بيجم ما ؞

Ita kūa sai ta tāshi, ta dauki kworianta,
ta fita, ta tafi dāji, wurin da māra ta ke,
ta iske māra, ta che mata, 'Kāka sūnanki?'
Sai māra ta che, 'Sūnana Shibshibtō mani.'
Ta che, 'Shibshibtō mani in jia.' Sai māra
ta rika zuba mata tūō, har kworianta
ta chika. [19] Ta daukō, ta tafō gida, ta dība,
ta ba shi, ya chi, da shi da maatansa guda, (sk)
su-ka-kōshi. Kulum hakanan, sai ranan ya che,
'Dōmin Ala ba ki kai ni wurinda ki ke sāmu
tūō nan.' Sai ta che masa, 'In garin Ala ya wāye
ka zō.' Yau, da gari ya wāye sai ya zō, su-ka-je wurin

She also got up, lifted her calabash (and) went out, and went off to the bush where the spoon was. She came to where he was and said to him, 'What is your name?' And the spoon said, 'My name is Help me.' She said, 'Help me that I may taste.' Thereupon the spoon commenced to pour out food for her until her calabash was full. She lifted it and went off home, took (the food) out and gave him. He ate, with his one wife. They were filled. And this happened again and again, till one day he said, 'For the sake of Allah will you not take me to where you are finding this food?' Then she said to him, 'When the dawn of Allah appears, come.' So when it was dawn, he came, and they went to the place

إِتَكُو؞ لَسْتُ تَتَّلْشْ؞ قَدُ رُكَ؞ كُمْ مِنْتْ؞ =

تَمْڢَتْ؞ تَنْتَبْ كَرَاجْ؞ وُرْنْدْ مَدْرَا تَنْجَكْمْ يِلَّا

تَمْ إِنْسْكَرْ مَدْرَا؞ تَڢْنْتَ؞ كَدَاكْ؞ اِسُو تَّڢْنْكْ

تَسْ مَدْرَا تَنْبْ؞ لِسُو ڢْدْرَ؞ تْشْبْشْبْ نْتُو مَرْ؞

تَنْبْ شْبْشْبْ نْتُو مَرْ؞ إِڢْجَرْ؞ لَسْ مَدْرَا؞ مَدْ

تَمْرْكْذْ بَاڢْتَ؞ تَڢُدُورْ؞ حَمْ كُمْ يَڢْتْ؞

تِّيشْ؞ تَدْ وُرْكُوا؞ تَنْبُڢُوا؞ غَدَا؞ تَمِّيبَا

تَبَاشْ؞ مِيثَا دْشِيمْ مَا؞ تَڢْنَسْ؞ غُدَا؞ لِيكْ

لُسْكُو يْسْ؞ يَعْلَمْ حَكْمْ؞ لَسْ رُ تَّمْرِيتْ

دُو تِمْرَالْ؞ بَاكِكَيْرْ؞ وُرْڢْدْ يَجْكْ لَسَامُوا؞

تَغْ وُ مْرْ؞ لَسْ تَڢْتْ مَسْ؞ نَا مْغْرْ بْالْ وَايِيرْ؞ يْكْ

كَذْرَا؞ مِيخُو دَغْمْ؞ مَبْوَاهْمْ؞ لَسْ مَڢُذْ؞ نْسْكُمْ؞ وُرْ

māra ta che, 'Gaishe ta.' Sai ya gaida māra. Sai
maatarsa ta che, 'Tanbaye ta mana, che, Kāka
sūnanki?' Sai ya che, 'Kāka sūnanki?'
Sai māra ta che, 'Sunana Shibshibtō mani.'
Sai [20] maatar kūa ta che masa, 'Che, Shibshibtō mani
in jia.' Sai ya che, 'Shibshibtō mani in jia.' Sai
māra kūa ta dinga zuba masu tūō, har
korainsu su-ka-chika. Su-ka-dauki, sa-ka-kā-
-wō gida, su-ka-chi. Da dare ya yi, sai mijin ya kōma,
ya dauke māra, ya kāwō gida, ya sainya
chikin [21] rufēwa. Idan yā ji yunwa, sai shi che maa-
-tansa ta shiga chikin rufēwa, ta gani me

---

where the spoon was. She said, 'Salute her,' so he saluted the spoon. Then his wife said, 'Ask her, can't you (her name)? say, What is your name?' So he said, 'What is your name?' And the spoon said, 'My name is Help me.' And the wife said to him, 'Say, Help me that I may taste.' And he said, 'Help me that I may taste.' Thereupon the spoon commenced to pour out food for them until their calabash was full; then they lifted it and took it home. They ate. When night came then the husband returned. He lifted up the spoon and came back to the house, and put the spoon inside the grain store. When he felt hungry then he told his wife to go into the grain store and see what

مَارَاتَقْشِ ؞ غَيْبْشِتَ ؞ لَسَنْ وَيَقْبْجِ مَارَا ؞ لَسَرْ

مَاقْمْ لَسَنْ ؞ قَجْبْ ؞ تَقْبْيِقْمَنْ ؞ ثْكَاكْ ؞

لَسُوشْكِ ؞ لَسَنْ يَبْ كَدَاكْ ؞ لُسُوشْكِ ؞

لَسَنْ مَارَا ؞ قَبْ لُسُوقْدَامُنْ ؞ لِشْبْشِبْتُو مَمِنْ

سَنْ مَاقْمْ كُوَ ؞ قَبْ مَسَنْ ؞ شْبْشِبْتُو مَمِنْ

إِقْجِنْ ؞ لَسَنْ يَبْ ؞ لِشْبْشِبْتُو مَمِنْ ؞ إِقْجِنْ لَسِنْ

مَارَاكُوَ ؞ تَدِنْغَ ؞ دُبَامَسَنْ ؞ قَدُوِنْ ؞ قَمْ

كُفُوِرْيَرْ لَسَنْ لَسُكَشِكْ ؞ لُسُكَدَّوْكِ ؞ لُسُكَكَا

وُوغِدَا ؞ لُسَكَشِ ؞ دَدَّبِرْ مَيَّبِنْ ؞ لَسَنْ مِجِمَّنْ ؞ يَكُوَمْ

؞ يَدَّوْكَمْ ؞ مَارَا ؞ يَكَاوُرْ ؞ غِدَا ؞ يَلَسْمُيِلَ ؞

ثِكُرْ وُجِمَوَا ؞ إِكَّمْرِيَاجِ ؞ يُفْنُوَ ؞ لَسَنْ لِشَبْ مَا

قَنْسَنْقَشِغَ فِكُمْ ؞ رُجِمَوَا ؞ قَغَنِمْ ؞ مَبِنْ

ke chiki. Sai ta shiga rufēwa, ta iske māra.
Ta che, 'Kāka sūnanki?' Sai māra ta che,
'Sunana Shibshibtō mani.' Sai ta che, 'Shibshibtō
mani in jia.' Sai māra ta chika mata kworia
da tūō. Ba su bai wachan maata da ta gwoda masa.
Ita kūa ba ta sāmun abinchi, hakanan kulum.
Sai ranan maatansa wa(n)da shi ke sō, mai-gida
ba shi gida, ya je dāji. Sai ta dauki
mārá ta kai raafi, ta-na-wanki. Sai [22] mātan
sarki su-ka-zō, su-ka-gaishe ta, su-ka-che
'Me ki ke yi?' Ta che, 'Gā shi dai.' Sai su-ka-kyale.
Sai ta che, 'Ba ku gaishe ta?' Sai su-ka-che, 'Sannu, sannu.'

---

was inside. When she entered the store she met the spoon. She said, 'What is your name?' Then he said, 'My name is Help me.' And she said, 'Help me that I may taste.' And the spoon filled her calabash with food. And they did not give that wife who had told him all about it. She also did not find any food. It was always so, until one day his wife, the one the man loved, when the husband was not at home, he had gone to the bush, took the spoon. She came to the stream and was washing it, when the chief's wife came and greeted her and said, 'What are you doing?' She said, 'Look at that.' Then they said nothing more. Then she said, 'Are you not going to salute her?' And they said, 'Greetings, greetings.'

بكيثكيم ؞ اسم قشغر ربو ؞ قد اسكي مدار ؞

تث كاك ؞ سوقنك ؞ سم مدار ؞ قث ؞

سوقد امن ؞ لشبشبنو من ؞ سع قث شبشبنو

من ؞ إقجن ؞ سع مدار ؞ قتشكامت ؞ كرين ؞

دنحو و ؞ بماسبين ؞ وقمر ماثد قتقد امسن اب

انكو ؞ بد تمسد امن ؞ ابقث ؞ تحكمن ؞ كلم

سن وقمر ؞ ماتنس ؞ وقد شبكسو ؞ مينقد ا

؞ بد يشغد ؞ يماجن ؞ دراج ؞ اسن قدو ك

مدار ؞ نكن ؞ راقم ؞ قتمد وقنك ؞ اسن ما تمر

سن كم ؞ سككو ؞ سكغيبثت ؞ سكث

بمككبن ؞ قثب ؞ نمد شدمن ؞ اسن سكبلو

اسن قلث ؞ بد كغيبثت ؞ اسن مكث لسنقو السنو ..

Ta amsa gaisua. Sai maatar nan ta che, 'Ku tanbaye ta ku che, Kāka sūnanki?' Ta che, 'Sūnana shibshibtō mani.' Sai su-ka-che, 'Wani abu kuma aka-che masa Shibshibtō mani?' Sai maata nan ta che, 'Ku che, Shibshibtō mani in jia.' Sai su-ka-che, 'Shibshibtō mani in jia. Sai māra ta dinga zuba masu tūo. Wadansu sun dēbi rūa, sai su-ka-zuba, su-ka-kāwō, ta zuba masu tūō, su-ka-dauki, su-ka-kai gida, Sarki ya tanbaye su. 'Ana ku-ka-sāmu abin nan?' Sai su-ka-che, 'Raafi mu-ka-je, mu-ka-ishe maatar wāne, sai ta che, Ba ku gani ina wanki māra ba? Mu-ka-che, Mun gani. Sai ta che, Ba ku gaishe ta?

It answered the salute. Then this wife said, 'Ask, What is your name?' It answered, 'My name is Help me.' Then they said, 'What sort of a thing now do they call Help me?' Then this woman said, 'You say, Help me that I may taste.' And they said, 'Help me that I may taste.' Thereupon the spoon kept pouring out food for them. Some have (had) drawn water, but they poured it out, and brought (their calabashes), and the spoon poured in food for them, and they lifted it and took it home. And the chief asked, 'Where did you get this thing?' And they said, 'We went to the stream and we met there the wife of So-and-so, and she said, Don't you see I am washing a spoon? We said, We have seen, and she said, Will you not salute it?

تَأَمْسَ نَمِيْنسُوَا ؛ لَسَرْ مَا اَقْتَرْ قَمَّنْ ؛ قَتْبُ كُتَنَقْبَتْ
كُتْبُ كَدَاكَ ؛ لسُوقَنْكِ ؛ قَتْبُ لسُومَاقَمَن ؛
ثْبِنْبِشْبُو مَمِ ؛ لَسَرْ سُكَتْبُ ؛ وَزِنَا أَبُكَمّ ؛ أَكْتُبُ
قَمَسَ ؛ لِثْبْبِشْبُو مَمِ ؛ لَسَرْ مَا اَقْتَقَّنْ ؛ قَتَبُ كُتَبُ ؛
لِثْبِنْبِشْبُو مَمِ ؛ إِقْجَوَ ؛ لَسَرْ لُبكَنْبُ ؛ لِثْبِبِشْبُو مَمِ
إِقْمِجَ ؛ لَسَرْ قَدَارا ؛ قَحَى قْقْغَ ؛ دُبَا قَمَسَ ؛ قَتُوُو ؛
وَدْ قَمَسَ ؛ لَسْنَجَ مَفِ ؛ وُرُوا ؛ لَسَرْ لُسَكَنْ بَمْ ؛ لُسَكَادُو
قَدْ قَبَا قَمَسَ ؛ قَجَوُو ؛ لَسَكَرْ وَكِ ؛ لُسَكَكَنْ قَمَدَا
لَسَرْكِم ؛ يَتَنَبِيسُنْ ؛ أَقْدَاكُكَسَا مُوَا ؛ أَفِقَّمْ
لَسَرْ سُكَتْبُ ؛ وَأَفِجْ قَكَجَنْ ؛ قَكَاإِبشْنُ ؛ مَا اَقْتَرْ
وَاقْلُمْنْ ؛ لَسَرْ قَتْبُ بَكُغَنِم ؛ إِقَّدَا وَنْكِ ؛ قَدَا وَافِ
قَكْثُ ؛ قُنْغَنِم ؛ لَسَرْ قَتْبُ ؛ بَمَا كُغَيْبِنْتَ

Mu-ka-che, Sannu [23] abuya. Ta che, Sannu kade. Sai mu-ka-yi shirū, mu-na-kalō, sai maātar nan ta che, Ba ku tanbaya sūnanta? Sai mu kūa, mu ka che, Kāka sūnanki?
Ta che, Sunana Shibshibtō mani. Sai mu-ka-yi shirū, mu-na-dubanta, sai māatar nan ta che, Ku kāwō korainku, ku che, Shibshibtō mani in jia. Sai mu kūa mu-ka-che, Shibshibtō mani in jia, ta di-nga zubā muna tūō, ta chichika muna korai da tūō.' Sai sarki ya che, 'Ku je, ku kāwō ta, in gani.' Sai aka-tafi da fādāwa da dōgarai, aka-je, aka-tarda mutume nan, aka-che, 'Sarki ya che ka ba mu Shibshibtō mani, mu kāwō, shi gani.' Sai ya daukō ta dakansa, ya ba su. Shi na mai-bakin chiki

---

We said, Greetings, lady friend. And it said, Greetings to you. Next we were silent, we were gazing, when that woman said, Will you not ask its name? So we then said, What is your name? and it said, My name is Help me. Then we were silent (again), we were watching, when that woman said, Bring your calabashes and say, Help me that I may taste. And we too said, Help me that I may taste. And it kept pouring out food for us and filled up our calabashes with food.' Then the chief said, 'Go and bring it that I may see.' So they went off, the court officials and the chief's body-guard, and they went and met this person, and they said, 'The chief says, give us Help me, that we may bring it for him to see.' So he took it himself and gave them; he was black of heart

مُكَبْ لَسَنُو ؞ أَبِيَ ؞ تَبْ لَسَنُو كَجِيْ ؞ لَسَرْ مُكَسّ
شِرُو ؞ مُنَا كَلُو ؞ بَسَرْ مَا أَمَرْ قَسَّ ؞ بَا مُغَتَّبَيِّنْ ؞ سُو تَبْ
قَنْتَ ؞ لَسَرْ مُو كُوَّ ؞ مُكَبْ كَدَاكَ ؞ سُو فَنْكِ
تَبْ سُو قَلْ فَمَّ ؞ شِبِشْبِنُو مَمَ ؞ لَسَرْ مُكَسّ نِشْرُوا
مُقَادُو رُبَنْتَ ؞ لَسَرْ مَا أَمَرْ فَمَّ ؞ تَبْ كُكَلُو
كُوُرْبِكَ ؞ كُبْ شِنْشِبْنُو مَمَ ؞ إِفْجِّ ؞ لَسَسْ
مُو كُوَّ ؞ مُكَبْ شِبْشِبْنُو مَمَ ؞ إِفْجِّ ؞ قَمِ
نْغَ دُبَا مُمَ ؞ قُغُورُو ؞ تَنْشِكَا مُمَ ؞ كُغُورَرْ
دَ مُغُورُو ؞ لَسَرْ لَسَرْكِمْ بِبَثْ ؞ كُجِمْ كُكَلُو رُقَ
إِفْغَنِمْ ؞ لَسَرْ أَكَتِّفِ ؞ دَ بَادَ أَوَا ؞ دَ دُو غَمَرْ سْ
أَكَجِ ؞ أَكَتَمْرَ مُتَجَقَّرْ ؞ أَكَبْ لَسَرْكِمْ بِيَبْ ؞
كَبَامُ ؞ لِبِشْبِنُو مَمَ ؞ مُكَدَاوُرُو ؞ لِشْغَنِمْ ؞ أَلَسَ
بِدَّ وَكُوقَ ؞ دَكَنْلَسَ ؞ بَبَاسُ ؞ شِنَا مَبَكِنْشِكِ

Su-ka-karbe, su-ka-kai ma sarki, su-ka-che, 'Gā ta.'
Sarki ya che, 'Sannu, abuya,' sai ta amsa, sai ya che,
'Ku kāwō akushi.' Aka-kāwō akushi, ya che,
'Kāka sūnanki?' Ta che, 'Sūnana Shibshibtō mani.'
Sarki ya che, 'Shibshibtō mani.' Sai ta dinga zuba masa
tūō, ta chika masa akushi. Sai sarki
ya che, 'Wanan ya fi karfin gidan talaka.' Sai
sarki ya che akai ta gida. Aka-kai ta gida, ta-na-bai
gidan sarki abinchi. Shi kūa, wanda ke da māra,
shi-na-mutūa da yunwa. Ana-nan, ranan, maatansa,
wanda ta gwoda masa māra, ya dauke, ya bar ta,
sai ta je dāji, bidan abinchi. Sai ta gani tsumājīa,

They received (it) (from him), they brought (it) to the chief and said, 'Behold it.' The chief said, 'Hail, lady friend,' and it answered. And he said, 'Bring large wooden dishes,' and large wooden dishes were brought. Then he (the chief) said, 'What is your name?' and it said, 'My name is Help me.' And the chief said, 'Help me,' and it kept pouring out food and filled the wooden plates for him. And the chief said, 'This is too good a thing to be in a poor man's house.' So the chief ordered it to be brought to his house. It was brought to his house and it supplied the chief's house with food, but as for him who had the spoon (formerly) he was dying of hunger. Then one day his wife, the one who had shown him the spoon, when he had taken it and left her, went to the bush to look for food. And she saw a branch of a tree,

لسككم بي :: لسككيم لسركم :: لسكب غدمت ::

لسركم يمث :: لسنوا :: أبمن :: لسرقد مسن لسن يمث ::

ككدورن :: أكشم :: أككدورن :: أكشم :: يمث ::

كدك :: سوقنك :: قث لسوقدامن :: شبشبو

لسركم يمث :: شبشبو من :: لسرقدمخ :: دمدامسر

تمووت قشكدامسن :: أكشم :: لسن لسركم ::

يمث ونم بمدا في كمرجن غدمتلك :: لسر

لسركم :: أكيت غدا :: أككيت غدا :: قنداير يمث

غد قلسركم :: أمنث :: يشكو :: ونمدبكدمدارا

يشنا متو :: ديمو :: أمدا قمر :: وقمر :: مدا تمنسر

ومدتغدامسن مدارا :: يمدوبكمن :: يمبرمث ::

لسرتجمن داج مدمابمث :: لسرقفخم :: طعدابيا

wadansu su-ka-che, 'kurfū,' ta gani chikin dāji.
Ta che, 'Sannu.' Ta che, 'Sannu kade.' Maatar nan
ta che, 'Kāka sūnanki?' Kurfū ta che,
'Sūnana Sharsharbō mani. Sai maatar nan
ta che, 'Sharsharbō mani in jia.' Sai kurfū
ya dinga feadinta, sharb! sharb! ta-na-
-gudu, ta-na-kūwa, ta-ma-che, 'Wāyō [24] nā tūba,
nā bī ka, baa ni kārawa.' Kurfū kūa
shi-na-dukanta, har mutāne su-ka-zō, (sk)
su-ka-fāfēta. [25] Ta je gida; ta kirāwō mijinta;
ta kai shi wurin bulāla; ta che, '[26] Kā gani,
nā sāmu wani abu kuma mai-bāda abinchi.'

---

some say a whip; she saw it in the forest (bush). She said, 'Greetings,' and it said, 'Greetings to you.' And the wife said, 'What is your name?' and the whip said, 'My name is Whack me.' And the woman said, 'Whack me that I may feel.' Thereupon the whip kept flogging her, whack! whack! She was running away, she was yelling, she was saying, 'Alas, I am repentant, I shall follow you, I won't do it again.' But the whip flogged her until people came and rescued her. She went home and called her husband, and took him to where the whip was, and said, 'Have you seen, I have found another thing again for giving food.'

ءاد ءيقسن لسكّث كرفو :. تلخنت :. ثكرداج

تمث سننوا :. تمث سنوكجن :. ما تمرقن :.

تمث كاك :. لسوققنك :. كرفو تمث :.

سوقاقن :. لشرشر بومن :. لسن ما تمرقن :.

تمث لشرشر بومن :. إقجن :. لسن كرفو :.

بدفغ :. فدفتن :. لشرف :. لشرب :. تقلا

غمد :. تنكور :. تقلاب وبو :. قماقوب

قابيك :. بانكدار :. كرفو كوا :. =

شنادوكنت :. حم متامبن :. لسكذو :. اك

لسكا فكت :. تجن غدا :. تكرا او مجنت

تكيشن ورقبولان :. تمث كاغنم :.

قلسا موا :. وقاب غم :. مما داءمنث

Sai ta tsaya daga nīsa, ta che, ‘Gā shi chan.’ Sai miji ya tafi
da hamzari, farm! farm! sai ya tarda bulāla, ta-na-
[27]-kunche. Ya che, ‘Sannu, abōkīna.’ Bulāla ya che,
‘Sannu kade.’ Shi-na-tsamāni, kō abin kirki ne.
Sai ya che, ‘Kāka sūnanki?’ Sai kurfū ya che,
‘Sunana Sharsharbō mani in jia.’ Sai
mutume nan ya che, ‘Sharsharbō mani in jia.’ Sai
bulāla ya dinga dūkansa, har ya gaji. Ya kō-
-mō, ya [28] kunta kurum. Mutume nan shi kuma
ya tafi gida, ya kunta, shi-na-nīshi. Maatarsa wa(n)da
shi ke sō, ta zō, ta-na-fadi, ‘Me ya fāru?’ Bai
tanka ba. Shi-na-kurum, har ya sāmu sauki.

Then she stood afar off, she said, ‘There it is over there.’ Then the husband went off in haste, tramp! tramp! until he met the whip; it was lying down. He said, ‘Hail, friend,’ and the whip said, ‘Hail to you.’ He was all the time thinking it was something good. Then he said, ‘What is your name?’ and the whip said, ‘My name is Whack me that I may feel.’ Then this man said, ‘Whack me that I may feel.’ Thereupon the whip kept beating him until it was tired. And the whip went back and lay quite still, and the man too went home and lay down. And the wife he loved came along and said, ‘What has happened?’ And he did not answer. He lay quiet until he got better.

لسن قطكن . دخميلس . قنب غملش . شمر . لسنمج يتي

دحمد ر . فمم فمم . لسن يتم دبولان . قنا =

كنب . مب . لسنوا . ابو كينا . بولان يب .

لسنو فجر . شنا طعار . كوا ابنكم كنبر .

لسن مب . كدك سو شك . لسن كم فوا . يب

لسو قدافي . شمر شمر بجو قمر . افجي . لسن [redacted]

قتمتن . يب شمر شمر بجو قمر . افجي . لسن

بولان . ميج مغ . دو كنس حم يغج . يكو

موا . يكتع . كمم . متمتن شكم .

يتو غدا . يكتت شنا فيلش . هدقمرسل . وفد

شكسوا . قمغرا . قتنا قد . ميقار . بس

تنكاب . شنا كرم . حم يلام . سوكم

Sai ya tafi ya iske bulāla kunche. Sai ya di-
-nga kuntā. Shi-na-kuntō, har ya kai kusa
da ita. Sai ya zābura, ya taushe ta, ya kāwō gida,
ya sainya chikin runbu. Sai ya zamna kurum
har maatar nan da shi ke sō ta zō, ta che,
'Yau yunwa ni ke ji.' Sai ya che, 'Shiga chikin
runbū, ki gani me ke chiki.' Sai ta tāshi
maza maza, ta che, 'Me ka sāmu yau?' Ya che,
'Kedai shiga.' Sai ta che, 'In dauki koria?'
Ya che, 'ī.' Ta dauki koria, ta shiga chikin runbū.
Ya rufe, ya che, 'Me ki (ka) gani?' Sai ta che, 'Wani abu
nā gani mai-tsawō.' Ya che, 'Gaishe shi mana?' Ta che,

Then he went and came to where the whip was lying. Then he kept crouched down, he crouched down until he got near it, then he jumped and held it down, and took it home, and put it away in the grain store. Then he sat quietly until his favourite wife came. And she said, 'To-day I am feeling hungry.' Then he said, 'Go into the grain store and see what is inside.' Then she rose up in great haste, she said, 'What did you find to-day?' And he said, 'You yourself enter.' Then she said, 'Must I take a calabash?' He said, 'Yes.' She took a calabash and went into the grain store. He closed it. He said, 'What do you see?' And she said, 'Something I have seen which is long.' And he said, 'Greet it, cannot you?' She said,

لَسَنْ يَتَفِ ⁖ يَإِسْبَكِ مُوَلَآنْ ⁖ كُفْشْبْ ⁖ لَسَنْ يَجِ
مُغَ كُنْشُوا ⁖ لِشِفَا كُنْشُوا ⁖ حَمْ بَكَمْ ⁖ كُسَسْ
دَإِفَ ⁖ لَسَنْ يَجَ أُبِمَ ⁖ يَفُّوْلَبْشَتْ ⁖ يَبَكَدَاوُ وَعِدَا
يَلَسِفْيَا فِكِمْ وُفْبُوا ⁖ لَسَنْ يَدَّ مُمَنْ ⁖ كُمَ مَ ⁖
حَمْ مَا فَمْ قَّمْ ⁖ دِ شِبْكَسُلَّهُ ⁖ قَخُرْ ⁖ قَبْ
يَخُ يُفْمُو ⁖ فَجِ ⁖ لَسَنْ يَبْ شِغَ ⁖ ثِكِمْ
رُفْبُوا ⁖ كَغَنِمْ ⁖ مَبَكَيْثِكِمْ ⁖ لَسَمْ قَنَاشِ
مَغْ مَدْ ⁖ قَبْ مَبَّكَسَا مُوَايُّوْ ⁖ يَبْ
بَكَ دَ ئُ شِغْ ⁖ لَسَمْ قَبْ ⁖ إِفْمُ وُكِ كُمْ مَنْ ⁖
يَبَإِى ⁖ قَمَّوُكِ كُمْ مَنْ ⁖ قَشِغْ ثِكِمْ ⁖ رُفْبُو
يَمُ فِنْ ⁖ يَبْ مَكَكَغَنِمْ ⁖ لَسَمْ قَبْ وَنِلَّبُ ⁖
فَلَغَنِمْ ⁖ مَيْطَمُو ⁖ يَبْ غَمْبِسَنْثِمَنْ ⁖ قَبْ

'Sannu da fūtāwa.' Ta che, 'Kāka sūnanka?' Ya che, 'Sunana Sharsharbō mani.' Ta che, 'Sharsharbō mani in jia.' Sai bulāla ya dinga fīadinta, ta-na-kurūrūa. Mijinta da ya ji, sai ya sheka da gudu, ya yi dawa, maatarsa, wa(n)da ba shi sō, ita kuma sai ta fita, ta yi dawa, dōmin tsōrō. Ita kūa wachan, daket ta sāmu kafa, ta gudu. Su-ka-bar gida kangō. Da wuri māra da bulāla dāji su ke.

Mafārin zūansu gida ke nan.

[29] Kungurus kan kusu.

'I greet you (who are) resting,' (and) she said, 'What is your name?' It said, 'My name is Whack me,' and she said, 'Whack me that I may feel.' Thereupon the whip set about beating her, she was shouting. Her husband, when he heard, ran off to the forest, and his wife, the one he did not love, also ran out to the forest, through fear; and she also, the one who had entered the grain store, with difficulty she found a way of escape and ran off; and they left the house deserted. Long ago the spoon and the whip lived in the wilds, and this was the first time they made their appearance in the home. Off with the rat's head.

لسنوم فحو قداو ⁘ تبخ كداك ⁘ لسوقنك

يبخ لسو قدا قمن ⁘ لشم شم بجو مين ⁘ قبخ لشم شم

بو مين ⁘ افجي ⁘ لسن مو لالن ⁘ ميج منغ فياد منة

تقدا كم ورو ⁘ مجفت د بيج ⁘ لسن يبشك ⁘ د غم

بيم د و ⁘ هد قمر لسن رمد باشسو ⁘ اتكم

سم قفت ⁘ تم د و ⁘ د ومم دوو ⁘ اتكو ⁘

وقم ⁘ د بكت ⁘ قسام كبقا ⁘ تغد ⁘ سكبر غد ا

⁘ كنغو ⁘ د ر ⁘ مدوا ⁘ د بو لالن ⁘ د ابج لسكس

مبا وف ومسن غد ا بجنم ⁘

كنغم س ⁘ كنفوس

No. 6.

Wanàn tātsūnīar wani sarki che

[1] Gātanan, gātanan, ta je, ta kōmō. Wani sarki ana-che da shi Kurungu-mūgun-kīfi, ya tsū--fa chikin sarauta. Da ya kusa mutūa, shi-na da dīa dayawa, sai ya tāra su, ya che, 'Idan [2] naa mutu me zaa ku giyāra makōkina da shi?' Baban dansa ya che, 'Idan [3] kā mutu naa giyāra makōkinka da zāki.' Kōwa ya fadi abinda zaa shi yi. Autansa ya che, 'Idan kā mutu, ina-yin makōkinka da [4] kūra.' Yau ana-nan ba adade ba sai ya mutu. Kōwa ya kāwō abinda ya che. Sauran babansu da auta. Sai auta ya tafi dāji, shi-na-yāwō, sai ya [5] chintō

This is a story about a certain chief. A tale, a tale. Let it go and let it return. A certain chief, by name Kurungu-the-bad-fish, grew old in his kingdom, and when he was near to death—he had many children—he called them together and said, 'If I were to die what would you all do to observe my funeral?' His eldest child said, 'When you are dead I shall mourn for you by (slaughtering) a lion.' Each one said what he would do. His youngest said, 'When you are dead I shall mourn for you by killing a hyena.' And it came to pass that not long after he died, and each brought what he said; only the eldest and the youngest remained (to fulfil the promise). Then the youngest went to the bush, he was walking, and he came across

وقرنا طو فيير وفسركيث

غما قنّ غما قنن ∴ تجي تكو سو ∴ ولسركم ∴

أما ثبد لشي ∴ كرفغ ∴ موغم كيبقم ∴ يا طو

قد ∴ قكم لسر وقت ∴ دريكس متو ∴ لشنا د يمن

ديبو ∴ سنيمتا وآس ∴ يمث إدرقا مث ∴ بمداك

غيير ∴ محكو كم قداشي ∴ مبرد مس ∴ ريث

إدرنكا مث ∴ قا أغير محكو كنك ∴ درزاك

كو وا ميبجا بنغم ∴ دا أشن ∴ أوقنس يث ∴

إدركا مث ∴ إقا ينمحكو كنك ∴ دكورا ∴

يو أملقن ∴ مجا دبمب ∴ لسن يحث ∴ كورا ∴

يكا رو ∴ أبنغ ميث ∴ لسو ربيبس ∴ دا أوقس

لسر أوقم يتعد داج ∴ لشنا يد رو ∴ لسن يثنوا

[6] sānia, ya kāwō. Su-ka-yanka, su-ka-yi salka, su-ka-dauki kan sānia da [7] kafāhu, (sk) su-ka-tūra chikin salka. Sai ya je ya kirāwō kūra. Ta zo, ya che, 'Mun yi [8] watanda, ba ka nan, mu-ka-ajie nāka.' Su-ka-goda masa burgāme, su-ka-che, 'Gā shi nan, shiga, ka dauka.' Sai kūrā ta kuna kai, ta shiga. Sai auta ya yi maza maza, ya rufe bākin burgāme, su-ka-damre kūra chiki, su-ka-ja kūra, su-ka-kai bisa [9] kabarin ubansu. Su-na-duka har kirgi ya pashe. Kūra ta sāmu [10] kafa, ta fita, ta gudu. Sai auta ya ji haushi, ya che, 'Naa kāma ta kuma.' Ana-nan, wata raana kuma ya sāmu

---

a cow and brought it back. They slaughtered it and made a skin bag of it, and they took the cow's head and feet and pushed them into the bag. Then he went and called the hyena. She came (and) he (the man) said, 'We divided up the meat (when) you were not there, (and) we set aside your share.' They showed her (lit. him) the bag, they said, 'There it is, go in and lift (the meat).' Then the hyena put in her head and entered. Then the youngest son immediately closed the mouth of the bag (and) they tied it up, the hyena inside, and they dragged the hyena and brought her above their father's grave. And they kept flogging her until the skin burst. The hyena found an exit, got out, and ran off. Then the youngest son got angry and said, 'I shall catch her again.' And so another day he found

ثلقي ∴ يكراو ∴ سكينك ∴ سكن سلكن ∴
سكدرك ∴ كنشاقير ∴ دكبله ∴ اسك
سكتو ∴ قكن سلكن ∴ سن يجي ∴ يكراو ∴ كورا
مغدو ∴ يبث مفن وتقد ∴ بداكش ∴ مكا جيبي
ندك ∴ سكغدا مسن ∴ مرغدا مبي ∴ سكب
غدا شقن ∴ شغم ∴ كدرك ∴ سي كورا ∴
نكركن ∴ قمشغ ∴ لسن اوقلا ييقد هد ∴
يرقي ∴ بلكن بن غدا مكي ∴ سكد مرمن ∴
كورا ∴ ثك ∴ سكجي ∴ كورا ∴ سككن
بسركبر قلا مقنسن سنادوك ∴ قمركرغ
يفنبن ∴ كورا ∴ قسلام ∴ كبو ∴ تبقت تغد
سن اوقا ∴ يجي حوقس ∴ ميث فلا كدامان
كحم ∴ افا قمن ∴ وقدا قم كحم ∴ يسلام ∴

sānia, ya kāwō, ya yanka, ya bidi [11] dawō, ya līke idānunsa da shi, ya tafi dāji, ya gani kūra, ya che, 'Kūra, mun yi watanda ba ki nan, mu-ka-neme ki mu-ka-gaji, mu kūa māsurikō alkawali ne, gama uwāyenmu, da zaa su mutūa, su-ka-che mu rika bāya, kōwa ya sāmu wani abu, shi bidi dan uwansa.' Kūra ya che, 'Gaskīa ne, amā wani mutum yā zō nan ya rūdē ni, hakanan ya kai ni, shi-na-sō shi kashe ni.' Sai auta ya che, '[12] Asha kūra mutum shii kira dan uwansa dōmin shi kashe?' Kūra ta che, 'Mu tafi.' Su-ka-kāma hainya, su-na-zūa, sai kūra ta tsaya

---

a cow, he brought it back and killed (it), he searched for porridge and covered his eye with it and went off to the forest. He saw the hyena and said, 'Hyena, we have divided up the meat in your absence, we looked for you until we were tired. And as for us, we are a people who keep a promise to our parents, and when they were about to die they said we must continually give (gifts), and whoever found anything let him seek his brother (to share with him).' The hyena said, 'That is quite true, but some one has come here and deceived me. It was thus he enticed me away and he was wanting to kill me.' Then the youngest son said, 'Come now, hyena, would a man call his brother to kill (him)?' The hyena answered, 'Let us go.' They took the road, they were coming, when the hyena stood still

ثَافِيَمْ ؞ يَكَاوُو ؞ بِيَنْكَ ؞ بِجِ ؞ دُوو ؞ مِلِيقَشْ

إِدَّا مُقَنْسَ دَشِمْ ؞ بِمَتَّجِدَا إِمْ ؞ بِمَقِنْمْ كُوَرَا ؞ بِيَشْ

كُوَرَا شَ مُقَشَّ وُتَقَنْدَ بَاكِنَّشْ ؞ مُكَنْبَمْكِ ؞ =

مُكَقَجْ ؞ مُوكُو ؞ مَاسِمْ كُو ؞ أَلْكَوِلِيبَشْ

غَمَا ؞ غُوَاپِيمْ ؞ دَدَ أُسُ ؞ مُقُوَا ؞ لُسَكَشْ ؞

مُمِكْ مَبَاتِّ ؞ كُوَرَا ؞ بِبَسَامِ ؞ وَمَامِبْ ؞ شِبِجِ

دِنْغُوقَسَ ؞ كُوَرَا ؞ بِيشْ غَسْكِيَاقَبِّ ؞ أَمَّا

وِمُقُشَنْ بَادُرُقَّشْ ؞ بِقَمُودِمَسْ ؞ مَكَقَّشْ

يَكَيمْ ؞ لُشَقَا سُو ؞ لِشَكَشِبِمْ ؞ لَسَأُوقَمَّ

بِيَشْ أَشَا كُوَرَا شَ مُقَشَّ لِشَكِمْ ؞ مُغُقَّمُسَشْ

دُومِمَّ ؞ لِشَكَشِبُنْ ؞ كُوَرَا ؞ مَتَبْشْ مُتَنَبِجِ ؞ =

لُسَكَكَامَ مَقَتَّ ؞ سُنَا دُرَّ ؞ لَسَ كُوَرَا ؞ مَقَطَمَّ

ta che, 'Ai, jia wanda ya zō ya kirāye ni, kamanka shi ke, in ji bā kai bā ne.' Auta ya che, 'Mutume nan shi-na da [13] idānu gudā?' Kūra ya che, 'Mu tafi.' Su-ka-kāma hainya, su-na-tafia su-ka-kai gida. Sai auta ya goda masa wurin fāta sānia. Ya che, 'Shiga, akwai nāka chiki.' Sai kūra zaa shi kuna kai chiki, sai ya fitar ya che, 'Ai abōki, kad' ka zō ka yi mani kamar da dan uwa--nka ya yi mani.' Auta shi-na-tsaye. Sai ya che, 'Haba kūra, idan baa ka so [14] nāman ne, ka bari, [15] ka tafia(r)ka. Mutum shi kirāwō dan uwa--nsa dōmin shi chuche shi? Nāma na goda maka

---

and said, 'No, yesterday he who came to call me, like you was he, let me hear it was not you.' The youngest son said, 'This man, had he one eye?' The hyena said, 'Let us go on.' They took the road and were going on (and) they reached the house. Then the youngest son showed him (her) where the cow's hide was, and he said, 'Enter, your (share) is within.' Then the hyena, when he (she) was about to push in his (her) head, came out and said, 'No, friend, do not come and do to me as your brother did to me.' The youngest son was standing by, and he said, 'Come then, hyena, if it is that you do not want the meat, leave it, and go about your business. Does a man call his brother in order that he may do him harm? The meat I show you

تشا آ ؞ جنّ وقد ؞ يدو ؞ نبكرا يبي ؞ كمنك
شكن ؞ انج ماكيبن ؞ أوقاميث ؞ متبقّن
شنا د ؞ إدا قو ؞ غدا ؞ كورا يبث مقنف
سكا م قثن ؞ سنا تبقّن ؞ سكاكن غدا
لسن أوقا يبغدا امسّن ؞ وون ؞ قا ق ثا فيمن ؞
يبث شغ ؞ أكو يناك ثكيم ؞ لسن كورا ؞
دا اشكنرن كيم ؞ ثكيم ؞ لسن يقتن ؞ يبث آ ؞
أبوكيم ؞ تكد كذو ؞ كيّيقن ؞ كمّن د نغو
نك ؞ ييّصن ؞ أونن شنا طيبن ؞ لسن يث
تبن كورا ؞ إدّن ؞ ما كسو ؞ قا مقبن ؞
كبن ؞ كتقّيك ؞ منتن ؞ شغكرا اوا ؞ دنغو
فلسن ؞ د وقّن ؞ لشثو بشن ؞ قا م نغدا مك

in ba ka chi, ka bari, ka fita.' Sai kūra ya che, 'Aa ina-chi.' Sai ya tūra kai achiki, sai ya shiga. Kāmin shi daukō shi fitō, sai auta ya rufe kōfa, ya kāma bākin burgāme, ya rufe. Su-ka-tāru, su-ka-damre kūra, su-ka-ja, (sk) su-ka-kai bisa kabarin ubansu, [16] su-nā-dūka, su-ka-dūke ta har su-ka-pashe kirgi. Kūra ya sāmu kōfa, ya fita, ya gudu. Sai auta ya che, 'Naa [17] sāmō ta kuma.' Sai aka dede, kūra ta manche. Sai auta [18] ya sāmu bajinin sānia, ya kāwō. Su-ka-yanka, su-ka-fēde, su-ka-yi salka, su-ka-dauki katara na bāya, su-ka-sa

---

if you do not eat, leave it, and get out.' Then the hyena said, 'No, I am (going) to eat it.' So he (she) put his (her) head in and entered. As he (she) was going to lift the meat and then come out, then the youngest son seized the mouth of the bag and closed it. And they all came up and tied up the hyena and dragged it and brought it over their father's grave. They kept beating it, they beat it till the skin burst, and the hyena found an exit, and came out, and ran off. But the youngest son said, 'I will find and bring her back again.' Then some time passed and the hyena forgot. And the youngest son found a very large cow and brought it back. They slaughtered it, flayed it, and made a skin bag; they lifted a hind leg and put (it)

إِمْبَا كَحِفْ ⁖ كَيِمْ بَعَجِفْ ⁖ لَسْ كُوَرَا ⁖ يِمْبَا عَامْ ⁖

إِمَامْشِ ⁖ لَسْ مَتُورْكَمْ ⁖ أَتْكِمْ ⁖ لَسْ مَمِشْغْ ⁖

كَامِرْ ⁖ شَدُّ وْكُو ⁖ شِبِفْتُوَا ⁖ لَسْ أَوْقَلْ ⁖ يِرْفِي

كُوفَ ⁖ يَكَامْ بَاكِرْ بُرْ غَامُبُ ⁖ يِرْفِي ⁖ =

سُكَنْتَارْ ⁖ سُكَدُّمْبَرْ ⁖ كُوَرَا ⁖ سُكَجِنْ ⁖ سَكَ

سُكَكَنْ ⁖ نِبِسَ ⁖ كَيِبِمْ فُلَامْبُسْ ⁖ سُنَادُ وُكَ ⁖

سُكَدُّوبَتَ ⁖ حَمْ سُكَبَشُنْ ⁖ كِيرْغِ ⁖ كُوَرَا

⁖ مِبَسَادُ ⁖ كُوقَ ⁖ مِبِقَتَ ⁖ يَغْدُ سَرْ أَوْقَلْ

يِمْبَا فَاسَامُوتَكُمْ ⁖ لَسْ أَكَدْبُنْ ⁖ كُوَرَا ⁖

تَامْشُبْ ⁖ سَرْ أَوْقَلْ ⁖ مِسَلَامُ ⁖ بِجِنَنْ شَامِيَا

يَكَاوُرُ ⁖ سُكَيِّنْكَ ⁖ سُكَجَبُرُ ⁖ سُكَيَّنْ

سَلْكَنْ ⁖ سُكَدُّوكِ ⁖ كَتَرْ ⁖ قَبَالِ ⁖ سُكَسَ

chikin burgāme, su-ka-yi tarkō. Sai auta ya bidi dawō, ya tafi dāji, ya je kusa da rāme kūra. Sai ya dauki dawō, ya līke idānunsa, dada ba shi gani. Sai shi-na-kira, 'Inā wajen rāme(n) kūra, gā shi, ankashe sānia, tun jia aka-aje masa katara, bā agane shi ba.' Sai kūra ya ji, shi-na chikin rāme. Sai ta fitō, ta che, 'Gā ni.' Sai kūra ya che, 'Ina [19] nāman shi ke?' Sai auta ya mīka mata baban tsōka, ya che, 'Kin gani shaida.' Sai kūra ya karbi, ya hade nan da nan. Sai kūra ya che, 'Mu tafi maza maza.' Sai kūra ya tuna, sai ya tsaya, ya che,

---

in the bag, and made a trap. Then the youngest son got some porridge, went to the bush, came near the hole where the hyena was, then took the (*dawo*) porridge, and covered up his eyes; then he could not see. Then he called, 'Where is the hyena's den? Look at this, a cow has been slaughtered since yesterday, they put on one side a leg for him (her), and he (she) is not to be seen.' Then the hyena heard, he (she) was in the hole, so out he (she) came and said, 'Here I am.' And the hyena said, 'Where is the meat?' Then the youngest son held out to her a large piece of meat and said, 'You see the sign (that what I say is true).' Then the hyena took it and swallowed it right off, and the hyena said, 'Let us go at once.' Then the hyena remembered, and he (she) pulled up, and said,

ثكرن وبرن غدامس ∴ لسكن قمر كوا ∴ سن أوقم

ييجم دورن ∴ يقثف دابن ∴ يجبن كسن دوا مكورا

∴ لسن يدوك ∴ دورن ∴ يليفبن ∴ إدا أفنسن دم

بدا شغنم ∴ لسن شندا هكمن ∴ إمدا وجن زامس

∴ كورا ∴ غدا شن أنكشبن ∴ قدا فيدا ∴ قنجس

أكعجمس كنتن ∴ بدا غنبشي ∴ لسن كورا ∴

ييجم ∴ شندا ثكمن وامس ∴ سن قبقتوا ∴ قث

غدا ون ∴ سن كورا ∴ يقب إمدا قدا من ∴ شبكن ∴

سن أوقمن ∴ يميكا مقث ∴ مببن هوك ∴ ـ

يقب كنغنم ∴ شيكم ∴ لسن كورا ∴ يكرن ب

يمجم قندقمن ∴ سن كورا ∴ يقب مقتجم

مغ مغ ∴ لسن كورا ∴ يقترن ∴ سن يكمن ∴ يقب

لسم

'Abōkīna, wani dan uwanka, hakanan ya rūde ni, ya kai ni, shi-na-sō shi kashe ni.' Sai auta ya che, 'Haba kūra, kāka makāfō shi-ka-yi shi kashe wani?' Sai kūra ya che, 'Mu tafi.' Su-ka-kāma hainya, su-na-zūa, sai su-ka-kai wurin tarkō. Sai auta ya che, 'Kūra gā nāma nan.' Sai kūra ta gani katara mai-mai, kūra bai yi shāwara ba, sai ya zaabura, ya shiga, garin daukan nāma, bai san tarkō ba ne. Sai tarkō ya kāma shi. Sai kūra kūa shi-na-kūwa. Sai auta ya gudu, ya je gida, ya kirāwō yan uwansa. Su-ka-yi ta bugu kūra, har kūra ya galabaita. Su-ka-damre shi

---

'My friend, some one of your kindred, it was just thus he deceived me; he took me away and he wanted to kill me.' Then the youngest son said, 'Come now, hyena, how can a blind man manage to kill another person?' And the hyena said, 'Let us go on.' They took the road, they were coming, until they got to where the trap was. Then the youngest son said, 'Hyena, look at the meat there.' Then the hyena saw a very fat hind-quarter. The hyena, without a thought, leaped and went in, in order to lift the meat out; he (she) did not know it was a trap, till the trap caught him (her). Then the hyena began to shout, and the youngest son ran off and went home and called his brothers, (and) they flogged the hyena until the hyena became insensible. (And) they bound him (her)

أبُو كينا ؞ وَنْدَ مَعُونك ؞ قَكَنّ ؞ يَيرُوجس

يكيين ؞ شَنَا سُو ؞ شِكَ بَشُر ؞ لَسَنْ أَوْقَا ؞ يَيبْ

قَبْ كُورا ؞ كَاك ؞ مَكَا فُوا ؞ شِكَا يَن س

شِكَ بَشُر وَر ؞ لَسَنْ كُورا ؞ يَبْ مَتَقِم ؞ سُكَكَام

قَفَنْ ؞ سُنَا دُوَّ ؞ لَسَنْ سُكَكَنْ ؞ وُرفْتَنْ كُوا ؞

لَسَنْ أَوْقَن يَبْ ؞ كُورا ؞ غَمَ نَمَ مَقَّنْ ؞ لَسَنْ كُورا

تَفَقِم ؞ كَتَم ؞ قَيْقَمْ ؞ كُورَبِيَّنْ ؞ تَشَدَوَرا ب

؞ لَسَنْ يَدَ أُمَر ؞ يَشِغ غَمَ فَدَرْكَ ؞ مَدَام ؞ يَيْلَسَنْ

تَمْ كُوبَقَّن ؞ لَسَنْ فَمْ كُو ؞ يَكَا مَاشِنْ لَسَنْ

كُوا كُوَّ ؞ شِنَا غُو ؞ لَسَنْ أَوْقَن ؞ يَغُدَ

يَجَنْ غَدَا ؞ يَكَرَاوُ ؞ يَنْغُوفُلَسَنْ ؞ سُكَنّ تَمْبُغ

كُورا ؞ قَمْ كُورا ؞ يَفَمَا بِيَنْتَ ؞ سُكَدَ مَبْ مَقَر

su-ka-ja, su-ka-kai gun kushewan ubansu, su-ka-yanka, su-ka-fēde, su-ka-raba nāma, su-ka-chi. Dada su-ka-che, 'Kōwa ya gerta makōki ubanmu, saura babanmu.' Sai babansu ya dauki makēra, ya kai dāji. [21] Shi-na-kīra. Sai zāki ya zō, ya che, 'Abōkīna makēri in tafō in yi maka zuga.' Ya che, 'Ī.' Sai zāki ya tafō, shi-nā--yi masa zuga. Ashe makēri ya yi wani abu, ya bidō wani irin gainye, ya [22] danfara ga gū--tsunsa, sai ya dauki muntalaga, ya tūra wuta. Sai ya che, zāki shi yi zuga. Zāki shi-na-zuga har muntalaga ya yi ja. Sai

---

and dragged him (her), and brought him (her) to their father's grave, and (there) they cut (her throat), and skinned (her), and divided up the meat, and ate. Then they said, 'Each one has observed the funeral rites of our parent with the exception of our eldest brother.' Then their eldest brother lifted up an anvil, and took it to the bush; he was forging metal. Then the lion came, and said, 'Friend smith, let me come and work the bellows for you.' He said, 'Yes.' So the lion came and worked the bellows. Now of a truth the smith had done something, he had sought leaves of a certain kind and put (them) between his legs. Then he lifted the tongs and put (them) in the fire, and he told the lion to blow the bellows; and the lion blew them until the tongs were red hot. Then

لسكجن ۞ لسكسكن ۞ غمر كشبو فمأ بمسن ۞ =

لسكيتك ۞ لسكوجن ۞ لسكمر ومدام ۞ لسكث

در لسكث ۞ اكووا ۞ يما بجمرق ۞ امكوكم ۞

أبمهم ۞ السووا ابينهم ۞ السن وبنس ۞ ميدوك

مبكمرا ۞ يكن دام ۞ لشدا كيمر ۞ السن دراك ۞

يدو ۞ ويث أبو كيما ۞ مبكمري ۞ إن قبو

۞ إن يمك دغ ۞ إي ۞ اسن عراك يتقبو ۞ شدد — يث

يحسن ۞ دغ ۞ آبشي مكمري ۞ يماتر وفأب

يماجد وا ۞ وفإ ون ۞ غشبين ۞ ميد بجرا ۞ غفو

طفس ۞ لسن ميدوك ۞ مفتلغ ۞ ميثور ۞

وقت ۞ اسن ميث ۞ دراك ۞ لشن غ ۞ دراك ۞

لشدا دغ ۞ حم مفتلغ ۞ يبن جكن ۞ لسس

makēri ya tāshi, ya yi gōfō, ya che ma zāki,
'Abōkīna tsūlīāta ta-na-yi mani kai kai.'
Ya dauki muntalaga ya tūra chikin gainye. Gainye
na-kōnēwa. Zāki shi-na-che tsūlīar
makēri che. Makēri kūa ya [23] kyale, har
muntalaga ya yi sainye. Daga nan zāki ya che,
'Kai dan kankane nan, kai ka yi karfin
hali hakanan?' Sai zāki shi ma ya sainya
muntalaga chikin wuta, shi-na-zuga har muntalaga
ya yi ja. Sai zāki ya che, 'Abōkīna
dauki, ni ma ka sainya mani.' Sai makēri
ya dauki muntalaga shi-na-[24] rāgada ma zāki

---

the smith got up and bent down and said to the lion, 'Friend, my anus is itching'; (and) he lifted the tongs and pushed them among the leaves, (and) the leaves were set on fire. The lion thought it was the smith's anus. The smith too left them there until the tongs were cold. After this the lion said, 'An insignificant person like you, you have strength of mind to do this?' Then the lion put the tongs into the fire, he was blowing the bellows until the tongs were red hot. Then the lion said, 'Friend, lift (them) and place them for me.' So the smith lifted the tongs, he worked them up and down the lion's

مَكِيرِ ؞ يَتَلَشِّ نَبِّ غُوڢَوْ ؞ يَبْ مَدَاكِ ؞

أَبُوكَيْنَا ؞ طُولِيَا قَمُ ؞ قَتَلَا يَبِّ ؞ عَيْكَمْ

يَدَّوْكِ ؞ مُنْتَلَغْ ؞ يَشُورُ تَكِنْ غُيُبُنْ ؞ عَيْبِ

ڢَدَاكُو ڢَكُوَا ؞ دَاكِ شَنَاڢْ ؞ طُولِيڢْ ؞

مَكِيرِ ڢْ ؞ مَكِيرِ كُوَّ ؞ يَكِّلِرُ ؞ حَمْ

مُنْتَلَغْ ؞ يَبِّ لَسَنْيِبِّ ؞ دُعْمَنْ دَاكِ يَبْ ؞ دُ

كَنْدَعْ مُكَنْكَنْتَنْ ؞ كَنْكَوْ ؞ كَرْ ڢَرْ

قَلِمْ ؞ قَكَنْ ؞ لَسَنْ دَاكِ ؞ شَيْبَنْ ؞ يَلَسْ

مُنْتَلَغْ ؞ يَكِنْ رَتَمُ ؞ يَشَنَادُغْ ؞ حَمْ مُنْتَلَغْ

يَيِ ڢَنْ لَسَنْ دَاكِ ؞ يَبْ ؞ أَبُوكَيْنَا ؞

دُوكِ ؞ يَبَقَنْ ؞ كَسَنْيَا امُنْ ؞ سَنْ مَكِيرِ

يَعَزُوكِ ؞ مُنْتَلَغْ ؞ يَشَنَارَا اعْمَدَا اَمْدَاكِ

chikin shākira, har zāki ya sūma.
Sai makēri ya yi maza maza, ya tafi gida,
ya kirāwō kaninsa. Su-ka-zō, su-ka-ja,
su-ka-kai gida. Sai ya shiga gida
garin shi dēbō rūa, shi kāwō ma samāri.
Zāki na-kunche. Sai makēri ya dēbō
rūa, ya zō, mutāne sun tāru, su-na-kalō,
sai zāki ya falki, ya che, ‘Abōkīna,
haka ka yi mani?’ Sai makēri ya che,
‘Nā gani kā galabaita, dōmin hakanan
na kāwō ka gida dōmin in zubā
maka rūa.’ Sai zāki ya che, ‘Karīa ne.’

---

anus until the lion fainted. Then the smith with all speed went home and summoned his younger brothers, (and) they came (and) they pulled (the lion) (and) brought it home. Then he entered the house to get some water to bring for the young men—the lion is lying still. Then the smith drew the water (and) came, (and) the people gathered round and looked on, then the lion came round from his faint and said, ‘My friend, what are you doing to me?’ And the smith said, ‘I have seen you were weary, and so I brought you home to pour water on you.’ But the lion said, ‘You are a liar.’

ثكم شاكمرا ⁘ حمر داك ⁘ ميلسومن ⁘
سن مجمر ⁘ ميمد مد ⁘ ميتف غدا
يكم اوو ⁘ فينفس ⁘ لسكدو ⁘ لسكجن
لسكم ⁘ غدا ⁘ سن ميشغ غدا ⁘
غم فيشب مسبو ⁘ زو اشكاوو مسمار
داك ⁘ فالكنب ⁘ سن مجمر ⁘ ميجببو
زوايخو ⁘ متل مبن ⁘ لششدر ⁘ لسدكلو
سن داك ⁘ ميفلك ⁘ ميبث ابوكيبن
مك كيمرن سن مجمر يث ⁘
فل غمن ⁘ كل غمل مبين ⁘ دو مر وكمن
نكلووك ⁘ غدا ⁘ دو مر ⁘ اردمد ⁘
مك زوا ⁘ سن داك ⁘ ميث كم ميامن

Sai zāki ya zaabura, ya tāke shi, ya fashe.
Mafārin [25] gizō gizō ke nan, da ya tāke shi,
ya fashe, sai ya yi kafāfu dayawa.
Mafārin tautau ke nan, dā makēri ne.
[26] Kungurus kan kūsu.

And the lion leaped and trampled him and tore (him). That was the origin of the spider; when he (the lion) trampled on him (the smith), he broke up, and made many feet. That was the beginning of the spider; formerly he was a smith. Off with the rat's head.

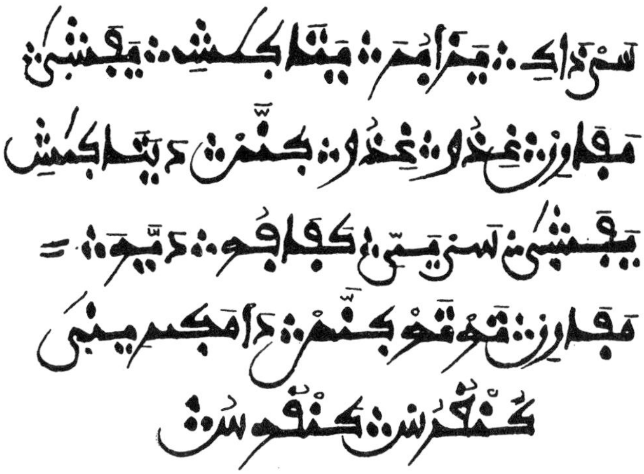

No. 7.

Wanan tātsūnīar marāyū che.

[1] Gātanan, gātanan, ta je, ta kōmō. Wani mutum
ke da [2] mātansa guda bīū. Ya mutu, ya bar su. Guda
daia chikin mātan ta sāmu chīwō. Ta gani
ta kusa mutūa. Sai ta che ma kīshiyanta, 'Dada
kin gani chīwō nan ba shi bari na, gā dīa
ta [3] nā bar taulafi garēki, dōmin Ala da anabi
ki dūba mani ita da ke(a)u.' Yau, mache ta mutu,
aka-bisna ta, su-na-nan da yārinya. Sai kulum
ta-na-gwoda mata wahala, har ranan yārinya,
chīwō ya ķāma ta. Ta-na-[4] kunche; [5] kīshia
uwa tata ta che, 'Tāshi ki tafi raafi.'

This is the story about orphans. A story, a story. Let it go, let it come. A certain man had wives, two in number. He died and left them. One among the wives fell ill. She saw she was near to death, so she said to the second wife, 'Now you have seen this illness will not leave me. There is my daughter, I have left her as a trust to you; for the sake of Allah and the prophets look after her well for me.' So the woman died and was buried, and they were left with the maid (her child). Now always they were showing her cruelty, until one day a sickness took hold of the maiden. She was lying down. Her step-mother said, 'Get up, (and) go to the stream.'

وقّرقا طوفيير مرا ميوف ::

ثما قنّر :: ثما اتنقر قجر تكومو :: وفنتر

بكر ما قنسر :: ثغدا ميو :: ميفت ييبرس :: غدا

ثمر :: تكر ما قنر :: تنسا م :: فيو :: تنغنم :: د

ثما كلسر فتو :: اسر فبثكيشينت :: ددر ::

كنغنم :: فيو قنر :: ما شبر ميبر :: غدا ديا

قا قولجم :: غمبك :: د وقر :: ال :: دام ب قا بر

كد ربا مر :: اقـ دبكو :: يوقب :: ثقت

اكبسنات :: سنا قنر :: ديا رفر :: اسر كلهم

تنا غدا امت :: وقل :: حر رقر ميا رف ::

فيو :: يكا قاف :: تقا كتب :: كيشين ::

غوا قت :: قب :: قا شر :: كنف :: واقم ::

Yārinya [6] ta tāshi, ta-na-nīshi, ta dauki
dan maburmi, ta kāma hainya. Ta tafi raafi,
ta dauko rūa, ta kāwō, ta che, '[7] Uma sabke ni.'
Sai kīshiar uwa tata ta che, 'Ba ki gani ina-[8]da-
-ka ba ne, sai nā gama?' Ta yi surfe, ta kāre,
ta-na-bākache, yārinya na-tasye. Yārinya
ta che, 'Uma sabke ni.' Sai kīshiar uwa tata
ta che, 'Ba ki gani ina-bākache ba ne sai nā gama?'
Yārinya na-tsaye, har ta gama, har ta wanke,
ba ta kula da yārinya ba. Yārinya ta che, 'Uma sabke ni.'
Ta che, 'Ba ki gani nā zuba hatsi turmi ba,
sai nā gama daka?' Yārinya nā-tsaye

The maid got up, she was groaning, she lifted a small calabash, (and) took the road. She went to the stream (and) drew water; she took it back (and) said, 'Mother, lift the calabash down for me.' But her step-mother said, 'Do you not see I am pounding? Not now, when I have finished.' She finished husking the grain, she was winnowing, the maiden was standing by. The maiden said, 'Mother, lift down the calabash for me.' But her step-mother said, 'Do you not see I am winnowing? (Not now), when I have finished.' The maiden stood by till she had finished, until she had washed; she paid no attention to the maiden. The maiden said, 'Mother, help me down (with the water-pot).' She said, 'Do you not see I am pouring grain into the mortar? (Not now), but when I have finished pounding.' The maiden kept standing by

يلوفم :. قمتالش :. قمنا فيبش :. قمعوكي :. =

د فمعبر مبم :. تكلام :. تمفي :. قتف :. وأوفي

قمد وكو :. زوا :. تكلاور :. قتبام :. اسبكس

اسي كيبشيم :. أوامت :. قبي بكغيم :. إقلاد

كلابني :. اسيفلا غمم :. قمي اسبفي :. تكلابي

قلدبلا كب :. يلوفم فلا طبين :. يلا فس

قتبام :. اسبكس اسي كيبشير عوامت :.

قتب بكغيم :. إقلا بكب بنبن :. اسيفلا غمم

:. يلوفم :. فلا طبين :. حير قفغم :. حير قمونكس

بتكلاد يلوفمب :. يلوفم قتبام :. اسبكس

:. قتب بكغيم :. قلا ذب :. قطم قتر فيبي :. =

اسي قلا غمم :. د كلا :. يلوفم فلا طبين =

har ta gama daka; ta yi ribidi, ta yi tankade, ta kāre, yārinya nā-tsaye. Yārinya ta che, 'Uma sabke ni.' Sai ta che, 'Ba ki gani ina-nasa fura ba, sai nā kāre?' Yārinya ta-na-tsaye har ta gama [9] nasa fura. Yārinya ta che, 'Uma sabke ni.' Sai ta che, 'In je garin sabke ki, fura ta [10] tsinbire, sai fura tā tafasa.' Fura ta tafasa, ta [11] tsāme, har ta kirba, ta dunkula, ta gama, ba ta che ma yārinya kōmi ba. Sai iska ya zō kamar gūgūa. Ya dauke yārinya, ya tafi da ita, ba agane ta ba. Iska ya kai ta dāji, bābu kōwa sai ita kadai. Ta-na-yāwō chikin dāji, sai ta gani buka. Sai ta je.

---

till she finished pounding; she re-pounded, she winnowed, she finished, the maiden was still standing. The maiden said, 'Mother, help me down,' but she said, 'Do you not see I am putting porridge in the pot? When I have finished.' The maiden kept standing by till she (the step-mother) had finished putting the porridge (in the pot). The maiden said, 'Mother, help me down,' but she said, 'If (I) come to help you down the porridge will get burned; (wait) till the porridge boils.' The porridge boiled, she took it out of the water, till (then) she pounded it, squeezed it, and finished. She did not say anything to the maid, till the wind came like a whirlwind; it lifted the maiden and went off with her (and) she was not seen. The wind took her to the forest (bush), there was no one but she alone. She was roaming in the forest till she saw a grass hut. Then she went (up to it).

تمر تغم دك ∴ قتي وجد ∴ تي قنكجن ∴

تكادبرن ∴ ميار فمر ∴ قما طيبن ∴ ميار فمر قتبا أم ∴

لسبكمن ∴ لسن قتب مكغنم ∴ إقما فسرقراب ∴

لسن قماكادبرن ∴ ميار فمر ∴ قما طيبن ∴ قمر تغم

قسفرا ∴ ميار فمر ∴ قتب أم ∴ لسبكمن ∴ لسن قتب ∴

إفجن غم فسبكم ∴ فراتي ∴ قطنبر برن ∴ لسن

فرا ∴ قما قبسن ∴ فرا قتبسن ∴ قطا برن ∴ =

تمر قكمرن ∴ تمر نكما ∴ تغم ∴ بتبثم ميار فمر

كموميتي ∴ لسن إلسك ∴ ميغو ∴ كمر غمو غمو ∴

ميدوكن ∴ ميار فمر ∴ ميتق ∴ دإق ∴ مإغبنتب ∴

إلسك ميكينا دإج ∴ بداب ∴ كموقا ∴ لسن إقتكدتن ∴

تقاميار ∴ نكمرداج ∴ لسن تغنم ∴ بك ∴ لسن ترو

Ta lēka, ta iske katara da kare ke chiki.
Sai ta kōma, sai katara ta che, 'Us! us!', sai kare
ya che, 'Wai ki kōmō.' Yārinya ta kōmō,
sai katara ta che, 'Us! us!', sai kare ya che, 'Wai ki shigō.'
Yārinya ta shiga buka, ta rusuna ta-na-gurfane,
sai katara ta che, 'Us! us!, sai kare ya che, 'Wai kin iya
tūō?' Yārinya ta che, 'Ī.' Sai su-ka-ba ta shinkā-
-fa kwāra guda, su-ka-che ta dafa. Ta dauki
shinkāfa kwāra guda. Ba ta yi gardama ba,
ta nasa chikin turmi, ta-na-daka, kāmin ta daka
ta kāre, shinkāfa ta chika turmi.
Ta susuka shinkāfa ta kāre, ta shėke.

She peeped in, (and) met a thigh-bone and a dog inside. Then she drew back, but the thigh-bone said, 'Us! us!', and the dog said, 'He says you are to come back.' The maiden came back, and the thigh-bone said, 'Us! us!', and the dog said, 'He says you are to enter.' The maiden entered the hut, and bowed down and prostrated herself, and the thigh-bone said, 'Us! us!', and the dog said, 'He says, Can you (cook) food?' And the maiden said, 'Yes.' So they gave her rice, one grain, and said she was to cook it. She picked up the single grain of rice. She did not grumble, she put it in the mortar and pounded, and when she had finished pounding, the rice filled the mortar. She dry pounded the rice and finished, and poured it from a height to let the wind blow away the chaff (*sheke*).

تلبفس قنا اسجس : كتتر : ء كبرن : بكشكي :

تسر تكوم : تسر كتتر : قتب أسر أسن : تسر كبرى

يبث : وبكسكوموا : يدوقس : تكوموا :

تسر كتتر تث : أسر أسن : تسر كبرى : يبث وبكتشكو

يدوقس تقتشيح بك : قتر سفس : قتا غمر قدابس

تسر كتتر : قتب أسر أسن : تسر كبر يبث : وبكنهى

قدوور : بدوقس قتب إء : تسر سكبدا ق : شنكا

قس : كوار : غدا : سكب قدق : قترك

شنكا قس : كوار : غدا : بتتي غمر دقمس :

تقتسر نبكر قمر مم : قتا دك : كا مسر قدك

تكا برن : شنكا قس : قشك قمر مم :

قلسك : شنكا قس : تكا برن : قشكس

Ta je raafi, ta wanke, ta kāwō gida, ta [12] sāsanwa,
ta zuba shinkāfa, kanda ajima shinkāfa
ta chika tukunia. Sai katara ta che, 'Us! us!', sai kare
ya che, 'Wai kin iya mia?' Yārinya ta che, 'Ī, nā iya.'
Katara ta che, 'Us! us!', sai kare ya tāshi, ya je
kan jibji, ya tōnō wani tsōfō kashi,
ya ba yārinya. Ta karbi, ta sainya tukunia.
Kāmin ajima kadan, sai nāma ya chika tukunia.
Sai nāma ya nuna, ta zuba gishiri da daudawa, ta zuba
kāyan mia duka. Mia ya nīna, ta shīde tukunia,
ta tūka tūō, ta kwāche, ta sainya ma
katara malmala gōma, ta sainya ma kare

She went to the stream and washed (it); she brought (it) back home, she set (the pot) on the fire, she poured in the rice and in a short time the rice filled the pot. Then the thigh-bone said, 'Us! us!', and the dog said, 'He says are you able (to make) soup?' The maiden said, 'Yes, I can.' The thigh-bone said, 'Us! us!', so the dog got up and went to a small refuse heap, (and) scraped up an old bone, and gave it to the maiden. She received it and put it in the pot. When a little while had passed, the meat filled the pot. When the meat was ready, she poured in salt and (*daudawa*) spice, (and) she put in all kinds of soup spices. When the soup was ready she took the pot off the fire, she served out the food and divided it up. Ten helpings she set aside for the thigh-bone, for the dog she set aside

تجر أفي ∴ تموتكي تكاووغدا ∴ تسا اسفو ∴

تمزب يشنكا قبي ∴ كند أيحم ∴ يشنكا قبي ∴ م

تيشك ∴ تكنيا ∴ تسغ كتر قب ∴ أسرأسن ∴ تسن كجرن

تيب ورتكيغ يميس ∴ يار فمس ∴ تقب إ ∴ فايعمن ∴ =

كتر قب ∴ أسرأسن ∴ تسن كجرن ∴ تيلا يشن يجس

كنيجم ∴ يتوفو ∴ ونطوفو ∴ كيشم ∴

تيبا ياد رفس ∴ تكغو ∴ تسنيس قكنيا ∴ =

كا مِن ∴ أجيم كغز ∴ السن فدام ∴ تبيك تكنيا

تسغ فام يفوون ∴ تذب غيشر ∴ دوداوا ∴ تذب

كا يسفيمن ∴ دك ∴ مِس يسنين ∴ قشيجن تكنيا

∴ تشوك ∴ تموون ∴ تكواشبن ∴ تسنيا م

كتر ∴ ملمن ∴ غوحم ∴ تسنيام ∴ كجرن

malmala tara, ta sainya ma kanta malmala bīū. Su-ka-chi, su-ka-kōshi. Tō, dōmin hakanan ne, idan bākō yā zō garēka, ka girmama shi, ka ba shi abinchi shi chi, saanan ka [13] jarabi hālinsa, ka gani mūgū ne, kō nagari ne. Yau, shi ke nan tāshin zanche, su-ka-kwāna, gari yā wāye, sai katara ta che, 'Us! us!', sai kare ya che ma yārinya, 'Wai kin iya fura?' Ta che, 'Ī.' Katara ta che, 'Us! us!' Sai kare ya tāshi, ya je, ya daukō kwāra hatsi guda daia, ya kāwō, ya bā ta. Ta karbi ta sainya chikin turmi, ta zuba rūa, ta dauki tabaria,

---

nine helpings, (and) she set out for herself two. They ate (and) were filled. So it is, because of this, if a stranger has come to you, honour him, give him food to eat. Meanwhile you study his nature, you see if (it) is bad or good. To return to the story. They went to sleep. At dawn the thigh-bone said, 'Us! us!', and the dog said to the maiden, 'He says, Can you make "fura" cakes?' She said, 'Yes.' The thigh-bone said, 'Us! us!' Then the dog got up (and) came (and) lifted one grain of corn; he brought it and gave her. She received it (and) put it in the mortar; she poured in water, she lifted the pestle,

هلملي تمر ∴ قسنبام ∴ كنت هلملي مبو

∴ سكني ∴ لسككوشم ∴ قو ∴ دو مرقكنّ

بمر ∴ إءّمر ∴ ملكوا ∴ بيادو غم بك ∴ كغرمها شم

كبا لشر ∴ أمنت ∴ شنت ∴ لسعقنّ ∴ كجمرب ∴

قد النسن كغنم موغوبمن ∴ كوغغمرين

∴ ييوشيكبقّن ∴ قاشر دغث ∴ لسككوا ون

غمر يموايكي ∴ لسركتم قثب ∴ ألسرألسن ∴ لسمر

كبرن ∴ ميشبيا رقم ∴ زيبكنكعن ∴ فمرا ∴ قثب

إي ∴ كتمر قثب ∴ ألسرألسن لسركبرن ميتا لشن

يجمن ∴ يدّ وكوا ∴ كوا رقطم ∴ غمدا دمرن

يكاورن ∴ مياف ∴ قنكرب ∴ قسنيا ∴ ثكسن

قثرمي ∴ قنخرب ∴ روا ∴ قدّوك ∴ قبريا ∴ =

ta-na-daka; kāmin ta surfe, hatsi ya yi
yawa. Ta kwāche, ta bākache, ta kai raafi,
ta wanke, ta kōmō, ta daka, ta kwāche,
ta bākache, ta kōmō, ta zuba, ta ribde, ta kwā-
-che, ta chibra, ta nasa tukunia, har ya tafasa,
ta sabke, ta tsāme, ta zuba turmi,
ta kirba, ta kwāche, ta dunkula, ta bai
wa katara dunkuli uku, ta ba kare
dunkuli bīū. Dada gari ya wāye
katara ta che, 'Us! us!', sai kare ya che,
'Wai kii tafi gida?' Ta che, [14] 'Naa tafi ama
ban san hainya ba.' Sai katara ta che, 'Us! us!',

---

she was pounding; as she (wet) pounded, the corn became much. She took it out, she winnowed, she took it to the water, she washed it, she returned, she pounded, she took it out, she winnowed, she returned, (and) poured (it in again). She pounded it very finely, she took it out, rolled it into cakes, and put it in the pot until it boiled. She took it off (the fire), set it down, poured it into the mortar, pounded, took it out, rolled it up into balls, and gave to the thigh-bone three balls, to the dog she gave two. When it was dawn the thigh-bone said, 'Us! us!', and the dog said, 'He says, Are you going home?' She said, 'I will go, but I do not know the way.' Then the thigh-bone said, 'Us! us!',

تَنَادَكَ ؞ نَكَامِنْ ؞ تَسُنْ فِيَ ؞ تَطِمْ ؞ يَامِّسْ

تَكُنْ رَاعِمْ ؞ تَبَاكُبْ ؞ تَكُوَابُشِنْ ؞ مِيوَّ ؞

تَوَنْبَكَنْ ؞ تَكُومُوَا ؞ تَمُدَكَ ؞ تُكُوَابُشِلْ

تَبَاكُبْ ؞ تَكُومْ ؞ تَمُدُبْ تَمْ بُجَنْ ؞ تَكُوَا

شِنْ ؞ تَشِبْمْ ؞ تَنَلَسْ ؞ تُكُنْيَا ؞ تَمْ يَتَبَسْ

تَسَبْكَنْ ؞ تَطَامِنْ ؞ تَمُدُبَ تُمْرِمْ ؞ ==

تَكِمْ بَ ؞ تَكُوَابُشِنْ ؞ تَمُنْكُلَا ؞ تَبِنْ

وَكِتَّمْ ؞ دُنْكُلِ ؞ أُكَ ؞ تَبَاكَبَنْ ؞

دُنْكُلِمْ ؞ بِيوُ ؞ دَدَغَمِ ؞ بِيوَابِيَنْ ؞

كَتَمْ تَبْ ؞ أُلْسَ أَلْسَنْ ؞ لَسْمْ كُمْرَ ؞ مِيبْ ؞

وَنْبِكَعْتَنْفِ غَدَا ؞ تَبْ مَأْتَبِجِمْ ؞ آمَّامَ

بُنْلَسْمَخُمْ بَ ؞ لَسْمْ كَتَّمْ ؞ تَبْ أُلْسَ أَلْسَنْ

sai kare ya tāshi; ya je, ya kāwō bāyi māsu-keau, ya kāwō shānu, da tumāki, dāwāki da kāji, da rākuma da dawāki, angarmu, da jiminu da rīguna, kōmi duka na dūnīa, kare ya kāwō ya bai wa yārinya. Ya che, 'Ga shi, katara ta che, in ba ki, ki yi guzūri, wai ta salame ki, ki tafi gida.' Sai yārinya ta che, 'Ban san hainya ba.' Sai kare ya gaia ma katara, sai katara ta che, 'Us! us!' Sai kare ya che, 'Wai mu tafi in gwoda maki hainya.' Sai kare ya wuche gaba, yārinya ta hau rākumi, ana-jan rākumi.

---

and the dog rose up; he went and brought slaves, beautiful ones, he brought cattle and sheep, horses and fowls, camels and war-horses, and ostriches, and robes, everything in the world, the dog brought and gave to the maiden. He said, 'There they are, the thigh-bone says I must give you (them); you will make them the provision for your journey. And he says he gives you leave to set out, and go to your home.' But the maiden said, 'I do not know the way.' So the dog told the thigh-bone, and the thigh-bone said, 'Us! us!' And the dog said, 'He says let us set out, (and) I must show you the way.' So the dog passed on in front, the maiden mounted a camel, the camel was led.

لسن كبرن ∴ يتناشن ∴ يجن يكاورن ∴ تبايم ∴

تد لسنقو ∴ يكاورن شانقو ∴ د قماكم ∴

داواكم ∴ دكاجم ∴ درافم ∴ دمدواكم ∴

أقغرموا ∴ دم بجنوا ∴ دريغن كوم

دك ∴ قدونيا ∴ كبرن يكاورن ∴ يبعرن ∴

يدوقم ∴ يبين غد لشكتر ∴ تبين إبداك ∴

كغدرون ∴ وقيتا لسلبك ∴ كتقي غدا ∴

لسن يدوقم ∴ تقين بنلسن ∴ حنياق ∴ بد

لسن كبرن ∴ يتخيام ∴ كتتر ∴ لسن عتترقب

ألن ألسن ∴ لسن كبرن تبين ∴ أريمتق ∴ إنقدا

تك حنن ∴ لسن كبرن يوقن ∴ غبن يدوقم

∴ تحو ∴ رافحم ∴ أقدا بتن ∴ رافيم ∴ بدا

Su-na-tafia. Kare ya kāwō su, har kusa da gida.
Kare ya kōmā. Ita kūa, ta aiki chikin gari
ta che, agaia ma sarki ita che ta zō. Sarki
ya che, ' Aje atarbō ta.' Aka-je, aka-tarbō ta.
Su-ka-sabka kōfan sarki. Sarki
ya ba su masabki, su-ka-sabka. Ta fi da ushuri,
ta ba sarki. Ta-na nan, har sarki
ya che shi-na-son ta aure. Su-ka-yi aure.
Ita kūa, wachan kīshiar uwa tata,
ta ji haushi, sai ta che dīar ta ta tafi
raafi, ta daukō mata rūa. Sai yārinya
ta che, ' Uma ni ba ni zūa.' Sai ta dauki kara

They were going along. The dog brought them till (they reached) close to (her) home. The dog turned back, but she herself sent into the town; she said, let the chief be told it was she who was come. The chief said, ' Let them go and meet her.' They went and met her. They drew up at the chief's doorway, the chief gave them permission to alight, they alighted. She took out one tenth and gave the chief. She stayed there until the chief said he wished her in marriage. They were married. She also, that step-mother of hers, (her late father's second wife) was envious, so she told her own daughter to go to the stream to draw water for her. But the little girl said, ' Mother, I am not going.' But she (the mother) lifted a reed

سنا تبجن ∴ كبرن ميكا أورسن ∴ جر كسن رغد ا ∴

كبرن تيكوهم ∴ إتكو ∴ ما أبك ∴ فكر غم

تمث أغيا مسنركم ∴ إمثب تخرون أسركم ∴

ينث أبكن ∴ أقمر بوق ∴ أكجن ∴ أكتر بوق

∴ سك سبك ∴ كوقر سركم ∴ سركم ∴

يجاسن ∴ مسبكم ∴ سك سبك ∴ تفجم عشر

∴ فبا سركم ∴ تغدا قمر ∴ جر سركم ∴ =

يث بشنا سنغ أورمن ∴ سكم أوربسن

إتكو ∴ وقمر ∴ كيشبير عوا أمت ∴

تبجم موشم ∴ سر فتب ميرق ∴ فتجم

رأفجيد وكوماخ وأ ∴ أسر يدرمن ∴

فثبأم ∴ فيبا فغرو ∴ أسرثرك ∴ كرا

ta kōrē ta, ta tafi raafi tīlas. Yau yārinya ta je raafi, ta dauko rūa, ta kāwō, ta iske uwa tata, ta-na-daka, ta che, 'Uma sabke ni.' Sai uwa tata ta che, 'Ina surfe, sai nā gama.' Ta gama surfe, yārinya ta che, 'Uma sabke ni.' Sai ta che, 'Zaa ni bākache ne, sai nā gama.' Ta gama bākache. Yārinya ta che, 'Uma sabke ni.' Ta che, 'Zaa ni daka ne, sai nā gama.' Kanda ta gama daka, sai ta nemi yārinya kasa da bisa, ba ta gane ta ba, iska yā dauke ta, ya kai dāji. Ya yar, ta-na nan, ta-na-yāwō chikin dāji, sai ta gani buka. Ta je ta lēka buka, sai ta gani

---

and drove her, (and) she went to the stream by compulsion. Now the girl went to the stream, drew water, and took (it) home. She came across her mother as she was pounding; she said, 'Mother, help me down (with the pot).' But her mother said, 'I am pounding, (wait) till I have finished.' She finished pounding, and the girl said, 'Mother, help me down.' But she answered, 'I am about to winnow, (wait) till I have finished.' She finished winnowing (and) the girl said, 'Mother, help me down (with the pot).' She replied, I am just going to pound—when I have finished.' When she had finished pounding then she sought the girl low and high; she did not see her, the wind has (had) lifted her (and) taken her to the bush. It cast her there, she was roaming in the forest, when she saw a grass hut. She went and peeped in the hut, and she saw

تكوبكت ⁖ تتقرأبم ⁖ قيلس يغ ⁖ يارس

⁖ قجس رأبم ⁖ تعر أكوزوا ⁖ تكدارو ⁖ قما إسبكس

غواقت ⁖ قعادك ⁖ قب أم ⁖ سبكس ⁖ =

لسغ غواقت ⁖ قب إقا اسروكس ⁖ لسغ قا غم

قغم سروكس ⁖ يدو قمر قب ⁖ أم لسبكس

⁖ لسغ قب دأ قبا كبقس ⁖ لسغ قا غم ⁖ قغم

با كب ⁖ يدو قمر قب ⁖ أم لسبكس ⁖ قب

دأ قعر كاقس ⁖ لسغ قا غم ⁖ كنغم قغم

دك ⁖ لسغ قبنم ⁖ يدو قمر ⁖ كلس ع يمس

⁖ يتغبتب ⁖ إسك ⁖ يدأ وبكت ⁖ يكس

دأم ⁖ يميم ⁖ قتنا قمر ⁖ قتنا يداوو ⁖ تكن دأم

لسغ قغنم بك ⁖ قجس قبليو بك ⁖ لسغ قغنم

katara da kare. Sai ta koma, sai katara ta che, 'Us! us!' Kare ya che, 'Wai ki zo.' Sai ta zo ta che, 'Gā ni.' Katara ta che, 'Us! us!' Kare ya che, (wk) 'Wai ki zamna.' Sai ta zamna ta che, 'Mu dai alhairi katara da magana, wani abu ne Us! us?' Sai su-ka-[16] kyale. Aka-jima katara ta che, 'Us! us!' Sai kare ya che, 'Wai kin iya tūō?' Sai ta che, 'Ai ana-mugunya shēkara, makwarwa tā ga dashe. Katara kuma, har ita da mai-gaio; nā iya, kū kuma hatsi ke garēku har ku na-tanbaya wai aniya tūō.' Su-ka-kyale, kare ya tāshi, ya dau--ko kwāra shinkāfa guda daia

---

a thigh-bone and a dog. Then she drew back, and the thigh-bone said, 'Us! us!' The dog said, 'He says you are to come.' So she came and said, 'Here I am.' The thigh-bone said, 'Us! us!' The dog said, 'He says you are to sit down.' So she sat down, (and) said, 'Mercy on us, a thigh-bone that talks. What sort of a thing is Us! us?' But they gave no answer. A short time after the thigh-bone said, 'Us!' us!' Then the dog said, 'He says, Can you (cook) food?' And she said, 'Ah, it 's a bad year when the partridge has seen them planting out the young trees (instead of sowing, when it could eat the seed). A thigh-bone, too, even it has an interpreter. I am able, you, I suppose, have the grain, when you are asking if people can cook food.' They gave no answer, (but) the dog got up; he lifted one single grain of rice

[illegible]
[illegible]
[illegible]
[illegible]
[illegible]
[illegible]
[illegible]
[illegible]
[illegible]
[illegible]
[illegible]
[illegible]

ya ba ta. Ta che, 'Gāsa, yau zaa ni gani
kaman da shinkāfa, kwāra guda daia,
ta ke yin tūō.' Kare ya che, 'Kedai yi hakanan,'
Ta dauki shinkāfa, ta nasa turmi,
ta-na-daka. Kanda ajima kadan, shinkāfa
ta yi yawa. Ta chāshe, ta kwāshe, ta shekē,
ta zuba rūa, ta dafa. Kanda
ta gama dafūa shinkāfa ta chika
tukunia. Ta-na-māmāki. Kare ya daukō
wani shekarare kashi, ya kāwō, ya ba ta.
Sai ta che, 'Kāka zaa ni yi da shi,
wanga shekarare kashi?' Kare ya che,

(and) gave her. 'What 's this?' she said, 'to-day I am about to see how one single grain of rice makes food.' The dog replied, 'As for you, make it thus.' She lifted the rice and put it in the mortar, she was pounding, and after a little while the rice became much. She dry pounded it, took it out, poured it out so as to blow away the chaff, poured on water, cooked it. By the time she had finished cooking it the rice filled the pot. She was amazed. The dog lifted up a year-old bone, brought it, and gave her. Then she said, 'What am I to do with it, this is a year-old bone?' The dog replied,

يباقّ ∴ قّب غداس ∴ ميو دأون ∴ غيم ∴ ك

كمر دشنكا ڢي ∴ كواو ∴ غداد مّن ∴

تبّيّن تغوو ∴ كجر ∴ ميش بكدر ∴ يحكقّس

تدّوك ∴ شنكا ڢي ∴ قنس ∴ شرمي ∴

تناد ك ∴ كند أجم ∴ كدّن ∴ شنكا ڢر

تّ ميو ∴ قنالبشي ∴ تكوالشي ∴ تشبكي

تدبوروتّ ∴ تحونجكي ∴ تسّرف ∴ كند ∴

تحم دڢوا ∴ شنكا ڢي ∴ تنك ∴

تكنيا ∴ تنمد مدك ∴ كمري يمّرڭو

ميباقّ ∴ يكداوو ∴ ككشي بر بشكر ∴ ر ∴

تسر تّب ∴ تكداك ∴ دأوجن دشم ∴

ونغ ∴ بشكر ور كشم ∴ كمري يث ∴

'Kedai yi kakanan.' Ta che, 'In ji ku māsu-
-sidabaru ne, [17] kashēdi, bābu rūāna mā-
-yū su chainye ni.' Kare na kurum, bai che
kōmi ba. Ta wanke kashi, ta nasa
tukunia. Kāmin ajima, tukunia ta chika
da nāma. Yārinya ta-na-māmāki. Sai ta tūka
tūō, ta kwāche, ta sabke mia, ta sainya ma
katara malmala uku, kare malmala bīū.
Sai kare ya yi fushi, dōmin ya gani
nāta dayawa, nāsu kadan kadan. Sai ya che,
'Haba.' Garin shi che, 'Haba,' sai ya che, 'Hab hab,'
dōmin da bai gaia ma katara ba. Da wuri kare bafāde ne

'As for you, make it thus.' She said, 'Are you supposed to be conjurers? I warn you; it is not my business that wizards should eat me.' The dog remained silent; not a thing did he say. She washed the bone and put it in the pot, and in a short time the pot was full of meat. The girl was amazed, but she stirred the food, she took it out (and) set the soup down. She put aside for the thigh-bone three helpings, for the dog two. But the dog was angry because he saw her share was large, theirs very small, and he said, 'What 's this?' When he would have said, 'Haba,' he could only say, 'Hab hab,' because he had not told the thigh-bone first before he spoke. Formerly the dog was a minister at court

بجد من : يحكنش قتجإقم : كوماش

سد بحر نبن : كشمد : بجاب وَأمن : ما

بيو : ستشيرن : كبرن : قاكرم : بيث

كومييب : قمونكبن : كشم : قفس

تكنيا : تكامن : أجحم : تكنبا : قاتك :

دقام : بجاوش : قمامامك : سن تنوك

قوور : تتكواشن : قسبكي حمن : تسنيام :

كتر ململ : دأك : كبرن : ململ : بجو :

سن كبرن : بيمن فشم : دومن : بياغيم :

نامث دبيو : قاسكد وكدرش سن بيث

تب : غمر فشث حب : سن بيث حب حب :

دوقمن : ع بيخم قم : كترام : دور : كبرن : بقاد مسنر

magana shi ke yi kamar mutum, da ya yi fushi
gaban sarki, shi ya sa shi ke yin 'Hab,
hab', idan ya tāshi zaa shi yin fada.
Dōmin hakanan ne yārō ba shi
fushi wurin da baba shi ke.
Yau, su-ka-chi abinchinsu, su-ka-kwāna.
Gari ya wāye katara ta che, 'Us! us!'
Dada kare bai iya ya yi magāna ba.
Sai ya je, ya kāwō makāfi mutāne,
da kutāre, da makāfi dawāki,
da gurgun jāki, da ragōgi,
rīguna da wanduna aka-ba ta, kare ya gwoda mata

---

and used to talk like a person, when (on this day) he got in a temper in front of the king, he condemned him to say 'Hab! hab!' if he rose up to quarrel. And the moral of this is, a youth must not lose his temper in the presence of an elder. Now they had eaten their food and slept. At dawn the thigh-bone said, 'Us! us!' Then the dog was not able to speak, but he went and brought blind men, and lepers, and blind horses, and lame asses, and sheep, robes and trousers were brought to her, (and) the dog showed her

مغرشجكن : يكمم متش دبي فشم ::

غمبر سمركم : لشم يبلسن : شكيمرجب

جمب : إدرن : يمتاشر : دأشيبجم : م

دومر : تحكنر فمرن : ميه ور : عباشن

فشم : ورفدم يمب : لشبكن : =

ميو : سكش : أمنشنسن : سكوان

غمر بيواين : كنتر قشأسراسن

دد : عجر بيعجن : ميان مغنافا ::

لسن قيجن : نيكاور : مكاجم مناين

دكناورن : دمكاجمر دوراكم ::

دغمرغمر : نجاكم : درغوغم ::

يرمغمر : دم وفدرن : آلجبا ق : كمريغر افة

hainya. Ya kāwō ta kusa da gida, ya kōma.
Sai katara ya kōre shi, sai ya kōmō
maza maza, ya chika da su, ya bi su har
su-ka-kāwō gida. Mafārin kare shi zō
gida ke nan, da wurin dawa shi ke. Tō, tāshin
zanche, da su-ka-kāwō kusa da gida, sai
ta aika kuturu guda daia chikin mutānenta,
shi na bisa makāfō dōki, wai shi je
shi gaya ma sarki tā zō. Sarki shi bari
atarbe ta. Sarki ya sa galadima
da mutāne dayawa aka-je, aka-tarbe su.
Da su-ka-zō fagashi, sai dwai ya chika gari.

---

the way. He brought her to near (her) home and turned back. But the thigh-bone drove him away, so he came back very quickly and joined them, and followed them until they reached the house. That is the first time the dog came to the house, formerly he was in the bush. Well, to continue, when they had got near the house, then she (the girl) sent one leper from among her retinue. He sat on a blind horse and his message was to tell the chief she has come. The chief allowed her to be met. The chief made the galadima and many people to go and meet them. When they reached the open space in front of the chief's house, then a stink filled the town.

تَفُنْ ∴ يَكَمْ وُوتَ ∴ كُسَعْ غِدَا ∴ بَكُو تَمْ ∴

سَنْ كَتَمْ ∴ يَكُو رَمَشِنْ ∴ سَنْ يَكُو مُو ∴

مَدْ مَدْ ∴ يَشِكْ دُسَو ∴ يَمِسِنْ قَمْ ∴

سُكَكَا وُرْ ∴ غِدَا ∴ فَقَا رِنْكَمْ ∴ شُدُو

غِدَا بِعَقِّنْ ∴ دُوُرْ ∴ دَ وَّشْبَكَنْ ∴ ثُوقَا شِنْ

دَفْثْ ∴ دُسُكَكَا وُرْ ∴ كُسَرْ دَغِدَا ∴ تَسْنْ

تَأَنْيَكْ ∴ كُتُمْ وُرْ ∴ غُدَا دَنَّ ∴ ثِكَمْ قَتَا بَنّتْ

شِقَا بِسَنْ ∴ قَكَا فُجُو ∴ دُوكِ ∴ وَمِثِجَنْ

∴ شِغَبَا تَمْ سَرْكِمْ ∴ قَادُرْ ∴ سَرْكِمْ شِبَمْ

أَقْرِبَتَا ∴ سَرْكِمْ ∴ بِلَنْ غَلَا دِ يَمَا ∴ ـــ

دَقْتَا بَنْ ∴ دَيَّجُو ∴ أَكَجِنْ أَكْتَمْ بِسَنْ ∴

دَسُكَذُرْ ∴ وَقُشِمْ ∴ تَسْدُ وَنْ ∴ يَثِكْ غَمْ

Sai sarki ya che akōma da su chan bayan gari.
Aka-kai su bayan gari, chan su-ka-yi gidāje su.
Uwar yārinya nan ta gani kakanan, sai ta yi
bakin chikin, ta mutu. Mafāri ke nan zanba,
ba ta da keau (chau). Kōwa ya yi zanba ga dan wani
ta-na-kōmāwa ga dansa, kaman da wani mālami
ya yi wākā, Ala shi jikainsa, ya che,
'Kōwa ya shibka zanba, ta na fita gōna [18] nasa.'
Wanan hakikan bābu wāwa kun jia?'

Shi ke nan, [19] kungurus
kan kusu.

Then the chief said they were to be taken far back to a distance behind the town. They were led behind the town, far away they were to make their houses. When the mother of this maiden saw all this, then she became black of heart, (and) died. That was the first appearance of wickedness, (which) is not a beautiful thing. Whoever commits a sin against another it comes back on himself, as a certain learned man sung, may Allah dispense mercy on him, he says, 'Whosoever sows evil it comes forth in his own garden. That is true without a doubt, have you heard?' That is all. Off with the rat's head.

سن سنركم ؞ يبا أكوم د سو ؞ ثم بايين غمر

أككيبس ؞ بايين غمر ؞ قم سكي ؞ غدا جس

عوزيار فيين ؞ تقغنم ؞ حكقن ؞ سوقن ؞ =

بكقشك ؞ تقوف ؞ مقار بكمشن ؞ دن ب

ماق دقو ؞ كوارا ؞ بي دقب ؞ غد قوت ؞

تنا كو مدارا ؞ غد قسش كمن د و نما آلم ؞

بي واك ؞ أن اشج كيس ؞ ميث ؞

كوار بيشبك ؞ دنب ؞ تنا فتا ؞ غو نم قسه

وقم ؞ حفيقا ؞ باب وار ؞ كقنجيا ؞

شيكنن ؞ ققخم سش

كحكوش

No. 8.

Wanan tātsūnīar [1] mayā che.

[2] Gātanan, gātanan, ta je, ta kōmō. Wata tsōfūa ta ke da yāyanta, budūri tara, sai [3] ta je dōka dāji ta zamna. Sai wadansu yāra, samāri, su tara, su-ka-tāshi daka gari-nsu, su-ka-tafi gidan mayā, wurin budūri. Su-ka-je. Budūri su-ka-ba su rūa, kōwa budūransa ta ba shi rūa ya sha. Sai karaminsu, karamar budūri ta kāwō rua, ta ba shi, sai ya ki sha. Dare ya yi, kōwa budūransa ta yi tūō, ta ba shi. Su-ka-chi. Autan budūri ta yi tūō, ta kāwō ma autan samāri, sai ya ki chi. Aka che, 'Kāka, da ka zō kōwa ya chi abinchi, sai kai daia ka ki chi?' Ya che, 'Idan

---

This is a story about a witch. A story, a story. Let it go, let it come. A certain old woman had children, nine girls, and she went far into the bush and lived (there). Now some boys, youths, there were nine of them too, set out from their village and went to the house of the witch, where the girls were. They came. The girls gave them water, each had a maid who gave him water to drink. Now the youngest (among the boys) the youngest maid brought water to (him) and gave him, but he refused to drink. When night came each of (the young men's) maids made food and gave him; (and) they ate. The youngest of the maidens made food and brought it to the youngest of the youths, but he refused to eat. They said, 'How is it when you come every one eats food, but you alone refuse to eat?' He said, 'If

وَقَمْ قَا طُو فِتِّيرْ مَيَا بْشَ

قَا قَمْ عَا قَمْ تِجَمْ تَكُو مُوا :. وَتَطُو بُجَوا :. تَبَلَكَم :.

يَا مَيْنْتَ :. بُدُرِ قَمْ :. لَسْ قَجُمْ دَرُ كَدَاجِ :. قَدْ مَسَ

لَسْ وَدْ قَلَسْ يَدَا وَرَا :. لَسَدَاوِ :. سَوْقَمْ :. سُكَتَا اِشْ دَكَمِ

قَسَ :. سُكَتَقِمْ :. نُجَدْ قَمْيَا :. وُرْ قَبُدُ وُرِ :. شُكَجَسْ

بُدُ وُرِ :. سُكَبَلَسْ وُرَا :. كُورَا :. بُدُرْ قَسَنْ

قَبَا اِشْ رُرَا :. مِيشَنْ :. لَسْ كَمْ مِنْسَ :. كَمْ قَمْ

بُدُ وُرِ :. تَكَا وُرُرَا :. قَبَا اِشْ :. سَرْ يَكِشْ :. دَبُرَ

بِيسِ :. كُورَا :. بُمْ رُقَسَ :. تَنْ قَمُوُرُ :. قَبَا اِشْ

سُكَشِ :. أُوقَمْ :. بُدُ وُرِ :. قَمْ قُوُرُ :. تَكَا وُرُ :.

مَا وُقَمْ سَدَاوِ :. لَسْ يَكِشِ :. آكُشْ :. كَدَاكَ :. دَكَدُو

كُورَا :. يَلِشِ أَمِنْشِ :. لَسْ كَمْ دَتَنْ :. عَكَشِ :. بَيْشَا اِدَوْ

samāri su-ka zō gidan budūri, su-na-chin abinchi, saanan sun zama samārin banza.' Aka che, 'Gaskīa ne.' [4] Wakatin kwāna ya zō, sai kōwa duka budrua tasa ta yi masa shinfida, su-ka-kwanta, su-na-kwāna. Autan samāri [5] ya tāshi, ya [6] kunche bantu nan waninsu, ya damra ma budūri. Ya fida rigunansu, ya sainya ma budūri, ya dauki fatalōli budūri, ya damra ma [7] mazan, ya dauki zannuan [8] mātan, ya damra masu. Aka-jima, ana-kwāna, sai tsōfūa nan ta zō. Idan ta lālaba, ta gani mai-rīga da bante. Sai ta yanke, hakanan har ta yanke dīanta duka, ta kōma, ta kwanta. Sai auta kūa shi-na-ganinta, bai yi kwāna ba. Ya tāshi, ya gina

---

young men come to the house of maidens and eat food, then they have become worthless young men.' And they said, 'That is true.' The time for sleep came, when for each and all his maiden prepared his couch, and they lay down and were sleeping. The youngest of the boys got up and unfastened the others' waist-cloths and tied them on the maidens. He took off their cloaks and put them on the maidens, he lifted the kerchiefs of the maidens and tied them on the boys. He took away the dresses of the girls and tied them on (the boys). A short time passed, they were asleep, when this old woman came. When she felt about with her hand, she discovered who had cloaks and who waist-cloths. Then she cut (their throats), and thus she did till she had cut off (the heads) of all her daughters; (then) she returned and lay down. But the baby of the family also had seen her, he had not slept. He got up, dug

لسحاري ؞ لسكغو ؞ غدول [redacted] و بحوري ؞ لسداشر أمنث

لسعقمن ؞ لسنذم ؞ لسمدو فبنغرا ؞ أكب غسكيلقبكي

رقتن كواقمن ؞ بيدوا ؞ لسن كوا ؞ يدك ؞ بحد رواقمس

تيمس شنعيد ؞ لسككنتا ؞ لسداكواقم ؞ أوقمن

لسحاري ؞ ميتداش ؞ يكنث ؞ بحتقمن رقمس ؞

مع قمرمعجوري ؞ بيقعرر يغقمس ؞ ميسقيا قبروري

ميداك ؞ بحقلولم ؞ بحوري ؞ ميد قمرمقمون ؞ ميدوك

دقمو قمداقمن ؞ بيقمرمسن ؞ أكجم أقداكواقمن

لسن طوبقوقمنن ؞ قدوا ؞ ادن ؞ قمالبه ؞ تقفيم

مبيرميغن ؞ دمنجن لسن قمنكن ؞ مكنمن ؞ حم قمبكي

ديمقت ذك ؞ تكوم ؞ تكقمن ؞ لسن أوقمر كوه ؞ =

شنا غنمتا ؞ بيمن كواقماب ؞ ميتداش ميقمن

rāmē tun daga [9] dākin da su ke kunche har dākin
uwansu. Sai auta ya tāda waninsa daga kwāna.
Su-ka-shiga chikin rāme, su-ka-tafi gida, su-ka-bar dīanta
kunche, [10] yankaki. Da gari ya wāye, tsōfūa ta zō.
Ta na murna, [11] zaa ta chin nāma, sai ta iske dīanta yankaki.
Sai ta chizi hannu, dōmin haushi, sai ta [12] kyale,
ta che, 'Naa rāma.' Wata rāna sai ta tafi chikin garin.
Ta zama [13] magarīa, sai yāra, mutun gōma sha bīar
su-ka-hau, su-na-zamne. Sai ta chire da su,
ta tafi gidanta da su. Uwayen yāra
su-na-kūka. Auta ya zō ya che, 'Ku bar kūka,
naa kāwō maku dīanku.' Ya tafi dāji, ya gani
sāniar tsōfūa nan, sai ya shiga chikin chikinta.

---

a hole from the house where they were lying to their mother's house. Then the baby of the family wakened the others from sleep. They entered the hole and went home and left her daughters lying (with their throats) cut. When day dawned the old woman came. She was rejoicing (because) she was about to eat meat, then she came across her daughters (with their throats) cut; then she ate her hand from vexation. Then she left off, and said, 'I shall be revenged.' Another day she went into the town (of the young men). (And) she turned herself into a *magaria* tree, then the boys, fifteen in number, climbed up and were sitting there. But she tore up (the tree) with them and went off to her house with them. The boys' parents were lamenting. The baby of the family came and said, 'Leave off crying, I shall bring you your children.' He went off to the bush, (and) he saw this old woman's cow, then he went inside its belly.

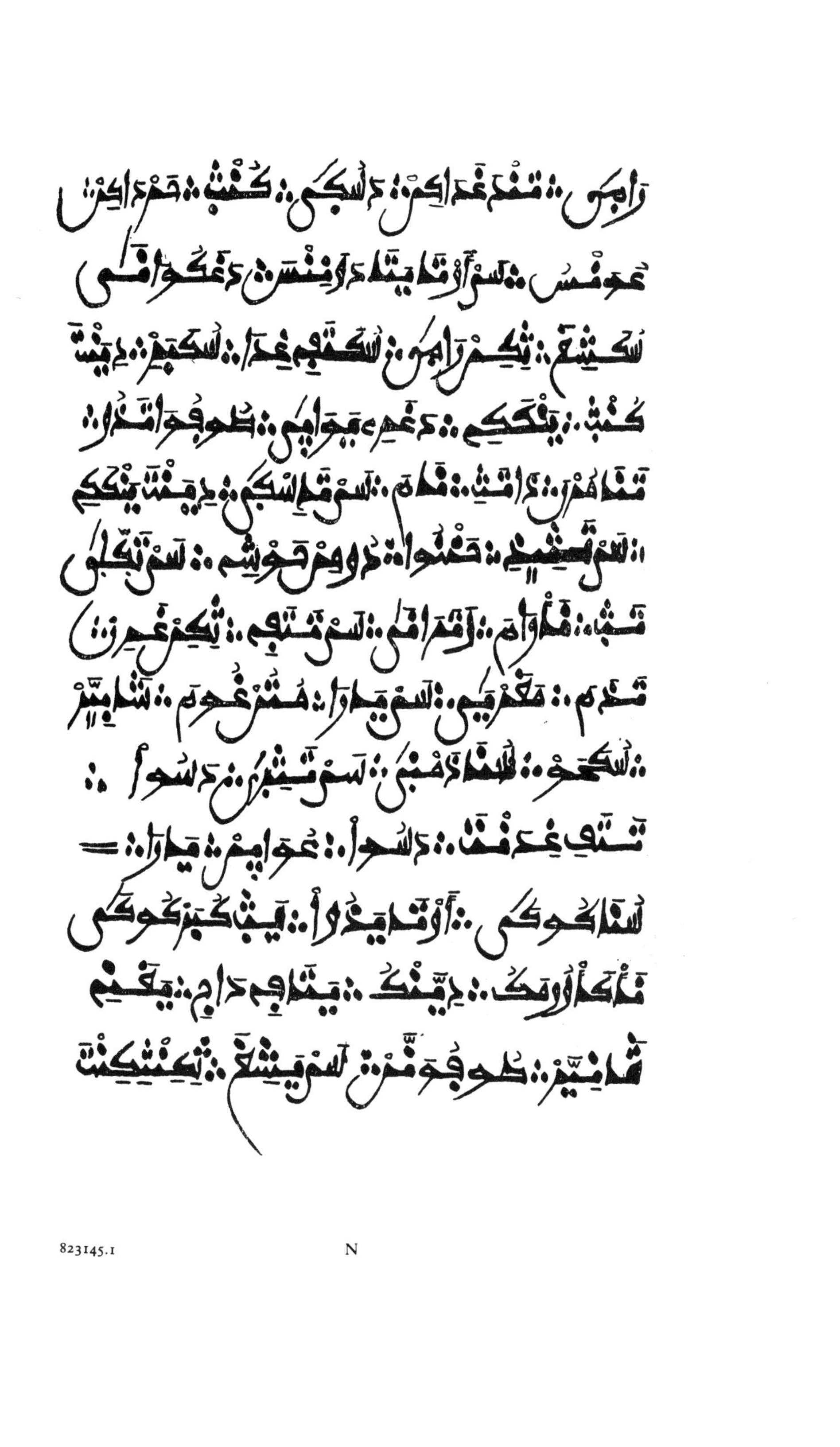

Da sānia ta kōmō gida, ta yi kamar mai-chiki.
Sai tsōfūa ta che sāniar nan tāwa, 'Idan
ki haifu namiji, [14] naa yanka ki, idan ki haifi
mache, naa bar ki.' Ananan, ranan, sai ta haifi
mache. Ashe auta ne, ya zama dan sānia.
Su-na nan, sai auta, idan tsōfūa tā yi
wanke kōrai, sai ya tuma, shi fāda achiki,
shi farfasa. Ranan ta wanke kōrainta,
ta shainya, sai [15] maraki sānia ta tuma, ta fāda
achiki, ta farfasa. Sai tsōfūa ta yi fushi,
ta che yāra nan su duka su tāshi, su tafi,
su kāmō shi, su yanka. Sai yāra
su-ka-tāshi, su ka bi maraka. Maraka ta shēka

When the cow came home, it was as if in calf. And the old woman said (to) this cow of hers, 'If you give birth to a son, I shall cut your throat; if you give birth to a daughter I shall leave you alone.' And it came to pass that one day the cow gave birth to a daughter. Now of a truth it was the baby of the family, he had turned into the child of a cow. They were living like this, when the baby of the family (who was now a calf), if the old woman washed her calabashes, jumped and fell among them and smashed them. One day she washed her calabashes and put them in the sun to dry, then the cow's calf jumped and fell on them and smashed them. And the old woman got in a rage, and said to these boys that they must all rise up, and go and catch and bring it, and cut (its throat). So the boys rose up (and) followed the calf. The calf ran off

دَقْدْ فِيَا :. تَكُو مُوا :. مُحَدَا :. نَسِ كَمَمْ مَيْشِكِ

لَسْنِ طُو فُجَوَا :. تَبْ ثَيَا فِيَرْ فَمّ :. قَدْوَّا :. إِدَّنْ

كِ[redacted]حَمِيُفْ نُمَجِ :. فَدْ بَيْكُمْ كُمْ :. إِدَّرْ كِ[redacted]حَمِيْهِ

مَثْ فَدْ بِمْ رَكِ :. أَفَدَّا فَمْرَ :. وَفَّمْ :. لَسَنْ فَحَمِيْبِ

مَثْ :. أَبْشَى أَوْ قَدْ فُبَى :. يَكَّمْ :. دَ مُقْتَا فِيَا :.

لَسَدَا فَمَّعْ :. لَسَنْ أَوْ قَمْ :. إِدَّرْ :. طُو فُجَوَا :. قَدَا دَسّ

وَنُكَبْ كُوُمْ :. لَسَرْ يُسَثَّمْ يِشْقِبَادَ :. أَنِكِـــمْ :.

شِبَقَرْ فَبَسَى :. وَفَّمْ تَحُو مُحْكُبْ :. كُوُرْتْ

مَشْتَيَا :. لَسَمْ مَمْرَكَنْ ثَدَا فِيَا :. مُسَثَّمْ :. قَبَادَ :.

أَنِكِـمْ :. فَقَبْ فَبَسَى :. لَسَرْ دُحُو فُجَوَا :. قَمْ فِيشِمْ

مَثْ :. يَدْوَ فَمَّرْ :. لَسُو دُكِ :. لَسَتَّاشِنْ لَسْنِجِمْ

لَسَكَا مُحُو لِشِمْ :. [redacted] لَسِيْنِكْ :. لَسَرْ يَدَوَا :. ==

لَسَكَتَاشِنْ لَسَكَبِ مَمْرَكُمْ :. مَمْرَكُمْ :. قَتْبَشِكْ

har chikin gari, yāra su-ka-bi ta. Sai maraka ta zama mutun, ashe auta ne. Sai ya che, 'Kōwa shi zō shi kāma dansa.' Sai kōwa ya fitō, ya kāma dansa, auta kūa sai ya tafi gidansu. Sai ta che, 'Naa kāma shi kuma.' Sai ta zama Bihilāta, ta dauki nōnō, ta kāwō chikin gari. Aka-che, kar kōwa shi dūba chikin nōnō, sai baban wan auta ya dūba, sai idānunsa ya fāda. Sai ta dauki nōnō ta, ta zama gūgūa, ta tafi da shi. Sai ya zō da wuri, ba shi gida. Aka che, 'Wata Bihilāta ta zō da nōnō, ta dauki idānu wanmu, ta tafi da su.' Sai auta ya che,

---

till (it came) right into the town; the boys followed it. Then the calf turned into a person, truly it was (he who was) the baby of the family. And he said, 'Let each come and catch his son.' So each one came out and caught his son, and the baby of the family he also went home. Now she (the old witch) said, 'I will catch him again.' So she turned into a Fulani woman, (and) took some milk, (and) brought it into the town. It was said that no one was to look into the milk. But one of the baby of the family's elder brothers looked in, and his eyes fell out. Then she took her milk, turned into a whirlwind, (and) went off with him. Then he (the baby of the family) came early, (and found his elder brother) was not at home. And they said, 'A certain Fulani woman came with milk and lifted the eyes of our elder brother and went off with them.' And the baby of the family said,

قَمْ ثِكِمْ نَغِمِ ى ∴ بَيْطْوَا ∴ لُسَكِيِيتْ ∴ لَسَنْ مَمَرْمَحَى ∴

قَغَمْ مُتَنْ ∴ أَنْشَى أَوْقَافُمْ ∴ لَسَنْ بَيْثْ كُوَرَا ∴

لِيثُغْ وَالِشَكَامْ ∴ دَفْلَسَنْ لَسَنْ كُوَاوَا بَيِمْتُوا ∴

بِكَامْ ∴ دَفْسَنْ أَوْقَا كُوَا ∴ لَسَنْ بَيْتَفِ يِغَعْ فَلَنْ

سَنْ قَتَبْ فَمَا أُكَامَا لِشُكَمْ ∴ لَسَنْ قَتَغَمْ بِيمَلَامْ ∴

قَتَرْأَكِ ∴ فُوفُوا ∴ تَكَاوُ ثِكِمْ نَغِمِ ى ∴ أَكَبْ

كَمْ كُوَرَا ∴ لِشَعْرُوبَ ∴ ثِكِمْ فُوفُوا ∴ لَسَنْ بَيْتَنْ

وَنْدَا أَوْقَمْ ∴ يَدُوبَ ∴ لَسَنْ إِدَا افُنْلَسَنْ ∴ بِيقَادَ ∴

سَنْ قَدَوْكِنُوفُوقَ ∴ قَغَمْ ∴ غُوغُوَ ∴ قَتَكِ

دِشَمْ ∴ لَسَنْ بِيغُوُ ∴ دَوُرِمَا لِشَغَدَا ∴ أَكَبْ وَقَ ∴

بِحِلَاقْ ∴ قَغَرَا ∴ دَفُوَانُو قَتَدَّرَاكِ ∴ إِدَافُو

وَفْفُمْ ∴ قَتَكِ دَسُوَا ∴ لَسَنْ أَوْقَمْ ∴ بَيْثْ [redacted]

'Naa karbō su.' Sai ya damra zane da fatala, ya tafi gidan tsōfūa. Da ta gane shi, ya yi kama da auta dīanta, sai ta che, 'Marhabi, marhabi.' Da auta shi kūa sai ya rika kūka, shi-na-kūka, shi-na-fadi, 'Laalātatu samāri sun zō, sun yi mani zanba, sun kashe mani wani.' Tsō-fūa kūa ta-na-che autan dīanta ne, sai ta che, 'Bari kūka auta, ai mu ma, [16] muu rāma.' Ta che, 'Ai ni ma, ga idānu babansu, [17] nā kāwō.' Sai auta ta che, 'Ba ni in gani [18] uma nāma in yi wāsa da su.' Sai tsōfuā ta dau-ki, ta ba shi, ba ta san shi ba ne. Shi-na-wāsa da su sai ta che, 'Zamna ki dūba gida, zaa ni raafi in kōmō.' Ta dauki tūlū, ta bāda bāya.

'I shall get them back.' So he fastened on a (girl's) dress and head kerchief, (and) went to the old woman's house. When she saw him, he was like her (own) youngest daughter, and she said, 'Welcome, welcome.' And the baby of the family he also began to cry, he was weeping and said, 'Bad boys came and sinned against me, they killed my elder sisters.' The old woman too was saying, 'It is the youngest of my daughters.' And she said, 'Cease crying, youngest of my children, as for us, we shall be revenged.' She said, 'As for me, see the eyes of the eldest of them I have brought.' And the baby of the family said, 'Give me that I may see, mother, the meat (eyes), (and) that I may play with them.' So the old woman took them, and gave him, she did not know it was he. He was playing with them, when she said, 'Sit and look after the house; I am going to the stream and shall return.' She lifted up the water-pot (and) turned her back.

نَاْ كَرْ بُجُوسُنْ لَسْوِيَدْ مَعْ طَنِبُنْ ۞ دَرِقِتَلِ ۞ مِتَقِ غَمَرِنْ

طُوبُوَا ۞ دَمَعْبِشِنْ ۞ يَايِكَصُ ۞ دَآوْتَادِيِنْ ۞

سَوْ مَثْ مَمْ حَبِ ۞ مَمْ حَبِ دَآوْتَا ۞ شِيكَهْ ۞ لَسْوِيَرِكْ ۞

كُوكَي ۞ شِنَا كُوكَنْ ۞ شِنَا قِجِ ۞ لَالَا اَمْتُوَا ۞ لَسَهَارِ

۞ لَسَنْدُوْ ۞ لَسِنْمَن ۞ دَفْبَ ۞ لَسَنْكَشْمَن ۞ وَفِمْ ۞ طُو

فُوَا كُوَا ۞ تَنَا اَفْ ۞ آوْتَمْ دِيَفَنْتَنِي ۞ لَسْ تَبْ ۞ بَمْ كُوكَي

آوْ تَنِ ۞ آءِ مُهْ مَعْنِ ۞ مُغُوْوَامْ ۞ تَبْ اَغَمْبِيَقُنْ ۞ غَدَا إِدَا اَنْتُو ۞

بَبَنْسُنْ ۞ فَدَكَدَاوْ ۞ لَسْ آوْتَدْ ۞ تَبْ بَدَفِي ۞ إِوْفِنَمْ

۞ اَمْ ۞ قَا مُوْ ۞ إِنْمُو وَاسَكِي ۞ دَسُو ۞ لَسْ طُوفُوَا ۞ تَدُو

كِ ۞ قَبَاشْ ۞ بَتَنْسَنْشِبَنُ ۞ شِنَا وَاسَكِنْ ۞ مَ سُوَا

لَسْ قَتْ ۞ دَمَشِي ۞ كَدُوبِ غَدَا ۞ دَاَفِي ۞ وَاَجِ ۞ بَ

إِنْكُومَوَا ۞ تَدَوْكِ ۞ فُوْلُوَا ۞ قَبَا دَبَابِي ۞ =

Sai auta ya tāshi, ya shēka da idānun wansu,
ya tafi da shi, ya bai wansu. Sai tsōfūa
ta kōmō, ta che, 'Ina auta?' Ba ta gani auta ba,
sai ta sabke rūa. Aka jima, sai yārinya ta zō,
tsōfūa ta che, 'Kāwō idānu, mu dafa.'
Yārinya ta che, 'Ai ba ki ba ni idānu ba.' Sai ta che,
'[19] La ila autansu ne ya zō ya rūde ni, ina-che
ke che, ama bābu laifi naa kāma shi.' Ta kyale.
Wata rāna auta ya tafi dāji, shi-na-farauta, sai
ya gamu da tsōfūa. Ta kāma shi, ta kai gidanta,
ta sainya rāme, ta rufe sai ta tafi raafi. Ta bar
dīanta karama, ta che ta jiran auta kada shi gudu.

Then the baby of the family rose up, and ran off with his brother's eyes; he went with it (them) (and) gave his elder brother. Then the old woman returned (from the stream) (and) said, 'Where is (my) youngest child?' She did not see her youngest child, and she set down the water. After a little while then the maiden came, and the old woman said, 'Bring the eyes that we may cook (them).' The maiden said, 'No, you did not give me any eyes.' And she said, '*La ila* it is the youngest of their family, he came and deceived me; I said (thought) it was you, but it cannot be helped, I shall catch him.' She ceased. Another day the baby of the family went to the bush. He was hunting when he met the old woman. She caught him, (and) took him to her house, put him in a hole, (and) covered (him) up, while she went to the stream. She left her youngest daughter and told her to wait and watch the baby of the family lest he ran away.

لسن أودمن :: يتنالشن يبشك :: د إم امنو فسن
يتقد يشم :: يججبت :: أوفسن لسن طوبوا :: =
تكومواء :: تفت إمن أودمن :: متغنم :: أودمب
:: لسن تتسبكن ورا :: أججم لسن يدومن :: تدوا ::
طوبوا امتبت :: كدور :: إدامو :: مدف ::
يدومن قتبت :: أي بكبدن :: إدامو مبن :: لسن متبت ::
لا إللمن :: أوتنسبن :: يغدوا :: ابير ودمرن :: إنداب
تجبت :: أمدابداب :: ليجم :: فلا أكدامدا شن تبجلن
:: ومترامن :: أودمن يتقد دام :: لشتا قدومت :: لسن
يغم :: د طوبوا :: تكدامدا ليش :: تكن غدمت
تلشبرا امن :: تنوبكن :: لسن متبجم وابم :: متبر
دي يبخت كدمن :: متب تبجرن :: أوقدا :: كدلشقد

Sai ta tafi raafi. Sai auta dianta ta je wurin auta wanda ke chikin rāme, ta che, 'Auta me ka ke chi?' Sai shi kua ya che, 'Mīkō [20] hannu(n)ki in ba ki, abinda ni ke chi.' Sai ta mīka hannu. Sai auta ya kāma hannunta ya ja ta, ya nasa rāme. Ta-na--chiki, ta-na-kūka. Auta ya rufe ta, kaman da uw(a)--nta ta rufe shi, ya dauki zane da fatala, ya damra. Shi-na nan, shi-na-wāsa, har tsōfūa ta zō. Ta che, 'In ji auta bai gudu ba.' Sai ya che, 'Shi-na-nan, bai gudu ba.' Ta dafa ruan zāfi, ya tafasa ta dauki ta che, 'Dan nema yau [21] shii gani.' Sai ta je wurin rāme, ta zuba, sai yārinya, da da ji zāfi

---

Then she went off to the stream. Then her (the witch's) youngest daughter came to the place where the baby of the family was in the pit (and) she said, 'Oh, baby of the family, what are you eating.' And he said, 'Stretch out your hand and I will give you what I am eating.' So she put out her hand, but the baby of the family seized her hand, (and) pulled her, (and) cast her into the pit; she was inside, she was crying. The baby of the family covered her up as her mother had covered him. He took (her) dress and kerchief and tied them on. He remained there, and was playing about until the old woman came. She said, 'Let me hear that the baby of the family has not run away,' and he replied, 'He is here, he has not run away.' She boiled hot water, it boiled, she took it up, and she said, 'Son of a profligate, to-day he will see.' Then she went to the hole and poured in (the water), and the maiden, when she felt the heat

لسن قتّي راوم ∴ لسن أوقاد يمّت ∴ فجو ورمدا أومّن

وفد بجيكن ∴ رابو ∴ قتّ أومّن ∴ مككجث ∴

لسن شيكو ∴ يجث ميكوا قشوك ∴ إنباك ∴

أمنغربكث ∴ لسن تجيك حشوا ∴ لسن أومّن ∴

يكام ∴ قشوقّ ∴ يجاق ∴ ينلسن رابو ∴ تقا

ثكي ∴ تقاكوكن ∴ أوقن يمرجت ∴ كمر دعو

فت ∴ قرجمشن يدرك طبّن ∴ د وجتلن ∴

يع مر ∴ ليشنا قمّر ∴ ليشنا والسن ∴ حمطوجوا ∴

تخوانقث إنج أوقن ∴ بيغدب ∴ لسن يث ∴

ليشنا قمّن ∴ بيغدب ∴ قدف ورمدا وم ∴ يتقس

تمّ ورك ∴ قث د فبّهن ∴ بّو ليشغنم ∴ لسن تجن

وورمد ابو ∴ نفغب ∴ لسن يدرفمن ∴ د فجّ داوم ∴

ta-na-kūwa, ta-na-fadi, 'Uma ni che, uma ni che.' Auta
shi-na-fadi, 'Karīa ka ke yi. Ala shi tsari uma ta haife ka,
Ala tsare ta ta haife ka.' Hakanan har ta mutu.
Ta dauko, ta [22] sasāre, ta nasa tukunia, ta dafa.
Yārinya ta nina, ta sainya daudawa da gishiri,
ta shīde tukunia, ta tsāme nāma, ta che, 'Auta
tafō, kedai mu chi dan nema.' Sai ya che, 'Aa
ni ba ni chi, yanzu kedai chi, ki kōshi.' Ta-na-
ham! ham! har ta kusa chinye nāma. Sai ta rage,
ta che. 'Gā nāki auta.' Auta ya che, 'Uma, idan ba ki kō-
-shi ba, ki chainye duka,' sai ta dauki saura, ta chi.
Ta rage kankane, ta aje, ta che, 'Gā nāki.'

---

kept shouting out, and saying, 'Mother, it is I, mother, it is I.' He, the baby of the family, said, 'It is a lie you are telling. May Allah guard mother from giving birth to such as you, may Allah guard her from giving birth to such as you,' and so on till she died. She (the old woman) lifted her out, cut (her) up in small pieces, put her in a pot and cooked her. When the girl was cooked she put in *daudawa* spice and salt, took the pot off the fire, took out the meat and said, 'Youngest daughter, come forward. You alone will eat the son of the profligate woman.' But he said, 'No, as for me I shall not eat, now you yourself eat and be filled.' She was crunching, crunch! crunch! until she had almost eaten (all) the meat. Then she ceased, and said, 'There is your share, little daughter.' The baby of the family replied, 'Mother, if you are not full eat up all,' and she (the old woman) took up what was left and ate. She left a small piece, put it aside, and said, 'There is yours.'

تَنَّا كُورْ :: تَنَّا قَبِ :: أُمْ فِيبْشْ :: أُمْ فِيبْغْ :: أَوْتْمِ

شْنَا قَبِ :: تْكَزْ يَا يْجِي :: أَلْشْطِمْ أُمْ :: تْجِيبْجِيكْ ::

أَلْطِمْ مَتْ :: تْجِيبْجِيكْ :: تَكَنْقْ تْكَنْقْ تَمْ قْمَتْ

تَدْوكْوَا :: تْلْسَلَسْ :: تْقَلَّسْ :: تْكْنِيَا :: تَعْقْ ::

يَا وُقْمْ :: تْقِيمْ :: تْلْسْقْ :: دُوكْدُوا :: دْغْشْلِي ::

تْشْبِجِي كُو :: تْكْنِيَا :: تْطَابُو :: قْدَمْ :: تْقْبْ أَوْتْمْ ::

تَجْوَا :: بْجَعْ نْ مْشْدْ قْنْجْمْ :: لَسْنْ مِيبْ :: عْمَاعْ ::

قِمْ بْدَاقْتْ :: بْنْغْ :: بْجَعْ :: قْكِكُوشْ :: تْنْدْ

لَهْقْهْمْ :: تَمْ تْكُسْنْ :: قْتْبِلْ :: قْدَمْ :: اَسْ قْمْ قِجْ

تْقْبْ :: عْمْدْ لَدْكِ :: أَوْتْمِ :: أَوْتْمِ يِبْ :: أُلْمْ إِكْرُو :: يْكِكُو

لْشْبْ :: يْكْشْبِي :: دْكْ :: لَسْقْ قْدْ وُكْ :: لَسْوَرْ :: تْقْتْ

تْرْعْجْ :: تْكْنْعْسْنْبْ :: تَأْبِي :: تْقْشْ عْمْدْلَكِ ::

Sai auta ya che, ‘Yau kin chainye dīanki duka, sauran ki chi kainki.’ Sai ya yāda zane, ya che, ‘Kin gane ni, ni ne auta, ba ki chi na.’ Sai ya shēka, ya tafō gida, ya gaya ma mutānen gidansu, ya che, ‘Mu gudu.’ Sai garin duka [23] ya tāshi, su-ka-gudu. Da su-ka-tafi, sai baban wansu [24] ya che yā yāda tākalminsa, ya che shi kōma, shi [25] daukō. Auta ya che, kar ka kōma. [26] Ya che, yaa kōma. Auta ya che, ‘Bari ni in kōma.’ Auta ya kōma, ya je, ya shiga dāki. Sai ta rufe shi, ya hau bisan dāki, ya kāma tanka. Sai ya che mata, ‘Idan ki-na-sō ki chainye ni, sai ki būde mani idānu, in ji tsōrō, in fādō, ki kāma ni.’ Sai ta tāda kainta bisa, ta bubūde

---

And he who was the youngest of the family said, ‘To-day you have eaten up all your daughters, and there only remains for you to eat yourself.’ Then he threw aside the cloak (and) said, ‘Do you see it is I, the baby of my family, you did not eat me.’ Then he ran off, and went home and told the people of his town (saying) ‘Flee’. And the whole town rose up and fled. When they had gone, then their elder brother said he has dropped his slipper; he said he would turn back and get it. The baby of the family said, ‘Do not go back,’ (but) he said he would return (for it). The baby of the family said, ‘Allow me to return.’ The baby of the family returned, he went and entered the house. And she (the old woman) came and closed (the door); he climbed on to the top of the house and caught hold of a beam. Then he said to her (the old witch), ‘If you are wanting to eat me up, you have only to open your eyes at me when I shall be afraid and fall down (on you) (and) you will catch me.’ Then she raised her head, and opened very widely

تَسِنْ أَوْتَمْ ∴ يَبْ يَبُو ∴ يَغْشِبِنْ دِ يَنْكِ دُكَ ∴ تَسُونْ

كِشْ ∴ كَبْكِ ∴ تَسِنْ يَبِيَادِ غَنْبِنْ ∴ يَبْ كِغَنْبِنْ ∴ فِيبُونْ

أَوْتَمْ ∴ بَدَكِشْغَنَا ∴ تَسِنْ يَبْشِكَ ∴ يَتَبْفُوغِدَا ∴ يَغْيَا

مَحْتَنَا فُجْبِنْ ∴ غِدْ فُلَسْ يَبْ مُغْدُ ∴ تَسِنْ غِمِ فُدِكَ

∴ يَتَنَالِشْ ∴ أَسْكَغُدُ ∴ دِ لُسْكَتِيفِ ∴ تَسِنْ يَتَبْنُو فُلَسْ ∴

يَبْ يَبَادِ تَاكَلِمِنْسْ يَبْ يِشْغَكُومْ ∴ لِشْدِ أَوْكُوَا

∴ أَوْتَمْ يَبْ ∴ كَرْكَكُومْ ∴ يَبْ يَأَكُومْ ∴ أَوْتَمْ

يَبْ تَبِ فِيمِ ∴ إِنْكُومْ ∴ أَوْتَمْ يَكُومْ ∴ يَجِنْ يَشِغْ ∴

دَاكِ ∴ تَسِنْ تَمْ فِشِ ∴ يَحَوْ بِتَسِنْ دَاكِ ∴ يَكَدَامْ

تَنْكُنْ ∴ تَسِنْ يَتَبْمَتْ ∴ إِدِّنْ ∴ كِنَدَا سُوَا ∴ كِبْشِيمْ

تَسِنْ كِبُو دِمِنْ ∴ إِدَا فُوَا ∴ إِفْجِ طُوُوَا ∴ إِفْقَادُوَا

يِكَدَاقَدَنْ تَسِنْ قَتَدَا دِكِيْنِ بِتَسِنْ قَتَبُو دِنْ

masa idānū. Shi kūa, akwai [27] tunka wurinsa nikake, sai ya wātsa mata ga idānu, sai ta rufe idānu. Ya sabkō, zāa shi fita, sai ta kāma kafansa, sai ya che, ‘Wāwa, kin kāma itāche, ki-na-che kafa na.’ Sai ta sake kafafunsa, ta kāma itāche. Sai ya fita ya kāma [28] kyaure, ya [29] kuble ya chūna ma dāki wuta. Tsōfūa ta kōne. Sai ya je, ya gaya ma sarki, kaman da su ka yi da tsōfūa, ya che, ‘Mu kōma gida.’ Sai su-ka-kōma gida. Sarki ya che, ‘Ayi gangami birni da kauye su tāru.’ Aka-yi gangami birni da kauye, duka su-ka-tāru. Sarki ya kāwō rīga dari, wandō dari, sānia dari, dōki dari,

---

her eyes at him. As for him, he had ground peppers with him, so he cast (them) at her eyes, and she closed (them) the eyes. He came down, and as he was about to go outside, she caught his foot. But he said, ‘Fool, you have caught a stick, and you think it is my foot.’ Then she let go his foot and caught hold of a post; and he came out, seized the door, shut it (and) set fire to the house. The old woman was burned. Then he went and told the chief what they (he) had done with the old woman, (and) he said, ‘Let us return home.’ So they returned home. And the chief said, ‘Let the drums be beaten in town and village and let them assemble.’ Drums were beaten in town and village and every one assembled. And the chief brought one hundred cloaks, one hundred trousers, one hundred cattle, one hundred horses,

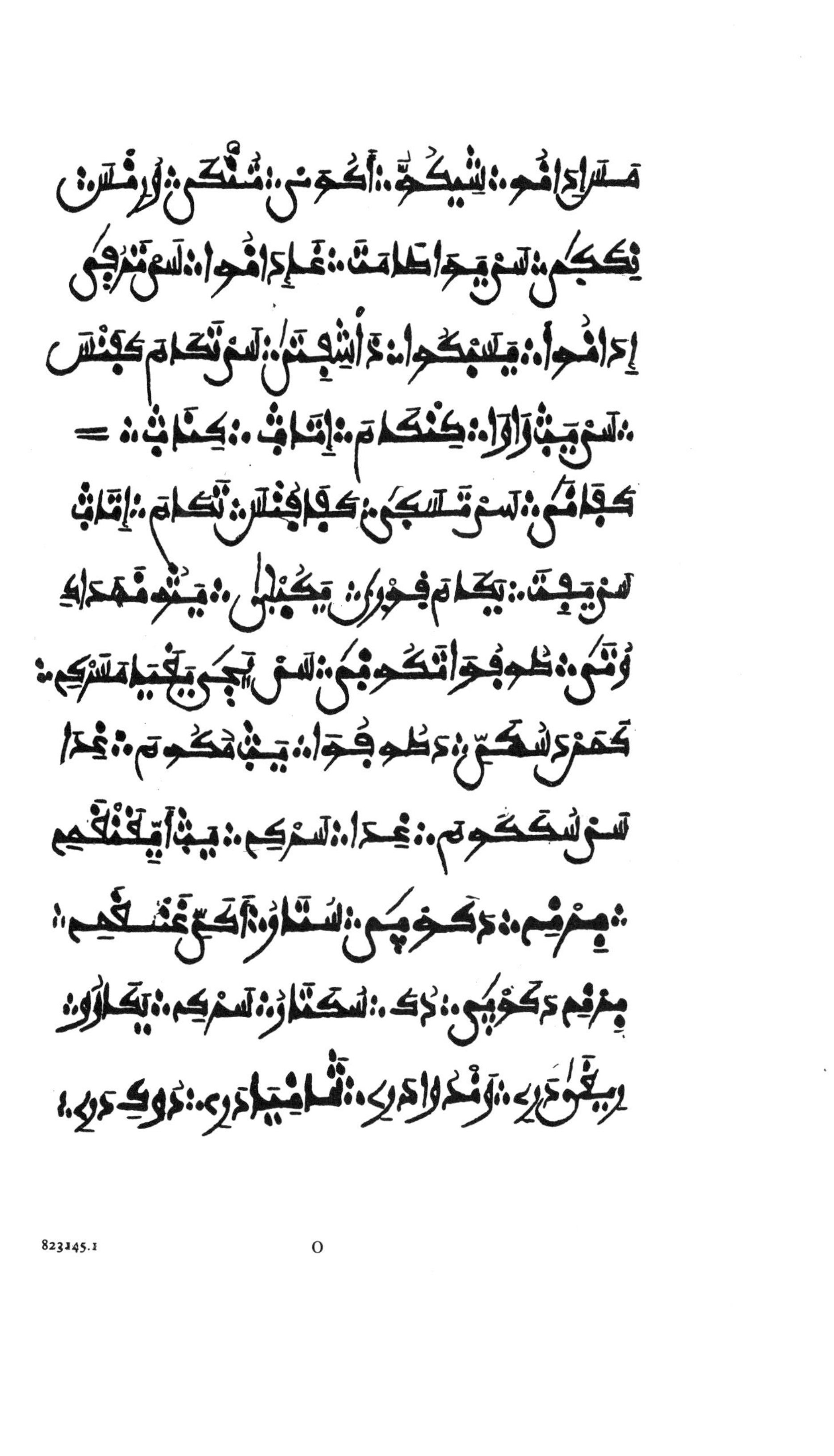

kōmi duka na dūnīa dari dari. [30] Ya che yā ba shi
rabin gari, abin nan da aka tāra duka sarki ya che yā baiwa
auta. Sai auta ya che, 'Sarki, gari, idan ba shi
da [31] tsari, banza ne, ka bari agina birni, tun mutāne
ba su wātse ba.' Sarki ya che, 'Bābu wanda ya iya ginin
birni.' Auta ya che, 'Ni naa gina, kai kadai ka taimake ni
da mutāne.' Sarki ya amsa, sai auta ya gina birni.
Mafārin ginin birni ke nan, auta ya fāra, kōwa
ya gani. [32] Kungurus kan kūsu.

---

of everything in the world one hundred of each. He said he gave him half his town (and) all the things which had been brought, the chief said he gave to the baby of the family. And the baby of the family said, 'Chief, a town, if it has not a protection, is worthless. Let a wall be built before the people have dispersed.' And the chief said, 'There is no one able to build a walled town.' And the baby of the family said, 'I shall build it; do you only give me assistance with the men.' The chief consented, so the baby of the family built a walled town. And that was the origin of walled towns, the baby of the family began that every one might see. Off with the rat's head.

كُومِ دِكَ ∴ مَكُو رِفِيَا ∴ كَرِي كَرِي ∴ بِيبَ يَا بَا يَشِ

وَبِنْكُمِ ∴ أَمِنْتُمْ دَ أَكَتَارْ دِكَ ∴ آسْرِكُمْ ∴ بِيبَ يَا بِبُو

آوْقُمْ ∴ آسَرْ أَوْقَلِ يِيبَ ∴ آسْرِكُمْ ∴ غَمِ ∴ إِدَّنْ ∴ مَدَ يَشِ

دِطَمِ ∴ بِنْدَ أَبِي ∴ كَبِر أَغِمْ بِرْفِمْ ∴ شُنْفُتَارْ فِي ∴

بَسْوَا بَطِي ∴ آسْرِكُمْ ∴ بِيشْ بِادَبْ ∴ آوْقَرْ مِيقِّي غِنْقَسْ

بِرْفِمْ ∴ آوْقُمْ بِيشْ ∴ فِنْتَا أُغِرَنْ كَنْكَمِ ∴ كَتِنْقَكَمِ

دِمَكَدَ أَبِي ∴ آسْرِكُمْ ∴ بِيَأَمْسَسِ ∴ آسَعْ أَوْقُمْ بِيَقِرْ بِرْفِمْ

مُقَارُنْ ∴ غِنْقَسْ بِرْفِمْ ∴ بِكْسِنْ أَوْقُمْ بِيَدَارْ ∴ كُوَرَا ∴

يِفَنِي ∴ فُنْغُرْسَنْ كَنْكُو سَنْ ∴

No. 9.

Wanan tātsūnīar [1] mālami che.

Wani mālami ya tāshi zūa Maka, dōmin shi dada lādansa shi yi yawa. Shi-na da kwarangaman gōdīansa. Ya hau, ya je tsakan dōkar dāji, sai ya gani [2] kūra. [3] Gōdīar tā gaji, sai kūra ta che, 'Mālam ina [4] zaa ka?' Mālami ya che, 'Zaa ni haji.' 'Me ya fāru?' Ya che, 'Gōdīa ta che ta gaza.' Ta che, 'Ita ke nan Kūra ta che, 'Ba ni ita, in yanke, in chainye, ka hau ni, mu tafi.' Mālami ya che, 'Hakanan?' Ta che, 'I.' Mālam ya che, 'Kar ki rūdē ni.' Ta che, '[5] Asha mālam, dōmin [6] nā gani ba ta iya tafia, dōmin hakanan ne; ni kūa, idan ka hau ni, yanzu yanzu naa kai ka Maka.' Mālam ya che, 'Bābu laifi, kāma, ki chainye.' Kūra

---

This is a story about a learned man. A certain doctor of learnin set out to go to Mecca in order to add to his rewards hereafter th they might be many. He had a very thin mare. He mounted, (an went deep into the forest when he saw a hyena. The mare was wear and the hyena said, 'Doctor, where are you going?' The doctor sai 'I am going the pilgrimage.' 'What is the matter?' (said the hyena He said, 'It is the mare, she is weary.' She (the hyena) said, 'Is th it?' the hyena said, 'Give her (the mare) to me, I shall kill her, and e her up. You will mount me and we shall set out.' The doctor said, 'So She (the hyena) said, 'Yes.' The doctor said, 'You must not decei me.' She replied, 'Come now, Doctor, because I have seen she wa unable to go on, it is because of that, (I speak thus) I for my par if you mount me, this instant will I carry you to Mecca.' The doct said, 'All right, catch (the mare) and eat (it) up.' The hyena

ونن تباطجو ميير ؞ مالميث

وفحا الم ؞ ببتاش دو ؞ مك ؞ دومن شدم ؞ الام مس

شبيو ؞ شنا نكر فغمن ؞ غمودي بيفس فحو ؞ يجي

طكن دو كر داج ؞ السم بغنم كوورا ؞ غمودي بيم ؞ تامج

سن كورا ؞ متب مالم ؞ إقادا أكن ؞ مالم ؞ ميب م ارن

بج ؞ ميقاو ؞ ميب غمودي يمي ماف ؞ تفح ؞ متب إتكتن

؞ كوورامتب ؞ بداوامة ؞ إفينكس ؞ إمشتين ؞ كحون

مشف ؞ مالم ؞ ميب حكتن متب إء ؞ مالم ميب

؞ كم كروح مص متب أش مالم ؞ دومن ؞ قاغنم ؞

باتحس ؞ ميجن دو ومن تكتن بين نبكو ؞ =

إدن كحون مينم مينم ؞ مأكنيك ؞ مك ؞ =

مالم ؞ ميب باب ابنجم ؞ كامن كتشين ؞ كووا

[7] ta kāma gōdīa, ta yāge, ta dībi nāma,
ta kai gida. Su ka chi da dīanta, su-ka-chainye nāma,
ta ki zakūa. Mālami ya zamna, ya gaji, bai gani
kūra tā zō ba. Ananan, sai [8] karen buki
ya zō, ya tarda mālam shi-na-zamne, karen buki
ya che, 'Mālam me ya fāru?' Mālami ya che, '[9] Nā tasō
daga gidana, zaa ni Maka, gōdīata ta gaji,
ina zamna, kūra ta tarshe ni, ta che, me ya fāru,
na che mata, Zaa ni Maka ne, gōdīata ta gaji,
shi ya sa ina zamne nan. Kūra ta che, Ai wanan
ba ta iya kai ka Maka, ba ni ita in chainye,
in ji dādi, in kāra [10] karfī, in kai ka Maka.

---

seized the mare, tore it up, picked up the meat (and) took it home. She ate it with her cubs (children), they ate up (all) the meat; (then) she refused to return. The doctor sat down (and) got tired (of waiting), he did not see that the hyena has (had) come back. Things were like this, when a jackal came and met the doctor sitting there. The jackal said, 'Doctor, what has happened?' The doctor said, 'I have set out from my home going to Mecca, my mare got tired, I was sitting down, the hyena came across me and asked what was the matter, and I said, I am going to Mecca, my mare got tired, and that is the cause of my sitting here. And the hyena said, Oh, this thing can never take you to Mecca. Give her to me to eat that I may feel joy, and increase my strength, so that I may carry you to Mecca.

تكدام غوديا ∴ تيا نجكن تدييب ∴ قدام ∴

تكن غدا ∴ سكف ∴ كديمت ∴ سكشتين قدام ∴

تك وفوا ∴ مدالم ∴ يدمن ∴ ينغج ∴ بتغنم

بجوا ∴ قادوب ∴ أقامقن ∴ لسن كج قبو ∴

تدو ∴ يترك مدالم ∴ لشقا كمبن ∴ كج قبو ∴

يش مدالم ∴ مبجار ∴ مدالم يب قاد قدا سوا ∴

كغفداقن ∴ كأنمك ∴ غودياق ∴ قغج ∴

إقاكمبن ∴ كجوا ∴ قترشن ∴ قتب مبجار ∴

قشقنه ∴ كأنمحكبن ∴ غودياق ∴ قغج ∴ =

شيتن ∴ إقاكمبتن كجورا ∴ قبآء وقمن

باقغن ∴ كيك ∴ قك ∴ بادرق ∴ إققشين

إنجادي ∴ إنكار ∴ كمرج ∴ إنكيك قك

Nī kūa na che, Kūra kar ki rūdē ni, ki chainye mani gōdīata, saanan ki gudu, ban gane ki ba. Ta che, Ina ake yin hakanan, da gaskīa na ke fadi, bābu karīa achiki. Ni kūa ina che gaskīa ne, na che ta kāma. Shi ke nan, kūra ta tafi, har yau ban gane ta ba.' Sai karen buki ya che, '[11] Kyale mālam [12] naa kāwō maka ita, yanzu.' Ya dauki sirdi da kāfu, da linzāme, da ragama, da kayāmai, da bulāla, ya tafi, ya sāmu tsōka nāma, ya tafi da shi. Shi-na-tafia, shi-na-yāda kayan dōki guda guda, har ya kai kusa da bākin rāminta, ya aje kāfu, ya wuche, ya je bākin rāmenta, ya tsaya, ya yi salama. Su-ka-kyale, da wuri kūa kūra tā gaya ma

---

I then said, Hyena, you must not deceive me, eat up my mare for me, and then run away, (and) I shall not see you again. She replied, Where do they do that sort of thing? it is the truth I told you, there is no lie in it, then I said (thought) it was true, (and) told her to catch (the mare). That is all, the hyena went off; till to-day I have not seen her.' And the jackal said, 'Leave off, Doctor, I will bring her to you now.' He lifted the saddle and saddle-cloth and bit and halter and spurs and whip and went off, and he got a lump of meat and took it. As he went he was dropping the horse furniture one by one until he got near the mouth of the hole (where the hyena) was. He put aside the saddle-cloth and passed on, and came to the mouth of her hole, and stood, and announced his arrival. No answer, for previous to this the hyena has told

نيكو ∴ قب كورا ∴ كم كم ودمم ∴ كتن يمن ∴

غود ميامق ∴ هحنن ∴ كغد ∴ بنغبكب ∴ قب

إمدا أجبين قحكنن ∴ دغسكيا مجقج ∴ عباب كمريكي

أنكم ∴ نيكو ∴ إمداف غسكيا مجل ∴ مثب تكادم

شيبكنن كورا ∴ تنف حم ميوا ∴ مننغبشب ∴

سن كم قبو ∴ ميث بكلين مدالم ∴ قدأ كداو وقك ∴ إف

ينغد ينغد وك ∴ لسرد ∴ دكاقجوا ∴ دلغ ابمي ∴ درعمى

∴ دكيامن ∴ دبوالل ∴ ينتق ∴ ينسادم ∴ طوكنادم

ينتقدشم ∴ شناقبن ∴ شنا ميادم ∴ كاميمن درك

غدا غدا ∴ حنر يكمن ∴ كسر مداكقرا منتا ∴ ياين

كاقجوا ∴ ميوقب ∴ نجن مداكن ∴ وامنتا ∴ مطن ∴

بين لسلم ∴ سكجلى ∴ دوركو ∴ كورا ∴ قاغيادم

dīanta ta che, 'Kōwa ya zō nan, shi-na-nema na, ku che ba ni nan.' Da dila ya yi salama, sai su ka che, 'Ba ta nan.' Dila ya che, 'Tir Ala wa maras arziki ana-neman mutāne da arziki tsīa ta-na-hana su, ga wani sānia yā mutu, [13] mamāya, [14] nā zō dōmin in kirāye ta, in gwodu mata, sai ku che, ba ta nan, bari in kōma.' Sai kūra ta che, 'Wa ke nema na?' Dila ya che, 'Ni ke nemanki, wata sānia ta mutu, māmāya, na yankō baba tsōka, nā kāwō maki, dōmin ki gani shi ne, yāranga su ka che, ba ki nan.' Sai kūra ta che, '[15] La ila, kā ga lalatatu, ina-kwāna, ana-bida na, ku che ba ni nan.' Sai kūra ta fitō.

---

her children saying, 'Whoever comes here looking for me, you m say I am not here.' So when the jackal hailed, they said, 'She is here.' And the jackal said, 'Allah curse her, she has no luck; m are sought for that they may get something good, and bad luck preve them from getting it. See, a cow has died, a very fat one, I have co to call her and show her, and you say, she is not here. Let me retur Then the hyena said, 'Who is seeking me?' The jackal said, 'I seeking you. Some cow died, a very fat one, I cut off a big lu and have brought it to you, but these boys are saying you are here.' And the hyena said, 'There is no God but Allah! y have seen, worthless fellows. I was asleep and was sought for, (ar you say I am not here.' So the hyena came out.

دِ يِمْنَّ ؞ مَنْبِ كُوكَرَا ؞ يِنْدِ وَقَّرْ ؞ لِشْنَا بِجَالَقِي ؞ كُبْ بِلَفِنَّرْ

كِ دِلَّ ؞ بِيِّ لَسْكِمْ ؞ لَسْ سُكُبْ ؞ بِدَا قَنَّرْ ؞ دِ لَامِيْبْ ؞ قِيرْ أَرّْ وَدَمْ

مَرْسَنْ أَرْزُفِمْ ؞ أَمَا بِجَرْ مُتَدَابِي ؞ دَأَرْزُفِمْ ؞ طِيبَ

قَمَا قَمَنَا لُسْ ؞ غَدَ وَفِتْنَا فِيَا ؞ بِيَا مُثْ ؞ مَجَا بِمِي ؞

تَمَا دُوَا ؞ دُو مِسّْنِ ؞ أَنْكِرَا مِثْ ؞ إِمْتُغَدَا مَثْ ؞

لَسْ كُبْ ؞ بِدَا قَنَّرْ ؞ بِمِ إِنْكُوِمْ ؞ لَسْ كُوكَرَا ؞

قَمْبْ ؞ وَاكِبْنَا قِمْ ؞ دِلَّامِبْ ؞ نِيكِبْنَنْكِ

وَقْتَا فِيَا ؞ تَمُثْ ؞ مَجَّا بِمِي ؞ فِيُنْكُوَا ؞ بِبْ

طُوكِ ؞ نَكَدَا وُمَكِ ؞ دُو وِمْ كِغَنِمْ ؞ شِيبِي

بِيَا وُمْغَ ؞ شْكَبِيْ بِدَا كُنَّرْ ؞ لَسْ كُوكَرَا ؞ قَمْبْ

لَالِأَلَيْ ؞ هَكَدَغَ ؞ لَالَامَسْتُو ؞ إِمَا كُوَا قِي ؞

أَمَا بِمَ أَقِي ؞ كُبْ بِلَفِنَّرْ ؞ لَسْ كُوكَرَا قِمْبُنُو ؞

Sai ta fitō ta che, 'Gā ni.' Dila ya che, 'Amshi, dandana.' Ta karbi, ta hade, ba ta bai dīanta. Ta che, 'Mu tafi.' Su-ka-kāma hainya, su-na-tafia, kūra ta-na-gaba gaba, dila na bāya. Sai ta che, 'Kai ba ka iya tāfia, hau ni, mu tafi maza maza.' Dila ya hau ta, su-na-tafia, su-ka-iske mashimfidi. Dila ya che, 'Bari in shifida abinga ga bāyanki, gāshin bāyanki shi-na--sūkāna.' Sai ta che, 'Yi maza maza mu tafi.' Dila ya dauki, ya shimfida, ya hau, su-na-tafia. Su-ka-iske linzāme, sai dila ya che, 'Bari in dauki abinan in sa maki bāki, kō naa ji dadi--n rikō.' Ta che, 'Sa maza maza mu tafi.' Dila ya sainya mata

---

When she came out she said, 'Here I am.' The jackal said, 'Take (it), taste.' She received (the meat), swallowed it; she did not give to her children. She said, 'Let us be off.' They took the road, they were going along; the hyena was in front a long way, the jackal behind. Then she said, 'You cannot walk, mount me (and) let us get along quickly.' The jackal mounted her, they were going along; they come across the saddle-cloth. The jackal said, 'Let me spread this thing on your back, the hair on your back is getting ruffled.' And she said, 'Do it quickly and let us get on.' The jackal lifted and spread it. He mounted, they were going along. They came across the bit, when the jackal said, 'Let me lift up this thing and put it in your mouth; perhaps it will be better for me to hold.' She said, 'Put it on quickly and let us get on.' The jackal put on

لسر تبيتوا :. قتب غدا فيه :. د لاميب آمشر د فد فمى

نكرب :. تحجر بجتمنر د يفتة :. قتب فتو :.

سعكام :. فتر سنا قبق :. كورا :. قتا غب

فب :. د لا فيا تر :. لسر قتب :. كرماك عر تبقر

قور :. فتو مع مد :. د لا يحوت :. سنا قبقر

سكا اسكر :. مشنبد :. د لاميب :. بمر لقشبح

أبعغ :. غبا ينك :. غما اشنبا ينك :. يشنا

سوكا فلر :. لسر قتب يبعد مد :. فتبح :.

د لا يد وك :. يشنبدا :. يحو :. لسنا قبق

سكا اسكر :. لبزا مر :. لسر د لاميب :. بمرا فد وك

أبقتر :. إفسا مك :. بجاكم :. كوفاج :. دادم

فر كوا :. قتب سا مع مد :. فتبح :. د لا يسنبا مق

lizāme, ya hau. Su-na-tafia, su-ka-iske kayāmai. Ya sabka, ya dauki kayāmai, ya sainya a-kafa, ya hau. Su-na-tafia, su-ka-kusa da mālami, sai kūra ta che, 'Kar mu bi nan. Dila ya che, 'Gurin da [16] nāman shi ke ke nan.' Kūra ta che, 'Mu karkata wajen haka.' Su-ka-karkata wani wuri da dila ya sani, sun kai dai dai da mālami, sai ya karkata lizāme zūa wurin mālami, ya kafa mata kaimi. Sai kūra ta zaabura, ta-na-che, 'Uu, uu.' Ba su zāme ba, sai wurin mālami. Dila ya zāme gaban mālami, ya sabka, ya che, 'Malam gā mabachinka, tāshi, ka hau, kar ka sabka, sai ka kai wurinda zaa ka.

---

the bit (and) mounted. They were going along; they came across the spurs. He dismounted, picked up the spurs, (and) put them on his feet, (and) mounted. They were going along, they were near the doctor, when the hyena said, 'You must not take this way.' The jackal replied, 'This is where the meat is.' The hyena said, 'Let us make a détour thus.' They have turned off another way, which the jackal knew, and got opposite to where the doctor was, when he turned the bit towards where the doctor was and struck her with the spurs. Then the hyena sprang forward, saying, 'Uu, uu.' They did not pull up till (they reached) where the doctor was. The jackal pulled up in front of the doctor, dismounted, and said, 'Doctor, behold your debtor. Rise up, mount, and do not get off until you reach where you are going.

لقرابى ؞ يحو لسنا تبى ؞ لسك النكو ؞ فيبا مى ؞
يسنبك ؞ يدوك فيبا من ؞ يلسميا اكق ؞
يحو لسنا تفى ؞ لسككسن ؞ د قدالم ؞ آسن
كحورا شقب كرفيسن ؞ دلا يبا ؞ اقم فدع قدامن
شبكبكتن دعحورا ؞ قبدعكر كتا ؞ ووبن قك
لسكنركتا منوفورى ؞ [redacted] ؞ دلا يبسن ؞ ت
لسكن ؞ مكنيم ون ؞ دم ما الم ؞ آسن يكنركتا لزابى
نرو ؞ ورفدالم ؞ يكقامت ؞ فنبيم ؞ آسن كحورا
؞ قدرابم ؞ قنافى ؞ عحوع ؞ عهوكم ؞ بشعابى
آسن ورفحدالم ؞ دللير ابى ؞ غعبن مالم ؞ ت
يقنبك ؞ يبث مالم ؞ غماقبثنك ؞ فالشن ؞ =
كعومكن كلسنبك ؞ آسن كاكن ؞ ورفعد اك

Idan kā sabka, kō rūa, kar ka che akai ta raafi.' Mālami ya che, '[17] Nā ji.' Mālami ya hau, bai sabka ba har ya kai Maka. Saanan ya sabka, ya ba yāra rikō, ya che, 'Kar ku hau, kar ku kai ta raafi.' Mālami ya shiga masalāchi, su-na-sala. Sai yāra su-ka-hau, su-ka-tafi da ita raafi. Da su-ka-fita bāyan gari, sai su-ka-yi sukūa. Kūra ta dauke su, ta shiga dawa da su, ta-na-gudu, har ta kāshe su, ta [18] tafianta. Mālami ya fitō masalāchi, bai gani yāra ba, bai gani kūra ba.

Shi ke nan, [19] kungurus kan kūsu.

If you dismount, even at the water, do not say she is to be taken to the stream.' The doctor replied, 'I have heard.' The doctor mounted, (and) did not get down till he had reached Mecca. Then he dismounted and gave (the hyena) to (some) boys to hold, saying, 'You must not mount, you must not take her to the stream.' The doctor entered the mosque, they were praying. Then the boys mounted, (and) went off with her to the stream. When they got behind the town then they galloped. The hyena carried them off, and entered the bush with them, and ran until she threw them and went her own way. (Then) the doctor came out of the mosque; he did not see the boys, he did not see the hyena. That is all. Off with the rat's head.

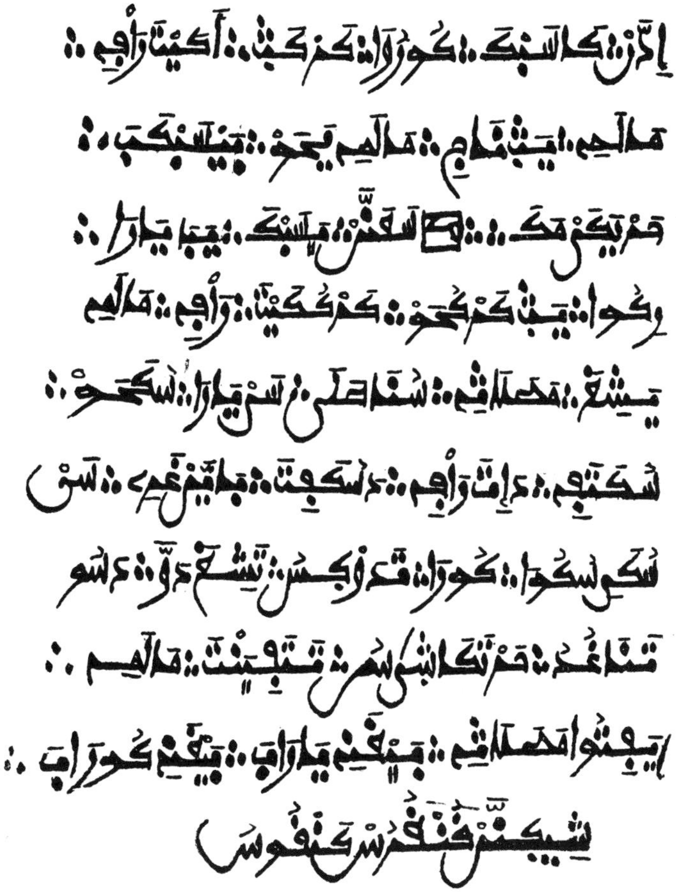

No. 10.

Wanan tātsūnīar [1] Garnakaki che.

Wani sarki ne mai-[2]karfī kwarai, wata rāna [3] ya fida sansani zaa shi yāki. Shi-na da wani mai-dafuwan tūō, shi-na da [4] maatans shi sarki nan, wada shi ke sō. Kōmi na sarki shi-na wurin maata nan ne. Mai-dafuwan tūō shi-na-neman maa--ta nan, ita kūa [5] ta-na-sō(n)sa, har wata rāna aka-kwar--mata ma sarki. Sarki ya kāma mai-dafuwan tūō, ya sainya shi kurkuku. Shi, sarkin, shi-na-sō mai-dafuwa nan kwarai, sai ya che afida shi. Aka-fishe shi, [6] aka-kāwō shi. Sarki ya che, 'Ama idan ka bar maata ta, ka kōma, ka-na-dafuwan tūō.' Sai ya che, '[7] Naa bar ta.' Ashe karīa ne.

This is a story about (a chief) Garnakaki. A certain very powerf chief one day struck camp to go to war. He had a certain coo (and) he had a wife, this chief, whom he loved. Everything the chi had was in this wife's possession. The cook was after this woma and she also loved him, until one day the chief was secretly informe The chief seized the cook (and) put him in prison. Now he, th chief, was very fond of the cook, so he said he was to be taken ou He was taken out and brought forward. The chief said, 'In spite all if you give up my wife, you may return and continue cookin food.' And he said, 'I shall leave her.' Truly it was a lie.

رنتنا طوفين عمر تكفيث ::

وفقر كيبن ميكر في كعمر : رقم افي : يجد لسغسنم ::
وأشياك : يشنا كر وفميذ فوقنتو وو : تشنا د ملا تنسن
شيسر كنترن ادشكسوا : كوبم تسر كم ::
شنا او فما قنتفن ميم فو فنتو ورن : شنا بعتما
قنن يا تكوا : فنا اسوا : سن : قمر وقم افي : اكيكم
قنا مسر كم : تسر كم يكا [redacted] م : ميكر فو فنتو ور
يتفيا اش كمر ككك : شيسر كمر شنا اسو : ميكر فو
قمر كم رن تسن يتبا فو د تشم : اكبشنشن : اكدا وو شي
تسر كم : يتبا اقدا ادركبر مدا قاف : ككو م ::
كنا د فوقنتو وو : تسر يتبا قدا بر ق

ابشر كمر يبا قبس

Shi-na nan, shi-na-dafa ma sarki tūō. Ashe su-na-
-tāre da [8] maatar nan, su-na-yi ma sarki [9] tānadi,
har su-ka-karbō māgani, su-ka-sainya wa sarki
achikin abinchi. Sarki ya chi, ya mutu. Maatar nan
ta dība kāyan sarki dayawa, da kurdin sar-
-ki dayawa, ta ba shi daga bōye, bābu
wanda ya sani, har aka gama kōmi duka. Saanan
ta fita, ta aure shi. Mafāri ke nan
aka-che, 'Sō mai-sonka, rabu da makīyinka,
kar shi ba ka māgani, ka chi, ka mutu.'
[10] Kungurus kan kūsu.

Time went on, (and) he was cooking food for the chief. Of a truth they were together, (he) and this woman, (and) they were sinning against the chief, until (one day) they got medicine, (and) put it in the chief's food. The chief ate and died. This woman took possession of much of the chief's property and much of the chief's money. She gave him (the cook) (them) secretly (and) no one knew, until they had finished taking everything. Then she came forward and married him. That was the origin of the saying, 'Love him who loves you, leave him who hates you, lest he give you medicine to eat (and) you die.' Off with the rat's head.

شنا قمن شناء فا مسن كم قمووا أبشي سنه

تدا برش د ما قتر قمش شنا يمسن كم قنا قمي

قم سككم بجوا ما غنم سككسنيد السركم

أشكنا منت سركم بيتي يمن ما قتر قمن

تدييب عا ببن سركم ديبو دكم كي قسر

كم دييو قبا اشن د غموبين مداب

وقد يمن قم اكغم كو ميدك اسكن

تبن قاوز [redacted] ن مقجاوي بكمن

اكبنا سو ميسنك وبكم مكينك

كم شباك ما غنم كشكمنا

فنقم سن كم كوسن

No. 11.

Wanan tātsūniar samāri che.

Wadansu samāri su-ka-tafi kauye wurin
budūri. Su-ka-je, su-ka-iske raafi, hainya bābu
rūa, rūa iyāka idānun sau. Su-ka-wuche.
Su-ka-isa gurin budūri, su-ka-je, su-ka-gaishe su,
su-ka-daukō su. Su-ka-zō wurin raafi, su-ka i-
-she, ya-chika da rūa. Sai su-ka-che, 'Af ai
mun wuche rūanga, bai kai haka ba.' Su-ka-che,
'Kāka ke nan?' Daia chikinsu ya che, 'Mu kōma.'
Saura su-ka-che, 'Aa ba mu kōmāwa.'
Su kūa, su uku ne, da dan sarkin kō-
-kūa, da dan sarkin mahalba, da dan limāmi.

This tale is about (some) youths. Certain young men went to an outlying village where some young girls were. They went on, and came to a stream; there was (practically) no water on the road; the water came (only) up to their ankles. They passed on. They came to where the maidens were, and came and greeted them, and carried them off. They came to the stream and found it full up with water. (Then) they said, 'Ah (when) we passed this water it was not so,' and they said, 'How is this?' One among them said, 'Let us turn back.' The rest said, 'No, we do not go back.' Now they were three, the king of wrestlers, the king of bowmen, and the king of prayer.

وقتر قنا طوفنيم اسحاوري ث

وقمس اسحاوري ٭ سكتنجي ٭ كحويي ٭ اورق

بحوري ٭ سكجي سكا اسكي ٭ واقم قنو ٭ باف

روا ٭ روا ٭ ابا كغ اد افر اسحو ٭ سكحوث ٭

سكا اسر ٭ غم قبحوري ٭ سكجي ٭ سكغيشس ٭

سكد وكوش سكدوا ٭ ورقم اقم ٭ سكا

ثس ٭ ميا قك ٭ د روا ٭ اسر سكث ٭ اف اي ٭

منوث ٭ ورقع ٭ جيكغ ٭ مكب ٭ سكث

كاك ٭ بحتر ٭ د تو نكغس ريث مكحوم ٭

اسحورا ٭ سكث ٭ عاع ٭ با مكحو ماوا ٭

اسوكحو ٭ اسوا كحتر ٭ د د قمحر كحر ٭ كحو ٭

كحو ٭ د د قاسر كحر ٭ مقابل ٭ د د قما يهام ٭

Su-ka-che, 'Kōwa shi yi dabāra gidansu, ta fishe shi.'
Su-ka-che, 'Dan limāmi shi fāra.' Sai [1] ya yi adua,
ya tōfa ga sandarsa, ya buga rūa, rūa ya tsāge,
da shi da budūra tasa su-ka-wuche. Sai rūa ya kōma wada shi ke.
Sai dan sarkin mahalba ya zazage kibau nasa
daga chikin [2] kori, ya jēra su bisa rūa, tun daga
wanan ganga har wanan ganga, ya kōmō, ya dau-
-ki budūra tasa. Su-ka-tāka kan kibau,
su-ka-wuche. Sai ya kōmō, ya tsinche kabausa.
Sauran dan sarkin kōkūa. Shi kūa
ya bidi wada zaa shi yi, ya rasa. Shi bi nan, shi rasa
gurin bi, shi yi wanan dabāra, shi rasa, har ya gaji.

(And) they said, 'Let each try and get out of the difficulty by resorting to his own particular skill.' They said, 'Let the one who is strong in prayer commence.' So he prostrated himself, spat on his staff (and) struck the water; (and) the water opened, and he with his maiden passed over. Then the water returned to where it was. Next the prince of bowmen drew out his arrows from his quiver, he set them in a line on the water, from one bank to another, he returned and lifted up his maiden. They stepped on the arrows, (and) passed over. Then he came back, (and) picked up his arrows. There remained the king of wrestlers. He too sought for what he should do; he could not find a way. He tried this way, (and) failed, he made that plan (and) failed, until he was weary.

لسكبث كحووا: شيتم بداو ىنغمد فسن: مَبثش

لسكتث: دم فلمايجام: شجاو: لسن بمّ آدعمن:

يتوق: غمسنغ رلسث ميبغ وراا: روا ابطلغمى

دلشم دمد روا اقسش لسن روا ابكوم: ود شكمى

لسن د فلسن كمن: معلبن بيدد غمن: كبو فلسن

دغمتكمن: كمح: شيجم السن بسن روا: تنغمغ

وقمن غمنغمن: قمن وقمن غمنقمى: بكو موا: بدو

ك: بمد روا اقسن لسكتاك: كنكبو: =

لسكوث: لسن بكو موا: بطمثب: كبو لسن

لسو وند فلسن كمن: غمكو كو: شيكو:

بيجم: ود د اشي: بيدمن: شيبقمن: لشم سن:

غمد فب: شي وقمن: د بداو: لشم سن: قمد بيجمع

Sai ya yi fushi, ya kāma budrua tasa, da kō-
-kūa ya nada mata hardīa, su-ka-tuma, su-ka-yi
bisa, ba su fādi ba, sai bākin ganga. Tō,
chikinsu wa ya fi dan uwansa? Idan ba-ka-san wanda
ya fi ba, shi ke nan. [3] Kungurus kan kūsu.

Then he got in a rage, (and) seized his maiden, and with a wrestling trick twisted his leg round hers (and) they jumped, (and) rose in the air, (and) did not fall, except on the edge of the (far) bank. Now among them who was better than another? If you do not know who was least, there you are. Off with the rat's head.

لَسْنِ بِيَّ ؞ فُشِ ؞ يِكَلَمْ ؞ بُدْ زُوا اَقَلْقَنْ ؞ كُو

كُو ؞ يِنْدَا اَمَتَ ؞ قَمْ دِيَا ؞ لُسَكُتُمْ ؞ لُسَكِّي

بِسَوْ بِسُقَامِ بَ ؞ لَسْنِ بَا كِمْ ؞ غَنْغَوَا ؞ تُو ؞ ء

ثُكِنْلُسْ وَبِيج نَغُوف لَسْ ؞ اِدَّرْ ؞ بَكَسُنُوفْ دَا ؞

يِبَ ؞ شِيبَكَنَّ فُنْغُرُسْ كَنْغُوسُ ؞

No. 12.

Wanan tātsūnīar dugun dāji che,

da shi da Namijin-Mijin-Maza.

[1] Gātanan, gātanan, ta je, ta kōmō. Wani mutun ne, sūnansa Namiji-Mijin-Maza, kulum idan [2] ya fitō dāji shi kan daukō itāche, shi tafō, shi yas, shi che, 'Ni Namiji-Mijin-Maza.' [3] Maatarsa ta che, 'Haba bari fadi kai namiji-mijin-maza, idan ka gani namiji-mijin-maza, [4] kaa gudu.' Sai shi che, 'Karīa ne.' Yau hakanan hakanan kulum, idan [5] yā kāwō itāche, sai shi yas da karfī, shi che, 'Ni Namiji-Mijin-Maza.' [6] Maatar ta che, 'Haba bari fadi hakanan, idan [7] kā gani

---

This story is about a forest giant, about him and a man called, A-Man-among-Men. A story, a story. Let it go, let it come. There was a certain man by name, A-Man-among-Men, always when he came from the bush he used to lift up a tree (and) come, (and) throw (it down), and say, 'I am A-Man-among-Men.' His wife said, 'Come now, leave off saying you are a-man-among-men; if you saw a-man-among-men you would run.' But he said, 'It is a lie.' Now it was always so, if he has brought in wood, then he would throw it down with force, (and) say, 'I am A-Man-among-Men.' The wife said, 'Come now, leave off saying so; if you have seen

وَقَرْ قَاطُوفِيَّرْ ؞ دُغُنْدَاجِبْ

دِشِمْ ؞ دَنَبِجِ ؞ مُجَنْمَدَا

غَمَا تَنَّرْ غَا تَنَّرْ قَجِي ؞ تَكُومُوا ؞ وَنِقَشْتُبْ

سُوقَنْلَسْ نَمِجِ مُجَنْمَدَا ؞ كُلُمْ ؞ إِدَّرْ ؞ يَجِقُوا ؞

دَاجِ ؞ شِكَنْدَرْ كُوا ؞ إِلَّمَاشْ ؞ شِتَّبُوا ؞ شِيَشْ

شِشْ قِبِنَمِجِ ؞ مُجَنْمَدَا ؞ مَاقْتَرْلَسْ ؞ مَشْ حَبَّ ؞

بَرِقَدِ ؞ كَيَنِمِ ؞ مُجَنْمَدَا ؞ إِدَّرْ ؞ كَقَنِمْ ؞

نَمِجِ ؞ مُجَنْمَدَا ؞ كَدَا قُدُمْ ؞ آسَرْ شِشْ ؞ قَرْ يَادِبِ

يَوْحَكَنَّرْ حَكَنَّرْ كُلُّمْ ؞ إِدَّرْ ؞ يَاكَدَاوُرِ امَادِبْ

آسَرْ شِبِشْ دَكَرْقِجِ ؞ شِشْ ؞ قِبَنَمِجِ ؞ مُجَنْمَدَا

؞ مَاقْتَرْ ؞ مَشْ حَبَّ ؞ بَرِقَحِ حَكَنَّرْ ؞ إِدَّرْ ؞ كَاقَنِمْ

namiji-mijin-maza, kaa gudu.' Sai shi che, 'Karīa ne.' Yau
ranan maatarsa ta tafi raafi, ta je gurin wata rījīa;
[8] wasakin rījīan mutun gōma ke jāwō shi.
Ta je, ta rasa rūa, sai ta kōma. Zaa ta gida, ta gamu
da wata mache, ta che, 'Ina zaa ki da kworīa, bābu rūa?'
Ta che, 'Nā je, nā gani gūga nan, ba ni iya jansa,
shi ya sa ina-kōmāwa gida.' Sai maatar nan,
da ke da yārō nan, ta che, 'Mu kōma ki sāmu.'
Ta che, 'Tō.' Sai su-ka-kōma tāre wurin rījīa.
Maatar nan, da ke da yārō, ta che yārō shi dauki
wasaki, shi dēbō rūa, [9] yāron kūa kankane ne,
bai wuche gōyō ba. Sai ya dauki gūga
nan da nan, ya nasa rījīa, ya jāwō rūa. Su-ka-chika

---

a man-among-men, you would run.' But he said, 'It is a lie.' Now one day his wife went to the stream. She came to a certain well; the well bucket, ten men were (necessary to) draw it up. She came, (but) had to do without the water, so she turned back. She was going home, when she met another woman (who) said, 'Where are you going with a calabash, with no water?' She said, 'I have come and seen a bucket there. I could not draw it; that is what caused me to turn back home.' And this (second) woman, who had this (a) son, said, 'Let us return that you may find (water).' She said, 'All right.' So they returned together to the well. This woman, who had the son, told the boy to lift the bucket and draw water. Now the boy was small, not past the age when he was carried on his mother's back. Then he lifted the bucket then and there, and put it in the well, (and) drew up the water. They filled

ثيمج ۞ مبمقدا ۞ يكا غُد ۞ سنى شبث فنريابفني ۞ تيو ۞
وقمن ۞ مدا فمرس ۞ قتفي وارقي ۞ فبجي غمر فمو قمر يجيبا
وسكمن ۞ وبجين ۞ متفمن غمو م ۞ بكجا وو شن ۞ مد
فجي قمر سن ۞ وو ا ۞ سنى تكو م ۞ دا فى غدا ۞ قفم ۞
دو قب مث ۞ قتبا فما دا رك ۞ دكمر يا ۞ بداب ورا ۞
قتبا قا دجي ۞ قا غمنيم ۞ غمو غتمن ۞ بدا فغي جنفس ۞
لقيم بيمس ۞ اقا كو ما وا ۞ غدا ۞ سنى تا فتر قمن ۞
دكمد يا وقمن ۞ قتبا مكو م ۞ كسا مو ا ۞
قتبا فمو ۞ سنى سكمكو م ۞ قتا ومن ۞ وو فم يجيا ۞
ما فتر قمن ۞ دكمد يا رو ۞ قتبا يا رو ۞ شدا رك ۞
وسفم ۞ شجم مبو ورا ۞ يا فكو ۞ كتكبني
بيوث ۞ غمو بيو ب ۞ سنى يدا رك ۞ غمو غمي ۞
تفد قمن ۞ بتلمس وبجيا ۞ بجا وورا ۞ سكنك

masukansu, su-ka-yi wanka, su-ka-wanke [10] zannua--nsu, su-ka-dauki rūa, zaa su gida. Wanan ta-na-mā--māki, sai ta gani wachan da ke da yārō, tā rātse, ta na shiga dāji. Sai wanan maatar Namiji-Mijin-Maza ta che, 'Ina zaa ki?' Ta che mata, 'Zaa ni gida ne.' Ta che, 'Hain gidanku ke nan?' Ta che, 'I.' Ta che, 'Gidan wa ke nan?' Ta che, 'Gidan Namiji-Mijin-Maza.' Sai ta yi kurum, ba ta che kōme ba, har ta je gida, ta gaia wa mijinta. Ya che gōbe ta kai shi. Ta che, 'Ala shi kai mu gōbe.' Da gari ya wāye, shi ya [11] rigāye ta tāshi daga kwāna, ya dauki kāyan shiga dājinsa. Ya rātaya, ya saba gātarinsa, ya tāshe ta daga kwāna, ya che, 'Tāshi mu tafi, ki kai ni, in gani

---

their large water-pots, they bathed, they washed their clothes, th lifted up the water to go home. This one was astonished. Then s saw that one who had the boy has turned off the path and w entering the bush. Then the wife of (him called) A-Man-amon Men said, 'Where are you going?' She said to her, 'I am goi home, where else?' She said, 'Is that the way to your home She said, 'Yes.' She said, 'Whose home is it?' She said, 'T home of A-Man-among-Men.' Then she was silent; she did not s anything till she got home. She told her husband. He said th to-morrow she must take him (there). She replied, 'May Allah gi us a to-morrow.' Next morning he was the first to get up fro sleep. He took the weapons of the chase and slung them over l shoulder. He put his axe on his shoulder and wakened her (his wi from sleep. He said, 'Get up, let us go. Take me that I may see,

مسكنسن : لسكتي : ونكي : لسكو فجكي : طلنو

فمسن لسكدوكي : ووا : دا سغدا : ونمر قتنامد

ماكي : لسن تغتم : وقمن : دبكدبيا زو : قدا واجلس

تنالشقو دام : لسن ونمن ما اقتنهم : مجنفدا :

تبا اقادا كي : قنب متن : دا رغدا بمي : تبا حمتي

ايدنكي : يكنن قتبا اي : تنبا غدقوا بكنن

تنبغدفنمج : مجنمدا : لسن قتي كدزم : بمتب

كوبتب : حم تجي غدا : قنبيدا وا : مجنمتن :

يبنا غوبي : نتكبيش : قتبا ان لشكيم غوبي

: دغمي : بمجوابي : لشم يبر غدا بيتن : قدا لشن دمغ

كوا امي : يبتم وكي : كدا يمنشكو : دا بنسن

يبدا قتيا : يلسب : غدا قتم فلسن يبنا بشتن : دغم

كوا امي : يبنب قدا شن متبحي : يكبين ازغمم

in gani Namiji-Mijin-Maza.' Ta tāshi, ta dauki masakinta, ta wuche gaba. Shi-na-binta har su-ka-kai, bākin rījīa. Su-ka-yi katar kūa. Su na zūa, maatar Namiji-Mijin-Maza ta zō, da ita da danta. Su-ka-gaishe ta, sai maatar wanan ta goda masa gūga, ta che, 'Dauki ka dēbō mani rūa.'
Sai ya je, ya dauki gūga, da fushi, ya nasa
chikin rījīa, sai gūga ta ja shi, zaa shi fāda rījīa,
sai yārō kankane, ya kāma shi, da shi da guga,
ya fisgō, ya yas waje. Sai yārō ya dauki gū-
-ga, ya sainya chikin rījīa, ya dēbō rūa. Su-ka-chika tūlunansu. Maatarsa ta che, 'Kā che ka-na-zūa ka gani Namiji-Mijin-Maza, kā gani maatarsa ke nan, da dansa, idan ka-na-zūa, ku je tāre, ni ba ni zūa.' Uwar yārō ta che,

---

that I may see the (one called) A-Man-among-Men.' She got up, lifted her large water-pot, and passed on in front. He was following her until they got to the edge of the well. Now they found what they sought indeed. (As) they were coming, the wife of A-Man-among-Men came up, both she and her son. They greeted her, and the wife of this one showed him the bucket (and) said, 'Lift it and draw water for me.' So he went and lifted the bucket in a rage and let it down the well; but the bucket pulled him, (and) he would have fallen into the well, when the little boy seized him, both him and the bucket, and drew (out) and threw them on one side. Then the boy lifted up the bucket, put it in the well, drew water, and filled their water-pots. His wife said, 'You have said you are going to see him called A-Man-among-Men. You have seen this is his wife and son. If you still want to go you can go together. As for me, I am not going.' The boy's mother said,

إلغنم ⁘ نمج ⁘ مجمفندا ⁘ متاش ⁘ قدوك ملسكنما ⁘

قوف ⁘ غب شنامنت ⁘ حرسككن ⁘ بدكنم ريجيا ⁘

سكن كترڭو ⁘ شفادور ⁘ ماقر نمج ⁘ مجنمدا ⁘ قدور ⁘

درات دمت ⁘ سكغيشت ⁘ سن ماقر وقن ⁘ تقدا

مسن غوغن ⁘ قب دوك ⁘ عج مبو من ⁘ وورا ⁘

سن يجن بيدوك ⁘ غوغن ⁘ دفشم ⁘ يقسن ⁘ =

تكنم ريجيا ⁘ سن غوغن ⁘ تجاشن دآش قادم ⁘ ريجيا

سن بيدور ⁘ فنفنبن ⁘ بيكد ماشن دشيد غوغن ⁘

بيفدغوا ⁘ بيبشن وبكن ⁘ سن بيدور ⁘ بيدوك ⁘ غو

غن ⁘ بيسفيا ⁘ تكن ريجيا ⁘ بيج مبوورا ⁘ سكيك

تولتسن مداقرس ⁘ قبكاد ش ⁘ يكنادور ⁘ يكغم

نمج ⁘ مجنمدا ⁘ تكاغم ⁘ مداقرس بكتن ⁘ ددمس

إدن ⁘ يكنادون كجتادرن ⁘ فيبامدور ⁘ عورباور قب

'A me ya fāru? Kad ka je.' [12] Ya che yaa je, ta che, 'Mu je.' Su-ka-tafi. Da su-ka-je, sai ta goda masa [13] rufēwa na māna, ya shiga. Shi kūa mai-gida ba shi gida; [14] yā tafi dāji. Ta che, 'Kā gani yā tafi dāji, ama kar ka yi mōtsi idan yā zō.' Ya zamna chiki, har marēche ya yi. Mai-gidan ya zō. Shi-na-fadi '[15] Ina-ji(n) wārin mutun.' Maatarsa ta che, 'Akwai wani mutun nan, ba ni ba?' Hakanan idan ya che shi-na-jin wārin mutun, sai ta che, 'Akwai wani mutun nan, ba ni ba? Idan ka-na-sō ka chinye ni ne, tō, bābu kōwa, sai ni.' Shi kūa kāto ne, magananṣa kamar hadari, gīwa gōma shi ke chi. Idan gari ya wāye, shi kare kumalō da guda daia, kāna

---

'Oh, what is the matter? You had better not come.' (But) he said he would come; and she said, 'Let us be off.' They set out. When they arrived (at the house) then she showed him a place for storing meat, (and) he got inside. Now he, the master of the house, was not at home; he has gone to the bush. She (his wife) said, 'You have seen he has gone to the bush; but you must not stir if he has come.' He sat inside till evening came. The master of the house came. He keeps saying, 'I smell the smell of a man.' His wife said, 'Is there another person here? It is not I.' Thus, if he said he smelled the smell of a man, then she would say, 'Is there another person here. Is it not I? If you want to eat me up, well and good, for there is no one else but I.' Now he was a huge man, his words like a tornado; ten elephants he would eat. When dawn came, he made his morning meal of one; then

عمد ابيا اقدارُ ∴ كد كجى ∴ ميث بيا اجو ∴ متبا مجس

سكتبم ∴ د لسكجى ∴ سن تقد امسن ∴ زبكوا ∴ =

منام ∴ ميشغ ∴ شيكو ∴ منفدون ∴ مد شغدا ∴

يداقفى دا ∴ متث كد عيم ∴ ميد اقفدا ∴ آمد كم

كم مو طم ∴ إدرن ∴ قيادرا ∴ ميغ ممن ∴ تكم ∴

تم صنز مث ∴ ميم مفدن ∴ يغدو ∴ يشنا قحى ∴

إندم ثوا ونفشن ∴ مترسن ∴ متث اكو بيو ففشن ∴

فنر يد فيب ∴ حكنم إدن ∴ يداث ∴ لشغد جن ∴ وار نفشن

سن قث ∴ اكو بيو نفشن ∴ فنر يد فيب ∴ إدن ∴

كندا السو ∴ كتشينبن ∴ نثو ∴ بدا في كورا ∴

سعبنم ∴ شيكو ∴ كدا قدوبن ∴ فغنس ∴ كمم

مدر ∴ غيوا ∴ غوم ∴ شبكش ∴ إدن غمر ميد

وابمن ∴ شكبر كملو ∴ دغدا ادتن ∴ كدان ∴ =

shi tafi dāji, idan [16] daa ya gani mutume nan, daa ya kashe shi.
Yau shi-na chikin runbu yā bōye. Maatar mai-gidan
ta gaia masa ta che, ' Kar ka yi mōtsi har shi yi kwāna,
idan kā gani wuri da dufu, bai yi kwāna ba, idan kā
gani wuri yā yi kashe, yā yi kwāna ke nan,
ka fita ka gudu.' Ana-nan sai ya gani wuri yā yi
haske kamar rāna. Sai ya fita. Shi-na-gudu, shi-na-
-gudu har gari ya wāye, shi-na-gudu, har rāna
ta fitō shi-na-gudu, bai tsāya ba. Sai mutume nan ya falka
daga kwāna, sai ya che, ' Ina-jin wārin mutun, ina-
-jin wārin mutun.' Ya tāshi, ya bi wurin da mutume nan
ya bi. Shi-na-gudu. Shi kuma, wa(n)chan, shi-na-gudu

---

he went to the bush, and if he should see a person there he would kill him. Now he (A Man-among-Men) was in the store-house, hidden. The man's wife told him, saying, 'You must not move till he is asleep. If you have seen the place dark, he is not asleep; if you have seen the place light, that is a sign he is asleep; come out and fly.' Shortly after he saw the place has become light like day, so he came out. He was running, he was running, until dawn, he was running, till the sun rose he was running, he did not stand. Then that man woke up from sleep and he said, ' I smell the smell of a man, I smell the smell of a man.' He rose up, he followed where the man had gone. He was running. He also, the other one, was running

شلبشكايد أم ؞ متبمنن يكغنم ؞ أد ن ر ؞ إدن ؞ داج شتف
نرغنمي مقم ؞ ميجوبيا ؞ أوبنفر نكيث ؞ أنشو يمو
نفاوكبشّ منم ؞ طومو كيكمّ كمي ؞ متين فمين ابيغت
كدرن إدا ؞ بفاوكتمبي ؞ فدم ؞ ؞ ير أو ؞ منغا كدرإ
نفمكي بفاوكبتمي ؞ نكسح ؞ ؞ تمّيم ير أو ؞ منغ
نتمّيم ؞ ؞ ير أو منغقيم سنل ؞ نمقا ؞ أمقا ؞ ؞ غكتي ؞ ؞ تجت
دنشل ؞ ؞ دغنش بجيم سنل ؞ وفمار مكن كبسح
ؤفار مح ؞ ؞ دغنش ؞ ؤبيم ؤبيم يغم محم ؞ ؞ دغم
هاقيم نتمبتم سنل ؞ ؞ بميطقم ؞ ؞ دغنش ؞ ؤاوتجت
ادفإ ؞ منشمر أرأو ؞ منجاد إ ؞ ثمي سنل ؞ مقاوكغد
منبقم مدفراو يبم نشلامي ؞ ؞ رمشمفاو رأو ؞ نجم
؞ ؞ دغنشل ؞ رمقوأ ؞ مكيبشل ؞ ؞ دغنش ؞ ؞ ببيم

har ya tarda masu-[17]sasabe, su-ka-che me ya fāru.
Ya che, 'Wani mutun ya kōrō ni.' Su-ka-che, 'Tsāye nan har
shi tafō.' Zūa anjima, sai iskansa ya zō,
shi-na-daukansu, shi-na-kaiyaswa. Sai ya che, 'Tō
iskansa ke nan, tukuna shi dakaisa bai zō ba,
idan ku-na-iyāwa ku gaia mani, idan ba ku iyāwa
ku gaia mani.' Su-ka-che, 'Yi gaba.' Sai ya shēka da gudu,
ya je ya iske wadansu, su-na-[18]fūda. Su-ka-che,
'Me ya kōrō ka?' Ya che, 'Wani mutun ya kōrō ni.'
Su-ka-che, 'Wani irin mutun ya kōrō kamanka.' Ya che,
'Wani ne wai shi Namiji-Mijin-Maza.' Su-ka-che,
'Ba Mijin-Maza ba, Mijin-Māta, tsāya har shi tafō.'
Ya tsaya. Shi-na-nan, iskansa ya zō, shi-na-tunḳude

---

till he met some people who were clearing the ground for a farm, (and) they asked what had happened. And he said, 'Some one chased (is chasing) me.' They said, 'Stand here till he comes.' A short time passed, and the wind caused by him came; it lifted them (and) cast them down. And he said, 'Yes, that is it, the wind he makes (running); he himself has not yet come. If you are able (to withstand him) tell me. If you are not able, say so.' And they said, 'Pass on.' So he ran off, and came and met some people hoeing. They said, 'What chased (is chasing) you?' He replied, 'Some one pursued (is pursuing) me.' They said, 'What kind of a man chased (is chasing) (one) such as you.' He said, 'Some one who says he is A-Man-among-Men. They said, 'Not a man-among-men, a man-among-women. Stand till he comes.' He stood. Here he was when the wind of him came, it was pushing about

حَمْ مَيْتَزْدَ ؞ مَدَاسُ لَسَسَبِي ؞ لُسَكِبْ ؞ مِيجَادُ ؞
مِيبْ وُفِنْشِ ؞ يَكُوزُورُ ؞ لُسَكِبْ ؞ طِيَاقِّمْ ؞ حَمْ
شِتَبُوا ؞ دُوَا ؞ أَنْجِحَ ؞ تَسَمْ إِسْكَفْشَ ؞ مِيخُوا ؞
شِنَادُ وُكَنْفَسْ ؞ شِنَاكَدِ مِيسْوَا ؞ لَسَرْ يَبْشُ ثُو
؞ إِسْكَفْلَسْ ؞ بِكَنْقَّمْ ؞ تُكُمْ ؞ شِمْ دَكِيسُ ؞ مِنْجُرَابْ
إِدَّرْ ؞ كُفَدَا عِيدَاوَا ؞ كُغِيَامِي ؞ إِدَّرْ ؞ مَدَاكُ عِيَاوَا
كُفِيَامِي ؞ لُسَكِبْ ؞ يَغِبْ ؞ لَسَمْ يِيشِكْ ؞ دَغْدُ
مَجِي مِيَا إِسْكُنْ ؞ وَدَمُسُ ؞ لُسَنَابُودَا ؞ لُسَكِبْ
مِيَكُووَرِكْ ؞ مَسُبْ وُقِّمْشِ ؞ يَكُوزُورُ ؞ لُسَـ
لُسَكِبْ ؞ وَبِيِوُ مُمْشِ ؞ مِيكُوزُوَا كَمْنْكَ ؞ يَبْ
وَبِنْبِي ؞ وَمِيشِمْ ؞ نَمِجِ ؞ مِجِنْمَدَا ؞ لُسَكِبْ
بَمْ مِجِنْمَدَابَ ؞ مِجِمْ مَاقَا ؞ طِيَاقَمْ ؞ شِنَبُو
بَطِجِ ؞ شِنَاقْمْ ؞ إِسْكَفْسَ ؞ مِخُوا ؞ شِنَاقْتُكُمْ بَرْ

māsu-nōma. Sai ya che, 'Kun gani iskansa ke nan,
19 takuna shi dakaisa bai tafō ba, idan ku-na-iyāwa,
ku gaia mani, idan ba ku iyāwa, ku gaia mani.' Sai su-ka-che,
'Yi gaba'; sai ya shēka da gudu. Shi-na-gudu ya iske māsu-
-shibka. Su-ka-che, 'Me ka kewa gudu?' Ya che, 'Wani ya kōrō
Su-ka-che, 'Wane irin mutun ne ya kōrō kamanka?' Ya che,
'Sunansa Namiji-Mijin-Maza.' Su-ka-che, 'Zamna nan
shi zō.' Yaa zamna. Aka-jima kadan sai iskansa ya zō.
Shi-na-daukansu, shi-na-kāyaswa. Sai su-ka-che, 'Wane irin
iska ne haka?' Shi, mutume nan da aka-kōrō shi,
ya che, 'Iskansa ke nan.' Sai su-ka-che, 'Yi gaba.' Su-ka-yāda
abin shibka, su-ka-shiga dāji, su-ka-bōye,

---

the men who were hoeing. So he said, 'You have seen, that is t wind he makes; he has not yet come himself. If you are a mat for him tell me; if not say so.' And they said, 'Pass on'; and off ran. He was running. He came across some people sowing; th said, 'What are you running for?' He said, 'Some one chased chasing) me.' And they said, 'What kind of a man is it who chas (is chasing) the like of you?' He said, 'His name is A-Man-amon Men.' They said, 'Sit here till he comes.' He sat down. In a sh time the wind he made came (and) it lifted them and cast them dow And they said, 'What kind of wind is that?' He, the man who w being pursued, said, 'It is his wind.' And they said, 'Pass o They threw away the sowing implements, (and) went into the bu (and) hid,

ماسفومو ؞ لسن ميغ كنغنيم ؞ إسكنسن بجقن ؞

تكندا لشم ؞ دكنيسن ؞ مينتقواب ؞ إدن ؞ كندا عيدارا ؞

كفيا مرن إدن ؞ مدكعيارا ؞ كقيا مرن ؞ لسن سكب ؞ بد

يغب ؞ لس بيشك ؞ دغد ؞ يشناغد ؞ بجلسكي ؞ مداس

شبك ؞ لسكب ؞ بككبواغد ؞ بيب وفيكورن ؞

لسكب ؞ وفدرن ؞ متغبن ؞ يكور وكمنك ؞ يب

موقفسن نعج ؞ معنفدا ؞ لسكب ؞ دمنا قمن ؞

شدوا ؞ يدمرن أكجم كدن ؞ لس إسكنسن ميدرا

قنادو كنسن شناكدا يسوا ؞ مس سكب ؞ وفدرن ؞

إسكافن ؞ فك ؞ شيفنجقن ؞ دآك كورشن =

ميب إسكنسن بجقن ؞ لس سكما ؞ يغب ؞ لسكيا د

أمنشبك ؞ لسكيشغ ؞ داج ؞ لسكبوبيس ؞ ==

shi kūa wanchan shi-na-gudu. Ya je, ya tarda wani gawurtache mutun, shi kadai gutsun kūka shi-na-zamne. Ya [20] kasō giwāye, shi-na-banda, shi kūa, gīwa ishirin shi ke chi, da sāfe shi karia kumalō da bīar. sūnansa, Dungun-Dāji. Sai ya tanbaye shi, ya che, 'Ina zaa ka da gudu?' Ya che, 'Namiji-Mijin-Maza ya kōrō ni.' Sai Dungun-Dāji ya che, 'Tafō, zamna har shi zō.' Ya zamna. Aka-jima iskan Namiji-Mijin-Maza ya zō, ya dauke shi, zaa shi da shi, sai Dungun-Dāji ya būga tsāwa ya che, 'Kōmō.' Ya che, 'Ba ni dakaina ke tafia ba, iskan mutume nan ke dauka na.' Sai Dungun-Dāji ya yi fushi. Ya tashi, ya kāmō [21] hannunsa, ya sainya karkashin

---

but that one was running on. He came (and) met a certain hu man; he was sitting alone at the foot of a baobab tree. He h killed elephants and was roasting them, as for him, twenty elepha he could eat; in the morning he broke his fast with five. I name was 'The Giant of the Forest.' Then he questioned h and said, 'Where are you going in all this haste?' And he sa 'A-Man-among-Men chased (is chasing) me.' And the Giant the Forest said, 'Come here, sit down till he comes.' He sat dov They waited a little while. Then a wind made by A-Man-amo Men came, and lifted him, (and) was about to carry him off, when Giant of the Forest shouted to him to come back. And he sa 'It is not I myself who am going off, the wind caused by the m is taking me away.' At that the Giant of the Forest got in a ra he got up and caught his hand, and placed it under

شيكو ∴ ورقشن شنا غد ∴ يجم يقتر د ∴ ورفغار رقبش

مقر ∴ شيكم سن ∴ غوطن ∴ كوك ∴ شنا دفين

ياكسوا ∴ خيوامي ∴ شنا بفد ∴ شيكو ∴ غيوا

عشمر ∴ شيكث ∴ داسدوق شكمر ∴ كملو ∴ ديم

سوفنس د فغم دراج ∴ اسن يتنبيش ∴ يث

إملاد أك ∴ د غد ∴ يث نمج مجنمدا ∴ يكوون =

سن د فغم دراج ∴ يث تقبوا د فنا ∴ حن شذوا ∴

يد ممر ∴ أكجم ∴ إسكر نمج مجنمدا ∴ يذوا ∴

يد وكمشن د أشد شم ∴ اسن د فغم دراج ∴ يبح

تطدوا ∴ يث كوموا ∴ يث بدفيد كيمقن بكنفياب

إسكر متبمقن ∴ بكد وكداوث سن د فغم دراج يس وقشي

يتداش ∴ يكاموا ∴ حننفسن يلسياكم كشمن

chinyasa. Shi-na-zamne har Namiji-Mijin-Maza ya zō, ya che, 'Kai wa ke zamne, masu-rai, kō masu--mutūa?' Sai Dungun-Dāji ya che, 'Karanbani garē--ka.' Sai Namiji-Mijin-Maza ya che, 'Idan ka-na-sō ka sāmu lāfia, ba ni ajiana.' Sai Dungun-Dāji ya che, 'Tafō ka dauki.' Sai ya yi fushi, ya zaabura, ya kāma shi. Su-na-kōkūa. Da su-ka-nada ma majuna hardia, su-ka-tuma, su-ka-yi bisa. Har wa yau su-na-chan, su-na-kōkūa. Idan sun gaji, su za--mna, su fūta, idan sun tāshi kōkūa, shi ne ka kan ji chida chikin samau, su ne su ke kō--kūa. Shi kūa, wanchan, ya sāmu kansa, ya je gida, shi-na-bāda lābāri. Sai maatarsa

---

his thigh. He was sitting until A-Man-among-Men came up and said, 'You sitting there, are you of the living, or of the dead?' And the Giant of the Forest said, 'You are interfering.' And A-Man-among-Men said, 'If you want to find health give up to me what you are keeping there.' And the Giant of the Forest said, 'Come and take (him).' And at that he flew into a rage and sprang and seized him. They were struggling together. When they had twisted their legs round one another they leaped up into the heavens. Till this day they are wrestling there; when they are tired out they sit down and rest; and if they rise up to struggle that is the thunder you are wont to hear in the sky; it is they struggling. He also, that other one, found himself (escaped), and went home, and told the tale. And his wife

ثيسن ننا دمبن ∴ قرنمج مجنمدا ∴ يدروا ∴
يبثكم ∴ واكد مبن ∴ مسوري ∴ كومسو
مثو ∴ سر د نغمراج ∴ يبثكم قبا لم ∴ غم
لك ∴ سرنمج ∴ نجنمدا ∴ يبث ادرن ∴ تجنا سو ∴
كسالم ∴ لاقو ∴ بدار ∴ اجيا قمن ∴ سر د نغمراج
يبث ∴ قبوا ∴ كدوك ∴ سريمي قبشم ∴ يبرا بمر ∴
يكا مداشن ∴ سنا كوكو ∴ دسمكندا مجومدا
قردها ∴ سكثم ∴ سكمصلن ∴ حمرويجوا ∴
سنا قمن ∴ سنا كوكو ∴ ادرن ∴ سنغج ∴ سخ
مرن سبقوت ∴ ادرن ∴ سنتاشن كوكو ∴ شيبن
ككنج ∴ شد ثكمن ∴ سمدا ∴ سوبمن ∴ سبكسكو
كو ∴ شيكو ∴ وقمن ميسالم ∴ ككنسن ∴
يجمنجدا ∴ مشنا بدا ∴ لابدارن ∴ سرها قمر من

ta che, 'Dōmin hakanan ni ke gaia maka, kulum kōmi ka ke yi, [22] dinga ragāwa. Idan [23] karfī, idan sarauta, idan kurdi, idan tsīa, ka ke takama, duka dai, wani ya fi ka, ka che, karīa ne, gā shi, [24] kā gani da idānunka.' [25] Kungurus kan kūsu.

---

said, 'That is why I was always telling you whatever you do, make little of it. Whether it be you excel in strength, or in power, or riches, or poverty, and are puffed up with pride, it is all the same; some one is better than you. You said, it was a lie. Behold, your own eyes have seen.' Off with the rat's head.

تشبد ومن ∴ تكنن ∴ قكغيا مك ∴ كلم ∴ كوم ∴
ككن ∴ د قغ رغكوا ∴ ادزن كرفي ∴ ادزن لسرق
ادزن كرد ∴ اعزن ديبا ∴ ككتا كها ∴ دكم ∴
وفيا فيك ∴ كش ∴ فريا بن غاش نكا غنم ∴
د ادا قنك ∴ فنقم سن كنقوس

No. 13.

Wanan tātsūnīar marāyu che.

[1] Gātanan, gātanan. Ta je, ta kōmō. Wani mutun [2] ya mutu ya bar dīansa bīū maza, da uwāyensu bīū mātā. Ana-nan chikin uwāye māta daia ta sāmu chīwō. Ta-na-jinya chiuta, ta ki karēwa. Da ta gani kamar [3] taa mutu, sai ta che da yar uwa tata, ai [4] kīshīa tata, wanche, ' Kin gani [5] chiutar nan tawa ta ki karē-wa, na san zaa ni mutūa ne, idan Ala taala [6] yā karbi rai na, ga danki nan, [7] nā bar maki taulafi, dōmin Ala da anabi.' Ta che, ' Tō, nā ji.' Ana-nan sai ranan ta mutu, yārō kūa ba shi da wāyō. Aka-yi kō-mi da kōmi aka-gama. Aka-yi kwānaki bāyan mutūanta, ana-nan danta da dan wachan su-na-

---

This story is about orphans. A story, a story. Let it go. Let it come. A certain man died and left two sons, and their mothers, two women. Then among the mothers one fell sick. She was taking medicine for her illness, (but) it refused to mend. When she saw she was apparently going to die; then she said to her sister, that one (her late husband's) second wife, 'You have seen this illness of mine will not go away. I know I am going to die, when Allah, the exalted one, has taken my life from me, behold there is a son (lit. your son) I have left to you and put in your charge, for the sake of Allah and the prophets.' She said, 'It is well, I have heard.' And it came to pass the day came when she died, and the boy had not reached an age when he had full knowledge. Then the funeral rites were completed. Some time passed after her death. Now her son and the son of the other (woman) possessed

وَقَّرْ قَا طُوفِيَّرْ ∴ مَرَابُوثْ

نَمَا قَمَّنْ ∴ نَغَا قَمَّنْ قُجِي تَكُومُوَا ∴ وَنَفُشَنْ يَمُنَا

يَجَرْ ∴ دِيَقَّسَنْ بِيُو مَدَا ∴ دَعُوَابِمُرْسُنْ بِيُو مَا قَدَا ∴

أَقَّا قَمَّرْ ∴ نِكُمْ ∴ عُوَابِّي مَا قَنَا ∴ دَسَّنْ ∴ قَسَّادُمْ ∴ قُيُو ∴

قَنَا جِمْنَى ∴ قِبُوقَلِي ∴ تَيكَا رُمَوَا ∴ دَقَغِيمْ ∴ كَمَرْ

تَأُمُثْ ∴ لَمْسِ قُبُثْ دَيَّبْرْ عُوَا قَمَثْ ∴ أَيْ كِيبِثَيَا قَمَثْ ∴

وَقُشَّنْ ∴ يَكُنْغَيمْ ∴ قِشُوقَّمْ قَمَّرْ ∴ قَدَاوْ ∴ قَدَاكِ ∴ كَدَابْ

بَوَا ∴ قَدَاسَمْ ∴ دَأُنْ ∴ مُشُوَاقَّي ∴ إِدَّرْنْ أَلَّثْ قَعَدَالِي

يَاكَرْبِ ∴ وَيْقَنَا ∴ غَمَادِ نَكُمَّنْ ∴ قَدَا بَرْمَكِ ∴ قُلُوَابِمْ

دُوَمَّنْ ∴ أَلَّثْ دَأَقَّبِ ∴ قَبَّثْ مُثُو ∴ قَدَاجِ ∴ أَقَّا قَمَّرْ ∴ لَسَنْ

رَقَمَّنْ ∴ تَمُثُ ∴ بِيَارُو كُحَوَّ ∴ بَدَاشِدَ وَرَابِيُوا ∴ أَقْمِي كُو

مِيمِ ∴ دَحُوَمِيمِ ∴ أَكَغَمَ ∴ أَكِي كُوَا قَكِيمِ ∴ بَدَايَّمْ

مُشُوقُمْتَ ∴ أَقَدَا قَمَّرْ ∴ عَمُثْ ∴ دَدَ مُقُو قَمَّرْ ∴ سُنَا

da kāji, su-na-kīwō, nasa guda, na marāya guda.
Ranan ta dauki sanda, ta buge na marāya da gangan,
ta kashe, ba shi gida. Da ya zō, ya gani kāza
tasa matachīa, bai che kōmi ba, sai ya che,
'Wayō Ala mai-girma yau kāzata tā mutu.'
Sai ya dauki, ya fīge, ya babake, ya gerta da keau,
ya dōra tukunia bisa wuta, ya dafa da keau,
ya dauki, ya kai kāsua. Kōwa ya zō, ya che
shi na sō shi saia, sai shi che, shi, ba shi
sairwa, sai dōki. Ana-nan dan sarki, wanda
shi ke sō, ya zō, shi kūa yārō ne kankane.
Shi-na bisa algarma, sai ya che, nāman kāza nan
shi ke sō sai asai masa. Marāya kūa ya che,

---

fowls, (and) were rearing them, he (had) one, (and) the orphan one. One day she lifted a stick, and hit the orphan's (fowl) on purpose, (and) killed it (when) he was not at home. When he returned he saw his hen dead; he did not say anything except 'Alas! Allah, the powerful one, to-day my hen has died.' Then he picked it up, (and) plucked it, (and) put it on the fire, and prepared it well, (and) placed a pot on the fire, (and) cooked it thoroughly. He took it up, (and) went (with it) to the market. Whoever came and said he wanted to buy it, he would answer he would not sell it, except for a horse. Then the chief's son came, the one the chief loved; he too was quite a little boy. He was mounted on a powerful horse; and he said the flesh of this hen was what he wanted and it must be sold to him. But the orphan said,

دكاجي ∴ سنا كيوو ∴ فاس غدا ∴ فمويا غدا ∴

رفم ∴ قمدّ ورك ∴ سندا ∴ تبغي ∴ فمادرم ∴ د غنغم

تكشي ∴ بدا شغدا ∴ د يدوا ∴ يغنم كدا دا

نمس ∴ متشيا ∴ بنب كوميي ∴ اسن يشب ∴

وميو ∴ ألّ ∴ مغيغم مو ∴ يوكدا ذات ∴ قامث ∴

بسن يدّورك ∴ يجيغي بيسبكي ∴ يغم قم ∴ د ثو

يدور ∴ تكنيا ∴ بسوقم ∴ يدّق ∴ د قو ∴ —

يدّ ورك ∴ يكن ∴ كد اسوا ∴ كوا يدوا ∴ يشب

شنا سوا ∴ شسيا ∴ سن شب ∴ شيبا شن

لسيزوا ∴ اسن د ورك ∴ أقّا قمّ ∴ د مسركم ∴ رقم

شبكمسوا ∴ يغوا ∴ شيكو ∴ يا زوبم ∴ فنفي

شنا بسن ∴ ألفزم ∴ اسن يشب ∴ قا مركا دقم

شبكسوا ∴ اسن أسيمسن ∴ مرليا كوّ ∴ يشب

idan ba dōki aka-ba shi ba, shi kūa bābu mai-chin nāmansa. Yau sai aka-ba shi dōki, aka-baiwa dan sarki nāma, shi kūa ya kāwō dōkinsa gida.
Sai uwa tasa ta che, ‘ Dauki dōkinka ka sainya achikin dākinga, ka līke da kasa, kāmin kwāna bakwoi, idan ka būde, sai ka gani yaa yi kiba, kamar zai pashe dākinsa. Zatonta idan ya yi hakanan sai shi mutu.’ Shi kūa yārō shi-na-zatō gaskīa ne. Sai ya sainya dōki chikin dāki, ya līke kōfa. Aka-kwāna kamar gōma, ya būde kōfa, sai ya gani dōkinsa ya yi kiba. Sai kīshiar uwa tasa ya yi bakin chiki dōmin da dōki

---

if he did not give him the horse, as for him, no one would eat his meat. So he was given the horse, (and) the chief's son the meat, and the former took his horse home. But his mother said, ‘Take your horse (and) put it in this house, and close up the door with earth ; in about seven days, if you open it, you will see it has become fat enough to burst its house.’ Her idea was if he did so it (the horse) would be dead. Now the boy thought this was true, so he put the horse in the house, and plastered up the door. When about ten days had elapsed, he opened the door, and he saw his horse had become fat. But his step-mother got black of heart because the horse

إِدَنْ ؞ مَادَّ زُكِ ؞ أَكَبَاشِبَ ؞ شِيكُوَّ ؞ بَادُ ؞ مِيثِسْ

قَامِنْسَنْ ؞ يِجُوسَنْ أَكَبَاشِدُ وُكِ ؞ أَكَبِنْوَ ؞ دُقْسَرْكِ

قَدَمْ ؞ يِشِيكُوَّ ؞ يَكَدُوْ ؞ دُوكِنْسَنْ غِدَا ؞ =

لَسَنْ عُوَاقُسَنْ ؞ قَبْشِ دَزُكِ ؞ دُوكِنْكَ ؞ كَلَسْنِيِ

أَشِكِنْدَ اكِنْغَ ؞ كَلِيفِنْ ؞ دَكُسَنْ ؞ كَدَامِنْ ؞ كُوَاقُنْ

بَكُمْنْ إِدَنْ كَبُوبَنْ ؞ لَسَنْ كَقَنِم ؞ قِيَامِّ ؞ كَبَ ؞

كَمَنْ ؞ دَيْقَشِنْ ؞ دَاكِنْسَنْ طَنُوقَ ؞ إِدَنْ ؞

يَامِّ ؞ قَكَنَّ ؞ لَسَنْ شِمُقُ ؞ شِيكُوَ ؞ قِدَارُ ؞ شِنَا

طَنُوغَ لِكِيَا قُنَّ ؞ لَسَنْ قِلَشْنَ ؞ دُوكِ ؞ ثِكَمْ دَاكِ

بَلِيفُنْ كُوقَ ؞ أَكَكُوَاقُنْ ؞ كَمَمْ غُومَ ؞ يَبُوبَنْ

كُوقَ ؞ لَسَنْ بَغَنِم ؞ دُوكِنْسَ ؞ بَاتَ كَبَ ؞ لَسَنْ .

كِيشِيَّرْ ؞ غُوَاقَلَسْ ؞ قَنَّ بَكَنْشِكِ ؞ دُوقِمْ ؞ دَدُو كِ

bai mutu ba. Yau ana-nan ranan ta che, 'Yau bābu karan da-fūa.' Shi saiar da dōkinsa, shi sayō kara. Sai ya che, 'Haba uwāna, ana wada ake sai da dōki, asai kara?' Ta che, 'Dōmin ba uwa(r) ka ni ke ba, dōmin hakanan ka ke gardama da ni?' Ya che, 'Ba gardama ni ke yi ba, naa tafi in bīdō kara.' Ta che, 'Bari idan ba ka sai da dōkinka ka bari.' Sai maraya ya che, 'Bābu laifi.' Ya je, ya sai da dōki, ya karbō kara. Ya kāwō mata. Ta kōne kara duka, ba ta rege kō kadan ba, sai yan guntāye guda uku su-ka-saura. Ya tsinche, ya dunka yar jaka, ya dūra su achiki. Sai wata rāna ya tāshi, ya je wani gari yāwō,

---

did not die. Well, things went on, and one day she said, 'To-day there are no grain-stalks to cook with.' He must sell his horse and buy stalks of grain. But he said, 'Oh my mother, why must the horse be sold to buy stalks of grain?' She said, 'Because I am not your mother, because of that do you argue with me?' He said, 'I am not disputing, I shall go and seek the grain stalks.' She said, 'Stop! If you do not sell the horse leave things as they are.' And the orphan said, 'It cannot be helped.' He went and sold the horse and received the grain stalks, (and) brought them to her. She burned all the stalks; she did not leave any at all, except three very small pieces which were left. He picked them up, sewed a little bag and tied them inside. Another day he rose up and went to another village for a walk,

بيقشب ؞ ييوأفاقم زقم ؞ تثبيوبدابم ؞ كرفم

بجوا ؞ لشسليم درو كقسش فشسليو ؞ كرا ؞ تسريهب

قب ؞ عوافم ؞ أفاوزأبكسيد دوك ؞ أسق

كرا ؞ قثبدوقم ؞ قاعوك ؞ نكب ؞ دوقم

قكنم ؞ ككجكم دم ؞ دفي ؞ ييثبقاغم دم ؞

نكسب ؞ نلأقي ؞ إقبدوا ؞ كرا ؞ قثبم ؞ إدن

قاكسيم ؞ دوكنك ؞ ككبم ؞ أسمرافم ؞ ميثب

قاب ليقم ؞ يجى ؞ يلسيم ؞ دوك ؞ يكرموكرا

يكلاوقة ؞ تكوفى ؞ كرادك ؞ بنتم بمن ؞ كو

كد قب ؞ أسم يقنقنلايمن ؞ غدا ؞ أك ؞ سكسور

يطلقب ؞ يدنك ؞ فيم بجكن قيدورالسم ؞ أتكم

أسم وقراقم ؞ يتنالشن قيجى ونغري ؞ قياو ؞

sai ya hau [8] matsāfa. Su-ka-gane shi, su-ka-kāma shi, su-ka-che, zaa su yanka shi. Sai ya che, ' Nā ji lābāri sarkinku ya makabche, dōmin hakanan na zō in yi masa māgani, idan ba ku sō, ku yanka ni.' Sai su-ka-che, 'Mu-na-so.' Sai aka-kai shi gidan sarki, aka-ba shi dāki. Dare ya yi, ya dauki karansa, saura-n bākin wuta nan. Ya kuna wuta ga guda, ya gewaiya bā-yan dākin sarki, kāmin shi mutu. Sai sarki ya fāra gani kadan kadan. Sai ya kuna guda kuma, kāmin wanan shi kāre, sai idānun sarki ya būde duka. Sai su-ka-girmama shi. Gari ya wāye, sarki ya tāra mutāne, ya che, [9] ' Kun ka gani yārō ya yi mani māgani.

---

and climbed up on the fetish altar. They saw him, (and) seized him, (and) said they would cut (his throat). But he said, ' I have heard the news that your chief is blind, and for that reason I came to make medicine for him. If you don't want (me to) then kill me.' But they said, ' We wish (it).' So he was brought to the chief's house and given a hut. When night came he lifted up his grain stalks; these which the fire had left. He set fire to one (stalk) and walked round the back of the chief's house till it died out. And the chiet began to see a very little. Then he lit another, when it was finished (burned out), then both the chief's eyes opened. Thereupon they gave him honour. At dawn the chiet assembled the people (and) said, ' You have seen the boy has made medicine for me.

لسن يحو ملاقي .: لسككغبش .: لسككلماش .:

لسكب .: دأس .: ينكاش .: لسن يخب .: فلاج للابار .:

لسركنك .: يلامكبث .: دوقمن مكتن .: فدرا .: =

إفيقس .: ماغنم .: إدفبا كسوا .: كينكار .: لسن

لسكب .: منداسوا .: لسن أككيش .: غم فلسركم .:

أكباش .: داك .: دبرميمق .: يمد وكرفس .: لسرور

نباكمن .: وقمن .: يكروند .: غغدا .: يغموتن .: نبا

يفدراكمن لسركم .: كدامر .: شمث .: لسن لسركم .: يقلار

غنم .: كدنكدر .: لسن يكرغداكم .: كدامر .: وقمن

شكبوكون .: لسراع افمر لسركم .: يجبوجمر دك .: =

لسن لسكغنز مماش .: غم ميخوامي .: لسركم .: يتلار

متلافين .: يخب كنكغنم .: يداور .: ميايمرش .: هلاغنم

Idānuna ya warke, ama naa ba shi rabin gari,
shi chi sarauta.' Sai ya che, 'Ni falke ne, ba ni chin sarauta.'
Su-ka-che, 'Idan ba ka chin sarauta, ka dībi abinda
ka ke sō, ka tafi.' Sai ya dēbi bāyi, da shānu,
da kōmi masu-chau, ya tafō da su, ya shigō
gari da su. Mutāne su-na-māmāki. Sai
kīshīar uwa tasa ta che, 'Tafō mu je hainya
rāfi, nā gani wani kūsū, yā shiga rāme,
ka gina mani, in yi mia.' Sai ya che, 'Haba uwana
wane irin nāma, ga zābi, ga kāji, ga rāguna?'
Sai ta che, 'Ansani ka-na da dūkīa, ni dai nā-
-man kūsu ni ke so.' Sai ya che, 'Bābu laifi
mu tafi ka gwoda mani.' Ashe tā gani rāmen kumurchi ne

My eyes are healed, and I shall give him half of the town to rule over.' But he (the boy) answered, 'I am only a trader, passing, and I do not rule.' They said, 'If you will not rule, take whatever you wish and go.' So he took slaves, and cattle, and everything beautiful, and went off with them, and entered (his) town with them. The people were astonished. But his step-mother said, 'Come, let us go to the road by the stream, I have seen a rat enter a hole; you dig it for me to make soup.' And he said, 'Come now, my mother, what kind of meat (is a rat's)? Behold guinea-fowls, and hens, and rams.' And she said, 'We all know you have wealth; as for me though, rat's meat is what I want.' So he said, 'There is no harm in that. Let us go, you show me.' Now really she has seen it was a snake's hole (but she told him this)

إِدَ اَفُوقَنِ ∴ يَاوْرْكَنْ ∴ اَمَّا قَمْبَادِشِ ∴ وَبِنْقَمِرِ ∴

يِشِ لَسَرْوُقَ ∴ لَسِنْ يَبْشِ ∴ فِمِ قَلْبَكَنِنْ ∴ بَمَا وْقِنْ لَسَرْوُقَ

∴ سَكَبْشِ ∴ اِدَّرِ ∴ بَدَ عَيِشْ لَسَرْوُقَ ∴ كَدِ مِيبِ ∴ اَبِنْدَ ∴

كَبَكَسُو ∴ كَتَفِ ∴ لَسِنْ يَدِ مَكِبِ ∴ بَدَ يِم ∴ دَ شَّدَنُو

دَ كُومِم ∴ مَكَسَ ∴ قُشْحُو ∴ يَتَبْقُوا دَسُوا ∴ يِيَشِقُحُو ∴

قَمِرِ ∴ دَسُوا ∴ قَتَابُكَن ∴ سَنَا قَمَا قَمَلِكِ ∴ لَسِنْ

كِيِشِيَرْ عُمَوَا قَسَ ∴ قَبْشْ تَبْقُوا ∴ مُجَمَنْ قَشِ ∴

رَا فِم ∴ قَمَا غَنِم ∴ وَنِكُوسَن ∴ يَدِشَغَ ∴ رَابَى

كَغَنَا قَمِن ∴ اِقَّمِحَ ∴ لَسِنْ يَبْشْ قَبَّا عُمَوَا قَمِ ∴

وَبَارِقَنَام ∴ غَمَا دَابِي ∴ غَمَا كَدَابِم ∴ غَمَا وَا غَمَس

∴ لَسِنْ تَبْشْ ∴ اَقْسَنِمِ ∴ كَقَنَا دَ دَوْرِكِيَا ∴ فِيَمِ ∴ قَمَ

مَنْكُوسَن ∴ نِكَسَوا ∴ لَسِنْ يَبْشْ بَدَ مِ لِنِجِم ∴ =

قَتَقِم ∴ كَغَدَا قَمَ مِن اَشِي قَمَا غَنِم ∴ وَابِنْكُمْ قَمِبَن

dōmin ta kai shi shi halaka. Sai baban bāwansa ya tāshi. Ta che, ‘Zamna, nā gane ka, mai bāyi, kai dakainka zaa mu da kai, idan ba ka zūa, ka bari.’ Sai ya che bāyinsa su zamna, shi shii tafi. Su-ka-zamna, su-ka-tafi tāre da kīshīar uwa tasa. Ta je, ta gwoda masa rāmen; zaa shi gina, sai ta che, ‘Ajie hauya, tūra hanunka.’ Sai ya tūra hanu. Sai ya jāwo kwandage. Ya che, ‘Ga shi.’ Ta che, ‘Ba shi ba, kūsu na che akwai shi nan.’ Sai ya tūra hannu kuma, sai ya zārō kwanda-ge na zīnāria. Sai ta yi fushi, ta kōma gida, ta kirāwo danta. Ya zō, sai ta che shi tūra hannu, shi kāmō mata kūsu. Da tūra hanunsa, kumurchi ya chīje hannunsa, sai aka-dauke shi

---

in order that she might bring him trouble. Now a big slave of his rose up (to accompany him). She said, ‘Sit down, I have seen you are the owner of slaves, but it is you alone we (I) will go with. If you will not come, then stay.’ So he told his slaves to sit down and he would go (alone). They sat down. They set off, (he) and his step-mother. She went and showed him the hole. When he was about to dig, then she said, ‘Put down your hoe (and) push in your hand.’ So he put in (his) hand and drew out a bracelet. He said, ‘There it is.’ She said, ‘That is not it. A rat, I said, was there.’ So he put in his hand again and drew out a golden bangle. But she got angry and went back home. She called her own son; he came, whereupon she said he must put in his hand and catch a rat for her. On putting in his hand a snake bit his hand, and they carried him

دُ وِرِّمْ تَكِيشْ يِشْعَلُو لَسْ يَبَّمْ بِدَا وُفْلَلِنْ

يِنْكَاشِنْ تَبْشْ دَ مْفِنِي قَدَا غَبَنْكَ هِيبَا يِمْ =

كَيْدِ كَنْكَ ذَ أُمْدَ كَحْ إِدْرَنْ بِدَا هَدْ رُ كَبِرْ

لَسْ يَبْشْ بِدَا يِفْلَلِنْ لُسْعَ فْمَرْ شِمْ شِنْفَمِ سُكَدْ فْمَرْ

سُكَنْفَمِ قَدَا رَمَدْ هِيشِيرْ عُوَا قَتَلَنْ تَجِرِ تَغْدَا

مَسَنْ وَامُوشْ دَاشِنْ غَمْنِي لَسْ قَتَبْشْ أَجِيبِي دَوِيدَ

شُورَ فْنَنْكَ لَسْ يَشُورْ دَفُوا لَسْ يَجَدَا وُرُ كُنْدَ غِمِي

شَيَبْشْ غَدَا شِنْ قَتَبْشْ بِدَا شِيبِي كُوسَنْ فَشَا أَكُو يِسَنْ

فَمْنْ لَسْ يَتُورْ دَفُوا كُمَّ لَسْ يَغْدَا اُورُ كُنْدَ

نَجُونْ مَنْدِ يِمَدَا رِيدَا لَسْ قَنْصِ فُشِمْ تَكُومْ يِمْدَا

تَكَمْ اُرْ دَ مْنْتَ يَدُوا لَسْ قَتَبْشْ يِشُورْ دَفْنُوا =

شِكَا مُوفْتَ كُوسَنْ دَ فُورْ دَشْنْلَلِنْ

كُمَّ قِمْ يَبْتِيجِي دَشْنْفَسَنْ لَسْ أَكَدَ اُوبْكِيشْ

zūa gida. Bai kai gida ba, sai ya mutu. Ita kūa kwā-
-nanta uku, sai ta mutu. Marāya ya gāde gida.
Mafāri ke nan akan-che, ‘Aki marāya da rīgan
būzu, agane shi da ta [10] karfē.’ Shi ke nan.
[11] Kungurus kan kūsu.

---

home. He died before they reached home. She also died in three days. The orphan inherited the house (property). This is the origin of the saying, ‘The orphan with the cloak of skin is hated, but when it is a metal one he is looked (favourably) on.’ That is all. Off with the rat's head.

دُوَّ ؞ غِدَا ؞ يَنْكَسْ ؞ غِدَابْ ؞ اسْرْيَمُتْ ؞ إِتْكُوَّ ؞ كُوَا

قَفْتَ ؞ أُكْ ؞ اسْرْتَمُتْ ؞ مَرَايِدْ ؞ يَغْلْ دْ مَغْدَا ؞

مَقْدَارِ ؞ بْجَقَّرْ ؞ أَكْنْتْ ؞ أَكْمْرَا مْ ؞ دْ رِيغْسْ

بُودْرَا ؞ أَغْنْبِشْ دْ تْكْرُوكْ ؞ شِيكْنَّرْ ؞

فُتْغُمْسْ ؞ كْنْقُوسْ ؞

No. 14.

Wanan tātsunīar makīsanchi che.

[1] Gātanan, gātanan, ta je, ta kōmō. Wani mutun shi-na chikin birni, sai [2] ya tāshi, ya kōma dāji dōmin kar anemi [3] maatansa, har wata rāna sar-kin [4] garin ya ji lābāri, sai ya che, 'Wanda ya je, ya nemi maatarsa, idan ya zō, [5] naa ba shi dōki, da rīga, da kurdi, zanba dari.' Sai wani mutun ya che shi [6] yaa tafi, ya kwāna da maatarsa, gaban idānunsa. Sai ya je ya bidi yāyan kūka. Ya fūde, ya ger-ta chikinsu da chau, ya nemi kurdi kankanāna, ya zuba chiki. Ya je, ya kai, ya ba shi keauta. Sai ya pasa, ya gani kankanānan kurdi ke chiki, ya pasa wani kuma. Hakanan ya pasa wani kuma hakanan.

This is a story about a jealous man. A story, a story. Let it go. Let it come. There was a certain man who used to live in a town, but afterwards he rose up and went to the bush, lest people might go after his wives, until one day the chief of the town heard about him) and he said, 'He who goes and seduces his wives, if he comes (to me) I will give him a horse, and a cloak, and one hundred thousand cowries.' Then a certain man said he would be the one to go and lie with his wife before his eyes. Then he went off and sought some baobab seeds. He opened them, (and) cleaned out the inside well; he sought for some very small pieces of money and poured them inside. He went, reached (the place where the man was) (and) gave him a present of them. When he broke (one) open he saw the small money inside. He broke another also, (and) in the same way broke open another.

ارقرقا طوفيز ∴ مكيبشيب

ثما اقتش ∴ ثما اقتش ∴ تجم تكوموا ∴ ونفشم

شناتكم ∴ مم تم ∴ لسوبتاش يكوم ∴ ما ج

دومن ∴ كم ابم ∴ ما اقتلس قم وقم امن اسم

كن غم فيج ∴ لا ابماو ∴ لس يبث ∴ وفم بجى ∴ =

يبنم ∴ ما اقم لس ان فيبذوا ∴ ما ابماش دوك ∴ م

وبعن ∴ دكمدي ∴ دفب دري ∴ لسم ونمشم يبث

شم يا تبم ∴ يكوا و ∴ م ما اقم لس غمبم اد افقلس

لسم بجن ∴ يبدي يا يمن ∴ كوك ∴ يفودن ∴ يغز

تث ∴ ثكفسن ∴ د ثو ∴ يبنم ∴ كمدي ∴ فمقفان

∴ يغب ∴ ثكم ∴ يجي لكن ∴ يباشن ∴ جكوثمن ∴ =

لسن مقبسن يغيم ∴ ففقاقمن ∴ كمدي ∴ بيثكم

يقبس ∴ ونكم ∴ مكثم ∴ مقبسن ونكم ∴ مكنم

Sai ya che, 'Abōki-na ba ka gwoda mani wurin da kūka nan ta ke?' Ya che, 'Wurin kūka nan shi-na da nīsa.' Ya che, 'Kai ni.' Ya che, 'Ba shi hauuwa sai da tsāni, bābu wanda ya san wurin da ta ke sai ni.' Sai ya dinga lālāshi, shi kūa kwar-tō, sai ya che, 'Mu tafi in kai ka, ama ba dōmin kai ba, ba ni kai kōwa.' Sai su-ka-tafi tāre da maatar-sa. Da su-ka-isa wurin kūka, sai kwartō ya daukō tsāni, ya dangana, ya che mai-maata shi hau. Sai ya hau. Da ya hau ya kāre, sai ya dauke tsāni, ya kai wani wuri, ya aje, ya kōmō, ya kāma maatar, ya kayas. Shi-na nasa abu, mai-maata shi-na gani, ba shi iya sabkōwa, sai ya che, 'Naa zuba maku miau, naa zuba maku miau.' Har su-ka-gama abinda su ke yi. Kwartō

And he said, 'My friend, will you not show me where this baobab tree is?' He replied, 'The place where this baobab tree is is far away.' (And) he said, 'Take me (to it).' And he said, 'It cannot be climbed except by a ladder, (and) no one knows where it is save me.' And he continued to entreat him; and at last the seducer said, 'Let us go, I will take you there, but if it was not for you, I would not show any one the place.' So they set out along with his wife. When they came to the baobab tree then the seducer lifted the ladder and placed it (against the tree), (and) told the woman's husband to climb up. So up he climbed. When he had finished climbing, then he lifted away the ladder, (and) carried it somewhere else (and) set it down, (and) came back. He seized the wife and threw her down. He did what he intended, the woman's husband looking on (and) not able to descend; but he said, 'I shall spit on you, I shall spit on you,' until they had finished what they were doing. The seducer

تسنِ قيتٌ أموكيناه :. بدا كحكد امين :. ورفد كوكنقن

تكن :. قيتٌ ورفكوكنقن :. شنّاد فيقسن :. قيتٌ كيين

قيتٌ بدا شعووا :. تسنِ دطلون :. قداف ورفد قيسن :. ورفد

تفكن تسينه :. تسنِ قيد فقغ :. لالاالشم :. شيكوكم

شوا :. تسنِ قيتٌ مقيه :. انكيك :. آمّا بادرمس :.

كينيت :. بدا انكيكووا :. تسنِ تسكتقيه :. تعاود ماقتم

تسنِ دتسكاسن ورفكوك :. تسنِ كمقو :. قيد وكو

طلون قيد فغنا :. قيتٌ قيقماقن :. شعحو :. تسنِ يعو

ديعو :. يكا رمن :. تسنِ قيدّ ويكن :. طلون :. يكم ورفوري

قيا جن :. يكومهو :. يكا تم :. ماقم :. يكا قيسن :.

بسنا فا سرابن :. قيقماقن :. بشنا غنيم :. بدا شعِنّ

تسبكووا :. تسنِ قيتٌ قنا ذبا مك :. مييو :. قنا ذبا

مّك :. مييو :. تم تسكغم :. أمند تسكنّ :. كمنو

ya yi [7] tafiasa. Ya je, ya gaia wa sarki kamar da su-ka-yi.
Sarki ya ba shi lāda tasa, ya kāra masa keauta.
Ya che, 'Māganinsa ke nan.' Shi kūa maatarsa
ta yi kōkari, ta daukō tsāni, ta kāwo masa,
ya sabka. Da zuansa gida, sai ya [8] tatara kāyansa,
ya kōmō chikin gari. Ya che, 'Kīshī-na
ya jāwō mani haka, idan ina-nan, mutāne su halaka ni.'
Shi ke nan. [9] Kungurus kan kūsu.

---

went his way. He came, (and) told the chief what they had done. The chief gave him his reward, and added to his gifts. He said, 'That's the medicine he required.' As for the (jealous) man, his wife with difficulty lifted the ladder, (and) brought it to him, (and) he descended. On his return home he collected all his goods, (and) returned (to live) in the town. He said, 'My jealousy dragged me into this ; if I remain here, people will destroy me.' That is the story. Off with the rat's head.

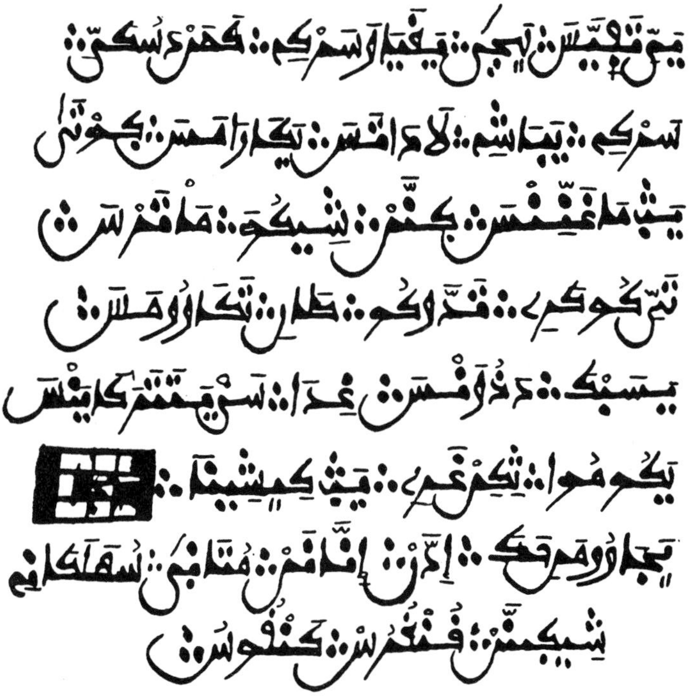

No. 15.

Wanan tātsunīar samāri che, abōki da abōki.
Wadansu yāra su-ka-yi abūta; su-na nan tāre ba su
rabūa. Su-na da buduri(n)su kauye. Kulum su kan tafi tāre,
su daukō su. Ranan dan uwansa bai je ba, sai guda
daia [1] ya tafi daukō [2] budurin. Da ya je, ya daukō buduri. Shi-na-
-zakua, sai su-ka-gamu da zāki, sai ya taushe budrua guda,
sai shi kūa, ya zāre takōbi, ya sāre kan zāki.
Zāki ya mutu, ya tāda budrua ba ta mutu ba, sai ya che ta kwanta karkashi
zāki tāre da shi, guda kūa ta je, ta gaia wa abōkinsa.
Sai ta che, 'Tō.' Ta shēka da gudu, ta iske shi [3] yā fāra kwāna.
Ta tāshe shi, ya che, 'Ana wāne da wānche?' Ta che, 'Su-na-chan,
zāki ya kashe su.' Sai ya tāshi, bai dauki kōmi ba,
ya tafi, ya je, ya tarda zāki, shi-na bisansu. Bai yi shāwara ba,
sai ya zābura, ya hau bissa zāki. Shi-na-che mai-rai ne, ashe matache ne.
Sai abōkinsa ya tāshi ya che, 'Tāshi wāne, [4] kā chika dā.' Sai su-ka-tāda
budrua, su-ka-tafō gida. Tō, chikinsu wa ya fi wani? Idan ba ka sani ba
shi ke nan. [5] Kungurus kan kūsu.

This story is about some young men who were friends. Some boy made a covenant of friendship; they lived together, (and) were inseparable They had their maidens in an outlying village. Always they used to g together (and) bring them. On one occasion, one of his friends did no go, so only one went to bring the maidens. When he went, he brough back the maids. (As) they were going along, they met a lion; and i knocked down and lay on one of the girls, but he, he drew his sword an cut at the lion's head. The lion died, and he found the maiden was no dead. And he told her to lie down beneath the lion along with him, an one of them was to go and tell his friend. So she consented, (and) ran o (and) found he has begun to sleep. She roused him, (and) he said, 'Wher are So-and-so and So-and-so?' And she said, 'They are out there, a lio has killed them.' And he rose up, he did not take anything with him he went along and came and reached (where) the lion was; it was above them. He did not hesitate, but sprang and climbed on the lion. H thought it was alive. Truly it was dead. Then his friend rose up an said, 'Rise, So-and-so, you have proved yourself (a free-born) man.' S they lifted up the maiden (and) went home. Now among them who wa better than another? If you do not know, there it is. Off with the rat' head.

وَمْرْنْ تَاطُوفِيَّمْ :. لسماري ف :. أبوكيم :. د أبوكم :.

ود فلس يدورا :. لسكي أبو تنو :. لسنا قمرن :. تدا برون :. تداس

رمبوا :. لسنا د مدرسن كوميون :. كلم :. لسكنعي تدا برن

لسد وكوسن وقمرن د مكوفسن بيمجب :. لسن غمدا

د تن :. يتنجي د ركو بمد رزن د يجي يد وكوبمد ري :. لشفا

د كوا :. لسن سكغم د داك :. لسن يتوشي :. يدروا غمدا :.

لسع شيكو :. يدا ارين تكوبي :. يلسدورن كغداك :.

داك يفت :. يتا د بدروا :. هتغتب :. لسن يبث تكنت :. كركشر

داك :. تدا برعرشي :. غدا كو :. تجي تغيا ور :. أبو كفسن

لسن قبث ثو :. تنبك د غد :. تا إسكشن يا قادر :. كرافي

تفا ليشش :. يبث أنا وا ابن يد وامث :. قبث لسنا ثرن =

داك :. يا كبشمسن لسن يتنا لش :. بيد وك :. كوميب :.

يتف :. يجي يترد داك :. لشنا بلسفسن :. يبتر شا و راب :.

لسن يزابر :. يجو بسن داك :. لشنا ث :. ميم ميمون أيشي متنهبر

لسن أبو كفسن يتلش :. يث تدا لش وا ابغ :. كدا لك د ا :. لسن سكتاد

بد روا :. سكتفو غدا :. فوتكنسن وبيجورن ادون تكلسين

شيجتن فنغمسن :. كرفوس

No. 16.

Wanan tātsunīar gwanāye che. [1] Gātanan, gātanan. Wani sarki [2] ya haifu dīansa uku maza. Ranan fāda--nchi ya tāru, ya che shi shi-na-sō shi gani gwani chikinsu. Akwai wata gāwurtata kūka fagashin sarki. Ya che shi-na-sō su hau dawāki, su zō, su gwoda gwaninta, wurin kūka nan. Sai su-ka-hau algarmu, su-ka-tafi da nīsa. Babansu ya yi sukūa, ya zō, ya nashi kūka nan da māshi. Māshi ya zarche, [3] ya bi ta kafar māshi nan da dōkinsa, ya wuche. Ma-bi baban ya tafō. Da ya kusa da kūka, sai ya kinkimi dōkinsa, sai ya tsalache kūka. Da autansa ya yi sukūa ya zō, sai ya chire

---

This story is about a (test of) skill. A story, a story. A certain chief begat children, three males. One day his councillors assembled. He said he himself wished to see the most skilled among them. There was a huge baobab tree (near) the entrance to the chief's house. He said he wanted them to mount (their) horses, (and) come (and) show their skill, where this baobab tree was. So they mounted their chargers, (and) went far away. The eldest galloped (and) came, (and) thrust that baobab with (his) spear. The spear went right through and he followed, passing through the hole made by the spear, with his horse. And he passed on. The next to follow the eldest came on. When he was near to the baobab tree he lifted his horse (on the bit) and jumped the baobab. When the youngest galloped, he came, (and) pulled

وفنر قا طوفيير ∴ غنا يث ∴ غا تنر غا قنن ∴

وفسنركم ∴ يحيف دينسراكي ∴ مغ ا ∴ وفنر ∴ قدام

فيثم ∴ قيا قداو ∴ ميث يثم يشنا اسوا ∴ يشكنم غنم

ثيكنسن اكوم ∴ وتنغا ورتت ∴ كوك ∴ قنغشن

تسنركم ∴ ميث يشنا اسو ∴ سعود واكم ∴ سغوا ∴

سفد ∴ غمنتنت ∴ ورنكو كنن ∴ تسن سكحو ∴

الفرموا ∴ سكتنج دفيلسو ∴ ببنشن يس

سكوا ∴ يغدا ميتشن كوكنن ∴ د مداشن ∴ مدايشن

يغرث ∴ ييب تكبز مداشتن ∴ د دوكمسن يوب

مسيم ببنن يتقبوا ∴ د يكلسن د كروك ∴ تسن

بينكم ∴ دويكنسن تسن يطلبث كوك ∴ =

داو تنسن يبر سكوا ∴ يغوا ∴ تسن يثبرك

kūka duka da sauyanta, ya je, ya yi ma ubansu jinjina. Sai [4] gūda ta gama wuri. Yanzu tanbaya ka na ke yi, chikinsu wa ya fi. Idan ba ka sani ba, shi ke nan. [5] Kungurus kan kūsu.

---

up the whole baobab, roots and all, and came on waving it aloft at his father, and the place rang with applause. Now I ask you who excelled among them. If you do not know, that is all. Off with the rat's head.

كُوتَكْ :: دُرْكْ :: دَرْسُويقْتْ :: يْجَرْ يمّ مَا أُبْنْسْ ::

يِنْجْرْ سَنْ غُوزْ :: تَغْمُونْ وُرْ :: يِمْدْ ::

تْنْبِيَّك :: نْكَّ نِكْنْسْ أُوبِجِي :: إِدّ نْ ::

بَكَلِينِيبْ :: يِشْيكْمْرْ :: فْنْغُرْ سْ :: كْنْفُوسْ ::

ه ه ه

ه

No. 17.

Wanan tātsunīar Gishiri che,
da [1] Daudawa, da Nari, da [2] Gabū,
da Tankūa, da [3] Daudawar
batsō.

[4] Gātanan, gātanan, ta je, ta kōmō. Gishiri, da Daudawa, da Nari, da Gabū, da Tankūa, da Daudawar batsō, su-ka-ji lābāri wani sarmāyi, sūnansa Daskandarīni. Shi kūa sarmāyi ne mai-chau (keau), dan Iblisai ne. Su-ka-tāshi su-ka-zama buduri masuchau, su-ka-tafi. Da [5] zaa su, Daudawar batsō [6] ta bi su. Su-ka-kore ta su-ka-che ta-na da wāri. Sai ta [7] make, har su-ka-tafi, ta dinga binsu bāya bāya, har su-ka-kai gurin wani rāfi. Su-ka-tarda tsōfūa, ta-na-wanka. Ta che, su chūda mata bā--yanta, sai wanan shi che, ‘Ala shi tsare ni in dauki hanu na

---

This story is about Salt, and Daudawa (sauce) and Nari (spice), and Onion-leaves, and Pepper and Daudawar-batso (a sauce). A story, a story! Let it go, let it come. Salt, and Daudawa, and Ground-nut, and Onion-leaves, and Pepper, and Daudawar-batso heard a report of a certain youth, by name Daskandarini. Now he was a beautiful youth, the son of the evil spirit. They (all) rose up, (and) turned into beautiful maidens, (and) they set off. As they (Salt, Onion-leaves, &c.) were going along, Daudawar-batso followed them. They drove her off, telling her she stank. But she crouched down until they had gone on. She kept following them behind, until they reached a certain stream. (There) they came across an old woman; she was bathing. She said they must rub down her back for her, but this one said, ‘May Allah save me that I should lift my hand

وَقَرْنَا طُو قِيَّرْ ؞ غِشَرِيفْ

دَدُوْدَوَرَا ؞ دَقَلِمْ ؞ دَغَبُوْ

دَقَنْكُوا ؞ دَدُوْدَوَرْ

بَطُولُهُ ؞

غَمَا قَمْرْ ؞ غَا اقَمْرْ قَجُرْ تَكُو هُوا ؞ غِشَرِ ؞ دَدُوْدَوَرَا ؞
دَقَلِمْ ؞ دَغَبُوْ ؞ دَقَنْكُوا ؞ دَدُوْدَوَرْ ؞ بَطُوا ؞ سُكِج لَابَارْ ؞
وَفِسَمْ مَيِّمْ ؞ سُو قَمْسَشْ دَسُكَنْدَرِ رِيمِنِي ؞ شِيكُو ؞
تَسَمْ هِيِينْ مَيْتُو ؞ دَمْ فِلِيسِيبَنِي سُكَتَا اشْ ؞ =
سُكَدَمْ ؞ فُدُرِ ؞ مَا اسْتُو ؞ سُكَتِيمِ ؞ دَدَأسْ ؞ دَدُوْدَوَ
بَطُوا ؞ قَبِيسْ ؞ سُكَكُو وُمَتَ ؞ سُكَبْ ؞ قَنَادَ وَارِي
تَسَرْ تَمَقُولْ ؞ قَمْ سُكَتِيمِ ؞ قَدِ فَغْ ؞ بِفَسْ بَدَسَى
بَاتَّرْ ؞ قَمْ سُكَكُمْ ؞ غَمْ فُو فِمْ رَاقِمْ ؞ سُكَتَمْ دَ ؞
طُو بُجُوا ؞ قَنَا وَفْكُرْ ؞ قَبْ سِيتُو دَاامَتَ ؞ بَا
يَمْنَا ؞ تَسَرْ وَقَمْ شَبْ ؞ آاَشْطَمْ مَمْ ؞ إفَدْ وُرِكِ تَنُو مَمْ

in taba bāyan tsōfūa.' Sai tsōfūa ta [8] kyale.
Su-ka-wuche, aka-jima, Daudawar batsō ta zō, ta ishe ta,
ta-na-wanka. Ta gaishe ta, ta amsa, ta che, 'Yārinya,
ina zaa ki?' Ta che, 'Zaa mu wurin wani sarmāyi ne.' Ta che, 'Chūda ma
bāyana.' Sai ta che, 'Tō.' Ta tsāya, ta chūda ta da chau.
Tsōfūa ta che, 'Ala shi yi maki albarka.' Ta che, 'Sarmāyi nan
da ku ke zūa wurinsa, kun san sūnansa?' Ta che,
'Aa ba mu san sūnansa ba.' Sai tsōfūa ta che, 'Dāna ne, sūnansa Daskandarīni, ama kar ki gaya
masu.' Ita kūa ta kyale, ta-na-binsu, bāya bāya,
har su-ka-kai wurin yārō. Zaa su shiga. Sai aka-che,
'Ku kōma, ku shigō daia daia.' Su-ka-che. 'Tō.'
Su-ka-kōma. Sai Gishiri ta zō, zaa ta shiga,

---

to touch an old woman's back.' And the old woman did not say anythin
more. They passed on, and soon Daudawar-batso came, (and) met h
washing. She greeted her, (and) she answered (and) said, 'Maiden, whe
are you going?' She replied, 'I am going to where a certain youth i
(And) she (the old woman) said, 'Rub my back for me.' 'She sai
'All right.' She stopped, (and) rubbed her back well for her. The o
woman said, 'May Allah bless you.' And she said, 'This youth to who
you are (all) going to, have you known his name?' She said, 'No, we d
not know his name.' Then the old woman said, 'He is my son, his nan
is Daskandarini, but you must not tell them.' Then she ceased. She w
following them far behind till they got to the place where the boy wa
They were about to enter, but he said, 'Go back, (and) enter one
a time.' They said, 'It is well,' and returned. And then Salt can
forward, (and) was about to enter,

إنتت ∴ بما ينطلوفوا ∴ أسن طوفوا ∴ تكّلين

سكوف ∴ أكجم ∴ د أردّور بطو ∴ تغزوا ∴ تد يشبت

تنداو نكي ∴ تغيشبشت ∴ تأمسن ∴ تبّ يارقي ∴ ـ

إقدا غ أك ∴ تبّ د أم ∴ أورفو نهن ميبيني ∴ تبّ يشو د أمس

بايا نغ ∴ أسن تبّ شو ∴ نقطي ∴ تيشو د أت ∴ كرقوت

طوفوا ∴ تبّ أل أشيهك ألجرك ∴ تبّ أسر ميبيش

تعجمد أو ∴ أورفس ∴ كفلسن ∴ أسوقّلسن ∴ تبّ

عاع ∴ يحسنسو نغلسب ∴ أسن طوفوا أتّي ∴ د أ

قدفي ∴ سوقّلسن ∴ د نسكنم رين ∴ أمّا كر كيا

مسش إنكو ∴ تكّلو ∴ قنا ينلسن ∴ با مو وباسي

تم سكلّن ∴ أورفيا روا ∴ د أسن ∴ شغو ∴ أسن أكبّ ∴

تكوتم ∴ كيشغوا ∴ د تم د مّ ∴ نسكب شو ∴

نسكوم ∴ أسن غيشم ∴ تغروا ∴ د أقشغو

aka-che, 'Wānene nan?' Ta che, 'Ni che.' 'Ke che wa?' 'Ni che Gishiri, mai mia da zāki.' Su-ka-che, 'Wānene sū-nā na?' Ta che, 'Ban san sūnanka ba dan yārō, ban san sūnanka ba.' Aka-che, 'Kōma da bāya yārinya, kōma da bāya.' Ta kōma. Sai Dau-dawa ta zō. Zaa ta shiga aka-che, 'Wacheche?' Ta che, 'Ni che.' 'Ke che wa? Wāne sūnanki?' 'Sūnana Daudawa, mai-mia da dādi.' Sai ya che, 'Wane sūnana?' Ta che, 'Ban san sūnanka ba dan yārō, ban san sūnanka ba.' Ya che, 'Kōma da bāya yārinya, kōma da bāya.' Ta kōma, ta zamna. Sai Nari ta tāsō, ta zō. Zaa ta shiga sai aka-che, 'Wānene nan yā-rinya? Wānene nan?' Ta che, 'Ni che ke gaisua dan yārō,

---

when she was addressed with, 'Who is there?' She said, 'It is I.' 'Who are you?' 'It is I, Salt, who make the soup tasty.' They (he) said, 'What is my name?' She said, 'I do not know your name, little boy, I do not know your name.' Then he said, 'Go back, little girl, go back.' She turned back. So Daudawa came forward. When she was about to enter, she was asked, 'Who are you?' She said, 'It is I.' 'Who are you? What is your name?' 'My name is Daudawa, who makes the soup sweet.' And he said, 'What is my name?' She said, 'I do not know your name, little boy, I do not know your name.' He said, 'Turn back, little girl, turn back.' She turned back, (and) sat down. Then Nari (spice) rose up and came forward, (and) she was about to enter when she was asked, 'Who is this little girl? Who is this?' She said, 'It is I who greet you, little boy,

أَكَبْ وَاقَّبُو قَّمْ ∴ قَبْ فِيبْ ∴ بِكْبُو ∴ فِيّبْ

فِشِرِ ∴ فِيمْ مِيّ ∴ دَدَاكِمْ ∴ سُكَبْ وَاقَّبُو لُسُو

فَدَافُو ∴ قَبْ بِنْسِنْ سُو نَّكَبَا ∴ دَفَيَا رُوَا ∴ =

بِنْسِنْسُو نَّكَبْ ∴ أَكَبْ كُوَمُو ∴ دَمَبَايِمْ ∴

يَارِفْمَنْ كُوَمُو ∴ دَمَبَايُمْ ∴ تَكُومُو ∴ سَرْدُوْ

دَوَّا ∴ مَدُوَا ∴ دَأَتْ شِقُو ∴ أَكَبْ وَاقْبَبْ ∴ قَبْ فِيبْ

كِبْوُ ∴ وَافُمْ سُو قَّنْكَ ∴ سُو فَدَاقُو ∴ دَوْدَوْرَا ∴

مَرْفِمّ ∴ دَدَادِ ∴ لَبْسُ قِبْ وَاقْبُمْ سُو فَدَافُمْ ∴ قَبْ

بِنْسِنْسُو نَّبَكَبَا ∴ دَفَيَا رُو ∴ بِنْسَنْسُو قَّنْكَبْ

فِيبْ كُوَمُو ∴ دَمَبَايَا ∴ مِيَارِفْمَنْ ∴ كُوَمَو

دَمَبَايَا ∴ تَكُومَ ∴ قَدَّ مُو ∴ لَسَنْ قِيمِ ∴ قَتَّا لَسُوَا

قَدُو ∴ دَأَقْ شِقُو ∴ لَسَرْ أَكَبْ ∴ وَاقْبَبْ قَمْ ∴ فِيدَ

رِفْمَنْ وَاقَّبُمْ قَّمْ ∴ قَبْ فِيبْ كَغَفِيسُوَا ∴ دَفَيَارُو

ni che ke gaisua.' 'Wāne sūnanki yārinya, wāne
sūnanki?' 'Sūnana Nari, mai-mia da gardi.'
'[9] Nā ji nāki sūna yārinya, nā ji nāki
sūna, fadi nāwa sūna.' Ta che, 'Ban san sūnanka ba
dan yārō, ban san sūnanka ba dan yaro ban san su-
-nanka ba.' 'Kōma da bāya yārinya, kōma
da bāya.' Sai ta kōma, ta zamna. Sai Gabū
ya tasō, sai ya kuna kai. Aka-che, 'Wānene nan yārinya,
wānene nan?' 'Ni che ke gaisua dan yārō, ni che
ke gaisua.' Wāne sūnanki yārinya, wāne
sūnanki?' 'Sūnana Gabū, dan yārō,
sūnana Gabū, mai-mia da kamshi.' Ya che, 'Naji
nāki sūna yārinya, ina nāwa sūna?'

---

it is I who greet you.' 'What is your name, little girl, what is your name?' 'My name is Nari, who makes the soup savoury.' 'I have heard your name, little girl, I have heard your name. Speak my name.' She said, 'I do not know your name, little boy, I do not know your name.' 'Turn back, little girl, turn back.' So she turned back, (and) sat down. Then Onion-leaves rose and came up, and she stuck her head (into the room) and was asked, 'Who is this little girl, who is this?' 'It is I who salute you, little boy, it is I who salute you.' 'What is your name, little girl, what is your name?' 'My name is Onion-leaves, who makes the soup smell nicely.' He said, 'I have heard your name, little girl. What is my name?'

نيب يكغيسوا ؞ والم لسو ننك ؞ يد رفم ؞ والم

سو ننك ؞ سو فلفم فسر ؞ مم ممن ؞ دغمدي ؞

فسام ؞ فلا ك سو فن ؞ يد رفن ؞ فام ناك

سو فن ؞ فجد نا و ؞ لسو فن ؞ قثب بنلسنسو ننكب

دفيا روا ؞ بنلسنسو ننكب دفيا روا ؞ بنلسنسو

ننكب ؞ كو مو د با يم ؞ يد رفن ؞ كو مو

د با مي ؞ سع تكو م ؞ فد مم ؞ سع غبوا ؞

يتا سوا ؞ سع يكم كون ؞ اكب وافن مم ؞ يد ون

وافن فم ؞ نيب كغيسوا ؞ د فيا ر ؞ فيب

كغيسوا ؞ وافن سو ننك ؞ يد رفن ؞ والم

سو ننك ؞ سو فلفن ؞ غبوا ؞ د فيا رو ؞

سو فلا غبوا ؞ مم مم د كفشم ؞ يثب فلا ج

ناك سو فلن ؞ يد رفن ؞ افلا و ؞ سو فلن ؞

Ta che, 'Ban san sūnanka ba dan yārō, ban san sūnanka ba.' 'Kōma da bāya dan yārō, kōma da bāya.' Sai ta kōma. Sai Tankua ya zō, ya che, 'Gāfaran [10] kudai dan yā-rō, gāfara kudai.' Aka-che, 'Wānene nan?' Ya che, 'Ni che, Tankua dan yārō, ni che tankua, mai-mia da yāji.' 'Nā ji nāki sūna yārinya, nā ji nāki sūna, fadi nāwa sūna yārinya, fadi nāwa sūna.' 'Ban san sūnanka ba dan yārō, ban san sū-nanka ba.' Aka-che, 'Kōma da bāya yārinya, kō-ma da bāya.' Sauran Daudawar batsō, sai aka-che, 'Ke ba ki zūa?' Ta che, 'Mu tafi gida, mutānen kirki sun tafi, ankōrō(n)su, bale ni mai-wāri.' Aka-che,

---

She said, 'I do not know your name, little boy, I do not know your name.' 'Turn back, little boy (girl), turn back.' So she turned back. Now Pepper came along; she said, 'Your pardon, little boy, your pardon.' She was asked who was there. She said, 'It is I, Pepper, little boy, it is I, Pepper, who make the soup hot.' 'I have heard your name, little girl, I have heard your name. Tell (me) my name, little girl, tell (me) my name.' 'I do not know your name, little boy, I do not know your name.' He said, 'Turn back, little maid, turn back.' There was only left Daudawar-batso, and they said, 'Are not you coming?' She said, 'Can I enter the house where such good people as you have gone, (and) been driven away? Would not they the sooner (drive) me out who stink?' They said,

تب بن لسن سو تنكبم ؞ دفيارو ؞ بن سن سو تنكب

كوموو ؞ دما ميا ؞ د نيارا ؞ كوممى ؞ دما ميى ؞ لسن

تكوم ؞ لسن تنكوا ؞ بيدو ؞ نيب غما فا رفكدى ؞ دنيا

روا ؞ غما فم كدى ؞ أكب ؞ وافنى فنم ؞ نيب نيب ؞

تنكوا ؞ دفيارا ؞ فيب تنكوا ؞ فبيمن ؞ دبام

فام ؞ فماكى ؞ لسو فمن ؞ نيارفمن ؞ فامى فماكى ؞

سو فمن ؞ فدى فماو ؞ سو فمن ؞ نيارفمن ؞ فدى فماو

سو فمن ؞ بن لسن سو تنكبا ؞ د نيارا ؞ بن لسن سو

تنكب ؞ أكب ؞ كوموو ؞ دما لن ؞ نيارفم ؞ كو

موو ؞ دما لن ؞ لسو ندورو ؞ بطوا ؞ لسن أكب

بكو ماكدورا ؞ تب مقتفي غدا ؞ مقتا فمر ؞ ككر

؞ سنتفي ؞ أنكوروسن ؞ بلو فسم فيوارى ؞ أكب

'Tāshi, ki tafi.' Sai ta tāshi, ta je. Aka che, 'Wānene nan
yārinya wānene nan?' Sai ta che, 'Ni che ke gaisua
dan yārō, ni ke gaisua.' 'Kāka sūnanki yārinya,
kāka sūnanki?' 'Sūnana Batsō, dan yārō,
sūnana Batsō, mai-mia da wāri.' Aka-ka che, 'Nā ji
nāki sūna yārinya, nā ji nāki sūna,
sauran nāwa sūna.' Ta che, 'Daskandarīni da-
-n yārō, Daskandarīni.' Sai aka che, 'Shigō.'
Aka-shinfida mata [11] kilīshi, aka-ba ta tufāfi,
aka-ba ta tākalmin zīnāria, dada sai
wadan da ke [12] kōran ta wanan shi che. '[13] Naa dinga
yi maki shāra.' Wanan shi che, 'Naa dinga yi maka daka.'

'Rise up (and) go.' So she got up (and) went. He asked her, 'Who is there, little girl, who is there?' And she said, 'It is I who am greeting you, little boy, it is I who am greeting you.' 'What is your name, little girl, what is your name?' 'My name is Batso, little boy, my name is Batso, which makes the soup smell.' He said, 'I have heard your name, little girl, I have heard your name. There remains my name to be told.' She said, 'Daskandarini, little boy, Daskandarini.' And he said, 'Enter.' A rug was spread for her, clothes were given to her, and slippers of gold; and then (of) these who had driven her away one said, 'I will always sweep for you'; another, 'I will pound for you.'

تاش ∴ كتنجم ∴ اسن متاش ∴ فجي ∴ أكب وافنبم فم

∴ يدار فم ∴ وافنبم فم ∴ اسن قب ∴ فيش كخيسوا

ديارار ∴ نيك خيسوا ∴ كاك ∴ اسوفنك يدار فم

كاك ∴ اسوفنك ∴ اسوفم ∴ مبطوا ∴ ديارار

اسوفم فا مبطوا ∴ فيجم ∴ درارى ∴ أكب ماجم

فاك ∴ اسوفم ∴ يدار فم ∴ فاجم فاك ∴ اسوفم

اسوار فناو ∴ اسوفم ∴ فب دسكفد ريم ∴ دم

فيادار ∴ دسكفد ريم ∴ اسن اكب شفوا ∴

آكشبجم امت ∴ كليشم ∴ آكبامت ∴ فباف

[redacted] ∴ أكبامت ∴ تاكلمن ∴ ع يتارش دد اسن

ودفم ∴ دبجكو رفت ∴ وفمر شب ∴ فا دفم

يمك ∴ شارا ∴ وفمر شب فا دفم ∴ يمك دمك

Wanan shi che, 'Naa dinga yi maki dauka rua.' Wanan shi che, 'Naa daka maki mia.' Wanan shi che, 'Naa tūka maki tūō.' Su duka su-ka-zama [14] kuyanginta. Dōmin hakanan, idan ka gani mutum talaka ne, kar ka rēna shi; ba ka sani ba wata rāna shi fi ka. Shi ke nan. [15] Kungurus kan kūsu.

Another said, 'I will see about drawing water for you'; and another, 'I will pound (the ingredients) of the soup'; and another, 'I will stir the food.' They all became her handmaids. And the moral of all this is, if you see a man is poor do not despise him; you do not know but that some day he may be better than you. That is all. Off with the rat's head.

وقم شب ؞ مادم فم يمك ؞ دم وكرا ؞ وقم شب ؞
مادم كامك ؞ مو ؞ وقم شب ؞ مأتو كامك ؞ =
تونور ؞ سودك ؞ لكدم ؞ كيفغشن ؞ دورقم
مكقن ؞ إدرن ؞ كاغشم ؞ فتم ؞ تلكقم ؞ كم
كم مقداش ؞ بكسيب ؞ وقم اقم ؞ شبيك ؞ =
شيكم فقغرس ؞ كم فوس ؞

No. 18.

Wanan tātsunīar [1] Mūsa che.

[2] Gātanan, gātanan, ta je, ta kōmō. Wani sarki [3] ya haifi dīansa guda biu, da mache da namiji. Su-ka-girma. Aka ba ta miji, ita mache, ta che ba ta sō, sai wanta ta ke sō. Idan aka-che, ta je, ta kirāwō Mūsa, sai ta je, ta che, '[4] Wāne wai ka zō.' Hakanan kulum, ranan sai wanta ya che, '[5] Naa yi māganinsa.' Akwai wata kōrama garinsu, yāra na wanka chiki, idan rāna ta yi; akwai wani itāche tsakan kōrama garin nasu, buduri na danri bante ne. Sai Mūsa ya [6] kyale, saada su-ka-zō, sun shiga achikin rua, su-na-wanka, su-ka-aje bantunansu gefē, sai ya zō ya kwā-che duka, ya je, ya hau itāchen tsakan [7] ruan

---

This story is about (a boy called) Musa. A story, a story. Let it go. Let it come. A certain chief begat children, two in number, a girl and a boy. They grew up. A husband was found for her, the daughter, (but) she said she did not want him; only her big brother she loved. If she was told to go and call Musa, then she went, (and) said, 'What's-your-name, they say you are to come.' And it was always so, (till) one day her brother said, 'I shall cure her of that.' (Lit. I shall make its medicine.) There was a small stream at their village, the children used to bathe in it when the sun was up; there was a tree in the middle of the stream at their village where the girls used to fasten their little loin-cloths. And Musa waited in the meantime. When they had come (and) entered the water (and) bathed they laid aside their loin-cloths at the water's edge. Then he (Musa), came and took them all away, and went and climbed the tree in the middle of the water

قرقا طوقيير :: موسب ::

و

غما اتنن غدا اقنن :: قجي تكو موا :: ور قسر كم :: يكيو

ديقلسن غدا ابيوا :: د مقب :: د نمج :: سكيقرم :: ا

اكبا قمج :: ات مقب :: مقب بدا قلسوا :: لسن ورقمة :: =

تكسوا :: ادن :: اكب قجي :: تكرا ور :: موسن :: لسي

قجي مقب :: را امن ور نكذوا :: حكنن :: كلم :: ورقن

لسن ورقة :: يقب قا ابدا غقلسن اكوبن :: ور تكورم

غمر قسن يدوا :: قد ور نكن :: نكم :: ادن :: رامر قم

اكومي :: رامر قاقب :: طكن :: كورم :: غمر نناس

بدر :: قاد قمر :: بقنبن :: سن موسن :: يكلبن ::

سعد سكذوا :: لسنشغ :: اتكرن :: روا :: سنا ور نكن

سكا بن :: بقنقنسن :: نجون سن يذوا :: يكو

بشن :: دك :: يبجن :: يجو امابقن :: حكن :: ورن ::

tsatsakin ruan, kōwa ya fitō bai gani bantensa ba,
sai shi dinga kūka. Sai Mūsa kūa shi-na bisa, shi-na-
-gani, har su duka su-ka-fitō, ya che, 'Ku duka gā
bantunanku wurina, kōwa ya kirāyi sūnana
naa ba shi bantensa, idan ba hakanan ba; ba ni ba ku.'
Sai wata ta zō, ta che, 'Kai; Mūsa, kai Mūsa, Mūsa
[8] gaia, Mūsa dan sarākai, dōmin Ala Mūsa ba ni
bantena.' Sai shi ba ta. Hakanan hakanan har su duka
su-ka-karbi bantunansu. Sauran kanua tasa.
Sai aka-che, 'Tafi ki karbi bantenki.' Ruan kūa
iyākan idānun sau shi ke. Sai ta shiga [9] ruan,
ta che, 'Kai Mūsa, Mūsan gaia Mūsa dan sarā-
-kai dōmin Ala Mūsa ba ni bantena.' Sai Mūsa ya che,

(middle of the water), each one who came out did not see his (her) cloth, whereupon he (she) began to cry. And Musa was up above and watching till they all came out. He said, 'All of you, see, your cloths are with me. Whoever calls out my name, I will give him (her) his (her) cloth; otherwise I will not give you.' Then one girl came forward. She said, 'You, Musa, you, Musa, Musa the spiteful one, Musa the son of chiefs, for Allah's sake, Musa, give me my loin-cloth.' And he gave her (it). And so on, and so on, until they all received from him their cloths, and there was only left his little sister. And she was told, 'Go and get your cloth.' Now the water was up to the ankles. Then she entered the water (and) said, 'You, Musa, Musa, the spiteful one, Musa the son of chiefs, for Allah's sake, Musa, give me my loin-cloth.' But Musa said,

كطكيس . زرّن كوا . يجثوا . مهكني . بنتنسب .
تسن شحي قمح . كوكن . تسن موتس كوا . شنا بلس . شنا
قمشم . قمر سودك . تسكجثوا . يتب كودم . غما
بشتنك . زوينا . كون يكراتن . سوقما قمو . =
قم بانش بنتنسن . إدرن بدا حكنا . ب بجا وبا ك
. تسن . زقتحدوا . تب كيموتسن كيموتسن . موتس
قميا . موتسن . د قلمرا كحن . دزمر أرن موتسن . بداو
بنتنا . تسن شبات . حكنن . حكمن . قمرسودك
تسكرب . بنتنسن . سوزففحوا امسن . ب
تسن أكبتقي . يكرب . بنبتنك . زرتكوا .
إياكرن . إدافنسوا . شكن . تسن تنشع . زورن
تب كيموتسن كيموتسن موتسن غميا . موتسن د قسرا
كنا . دوقمرن أأموتسن بدافنبتنا . تسن موتسن بيتة

‘Ba ni ba ki sai kin kāra fadi, saanan in ba ki.’ Ashe
tā manche ne da ta tuna sai ta che, ‘Kai wāne, kai wāne
wānen gaia, wāne dan sarākai, dōmin Ala wāne
ba ni bantena.’ Sai ya che, ‘[10] Nā ki ba ki, nā ki ba ki,
sai kin che, Kai Mūsa, kai Mūsa, Mūsan gaia, Mū-
-sa dan sarākai, dōmin Ala Mūsa ba ni bantena.’
Sai nan da nan rua ya kāma mata kwobri. Sai ta che,
‘Kai wāne, kai wāne, wāne(n) gaia, wāne dan sar-
-akai, dōmin Ala wāne ba ni bantena.’ Sai rua
ya kāma ta ga katara. Sai Mūsa ya che, ‘Na ki ba ki
sai kin che, Kai Mūsa, Mūsan gaia, Mūsa
dan sarākai, dōmin Ala Mūsa, ba ni bantena.’

‘I do not give it to you till you have said it again, then I will give it to you.’ Now she has forgotten (for a minute that she would not say his name); when she remembered, then she said, ‘You, What's-your-name, you, What's-your-name, What's-your-name the spiteful one, What's-your-name the son of chiefs, for the sake of Allah, What's-your-name, give me my cloth.’ But he said, ‘I have refused to give you, I have refused to give you, till you say, You, Musa, you, Musa, Musa the spiteful one, Musa the son of chiefs, for the sake of Allah, Musa, give me my cloth.’ Now by this time the water was up to her shins. Then she said, ‘You, What's-your-name, you, What's-your-name, What's-your-name the spiteful one, What's-your-name the son of chiefs, for Allah's sake, What's-your-name, give me my loin-cloth.’ But now the water had reached her thighs. But Musa said, ‘I have refused to give you unless you have said, You, Musa, Musa the spiteful one, Musa the son of chiefs, for the sake of Allah, Musa, give me my cloth.’

بار ببارك :. اسن كنكا وقحي :. سعقمن :. ابداك :. اقشن

تنا مقنبش بن :. دقشر :. السن تبش كي [redacted] ق

[redacted] دقسمر اكني :. دوموا آل [redacted]

بار قبنبتش :. اسن مبش قدارك بارك :. قدارك بارك

اسن كنشا :. كيمحوس :. كيمحوس :. موكسن :. غبيا :. مو

اسن :. دقسمر اكنم :. دومر آل موكسن :. مبار بنبنار :. =

اسن قمن دقمن :. زوار يكا اما مقا :. كبير :. اسن قتق

كيمحوس كيمحوس موكسن غميا موكسن دقسمر

اكنم دومرش آل موكسش مبار بقنبتش اسن زوار

يكا اما مقا :. كمكتمر :. اسن موكسن مبش :. قدارك بارك

اسن كنشا :. كيمحوس :. موكسن غميا :. موكسن :. =

دقسمر اكني :. دومر آل موكسش مبار بقنبتش =

Ta che, 'Kai wāne, kai wāne, wānen gaia, wāne dan sarā-
-kai, dōmin Ala wāne ba ni bantena.' Sai Mūsa
ya che, 'Nā ki ba ki, nā ki ba ki sai kin che, Kai Mū-
-sa, kai Mūsa, Mūsan gaia, Mūsa dan sarākai
dōmin Ala Mūsa ba ni bantena.' Sai rua ya kāma ta
ga kirji. Sai ta che, 'Kai wāne, kai wāne, wānen gaia,
wāne dan sarākai, dōmin Ala wāne ba ni bantena.'
Sai Mūsa ya che, 'Nā ki ba ki, sai kin kirāyi sū-
-nana.' Sai rua ya kāma ta ga wia. Aka-che, 'Ke fadi
sūnansa, idan ba ki fadi ba rua [11] yaa chi ki.'
Rua kua shi-na kōkari, shi kāma ta ga haba,
sai ta che, 'Kai Mūsa, kai Mūsa, Mūsan gaia

She said, 'You, What's-your-name, you, What's-your-name, What's-your-name, the spiteful one, What's-your-name the son of chiefs, for the sake of Allah, What's your name, give me my loin-cloth.' But Musa said, 'I have refused to give you, I have refused to give you, unless you say, You, Musa, you, Musa, Musa the spiteful one, Musa the son of chiefs, for the sake of Allah, Musa, give me my cloth.' And the water reached to her breasts, but she said, 'You, What's-your-name, you, What's-your-name, What's-your-name, the spiteful, What's-your-name the son of chiefs, for Allah's sake, What's-your-name, give me my cloth.' But Musa said, 'I have refused to give you till you have called out my name.' And the water was up to her neck. And they said, 'Speak his name; if you do not speak the water will swallow you up.' Now the water was trying hard to reach her chin. Then she said, 'You, Musa, you, Musa, Musa the spiteful one,

قب كيو ابي : كيو ابي : وابر غميا : وابي د قسرا

كم : د ومر : اآل وابي : بار بنشنو : سر موسر :

بيب قماك باك : قماك باك : اسر كنبا : كيمو

سر : كيمو سر : موسر غميا : موسر د قسرا كم :

د ومر اآل موسر : بار : بمر تمني : سر ورا : يكامات

غكر جب : سر قب كيو ابي : كيو ابي : وابر غميا

وابي د قسرا كم : د ومر : اآل وابي : بار : بمر تمني

سر موسر : بيب : قماك باك : اسر كنكرابي : اسو

قداقمو : سر ورا : يكامات : غمو تر : اكب بكج

سو قنلسر : اكر بك قج ميا : ورا : بيا اتيك

: وراكو : شندا كو كر : شكامات غميب

اسع تب : كيمو سر : كيمو سر : موسر غميا

Mūsa dan sarākai dōmin Ala Mūsa ba ni bantena.'
Sai ya che, 'Kāra fadi.' Ta fadi. Ya che, 'Kāra.' Ta kāra har uku
Ya che, 'Kii kāra fadi ni mijinki?' Ta che, 'Aa.'
'Ki-na sō mijin da aka-ba ki?' Ta che, 'I.' Mafāri
ke nan, wa ba shi auren kanua. Shi ke nan.
[12] Kungurus kan kūsu.

Musa the son of chiefs, for the sake of Allah, Musa, give me my cloth.' But he said, 'Repeat it.' She said it (again). He said 'Again.' She repeated it, until three times. He said, 'Are you going to say again that I am your husband?' She said, 'No.' 'Do you want the husband whom you have been given?' She said 'Yes.' This was the beginning (of the custom) that a brother should not marry his sister. That is all. Off with the rat's head.

مُولسِ دِ فْلسَرا اكُمْ :: رِقَمْ :: آلْ مُولسِ :: قَدا :: مَمْ قَنْ

سَنْ يجٓبْ كَارْفِجِ :: قَبْجِ :: ييْبْ كَدرا :: تَكَدا :: قَمْراكْ

ييْبْ كَدرا :: يكْمَكَارْ :: فِجِ نِيمِجِنْكِ :: قَتَنْبْ عَدَاعْ ::

كِنْدا سُوا :: مِجِمْرْ آكَبْداكِ :: مَتَنْبْ إيْ :: مَقَدارِي ::

بِكَتَّنْ :: قَوْ :: بَدا اِشَعَوْ :: مُخَمْوِ :: شِيبِكَتَّنْ ::

فُنْغُمْسِ :: كَمْ فُوسِ

No. 19.

Wanan tātsunīar mahalbi che
da sarki.

Wani mutun ne, ba shi da aiki kōmi sai halbi,
da shi da dansa. Ranan su-ka-tafi dāji, da dansa,
ba su sāmu kōmi ba, sai kūsu. Sai
dansa [1] ya yāda kūsu. Sai su-ka-ji yunwa. Uban
ya che, '[2] Gasa muna kūsunmu, mu chi.' Yārō ya che,
'Ai [3] nā yas.' Uban ya che, 'Ka ga dan durun uwa.'
Uban ya dauki gātari, ya buge yārō,
ya sūma. Ya [4] tafia(r)sa, ya bar shi. Yārō
ya falka, ya tāshi, ya tafō gida da dare.
Ya iske sun yi kwāna, sai ya shiga dā-
-kinsa, ya dauki tarkachensa, ya kāma hainya,

This tale is about a hunter (lit. a shooter) and a chief. There was once a certain man who had no other work but hunting, both he and his son. One day (he) they went to the bush with his son. They did not find anything but a rat, and his son threw the rat away. But they became hungry (and) the father said, 'Roast our rat for me, (and) let us eat.' The boy said, 'Oh, but I have thrown it away.' The father said, '. . .' (cursing him), (and) the father lifted (his) axe and struck the boy; he fainted. He (the father) went his way, (and) left him. The boy came round, he rose up, and went home by night. He found them asleep, so he entered the room and lifted his belongings. He took the road,

وَنَّمْرَ قَدَا كُوفِيمْرُ ⁖ مَمْلِبِهِ ثْ

دَ لَسْرَكِمْ ⁖

وَنِمُشْتُبُنْ بَدَاشِدَ آيْكِ ⁖ كُوهِمْ ⁖ لَسْرَ قَلْبِ ⁖

دَ لِشِمْ ⁖ دَدَ فَسَنْ رَفَّمْنْ لَسَكَتَبِمْ ⁖ دَرَاجِ ⁖ دَدَ فَسْ

بَجُنْ لَسَامْ ⁖ كُوهِمْ بَ ⁖ لَسْرَ كُوسُنْ لَسَ

دَ فْسَنْ بَمِيَادِ ⁖ كُوسُنْ لَسْرَ لَسَكِمْ ⁖ يُفُو ⁖ أَبْمَ

يَبْ غَسَمْ مُرَ ⁖ كُوسَفَمْ ⁖ مَثْ ⁖ يَدَارُ وِيَثْ

أَ فَدَامِيَسْنْ أَبْمَرِيَثْ ⁖ كَدَاغَدَ مُدُرُورْ نُفُوَّ ⁖

أَبْمَرِيَدْ وْكِ ⁖ غَدَاقَمِرُ ⁖ يُيَبْغُنْ يَدَارُونْ ⁖ ب

يَسُومَمُنْ يَتَّبِيَّسَنْ يَمِجْمَرْشِنْ يَدَارُونْ ⁖ ب

يَبَلْكِ ⁖ يَتَّاشُنْ يَتَّبُو ⁖ غَدَا ⁖ دَدَ بَرِسْ

يَدِاسْكُنْ لَسْمُنْ كُوَامُنْ لَسْرُ ⁖ يَشْغُ ⁖ دَرَ و

كِفْسَنْ يَدَّ وْكِ ⁖ تَمْرَ كِبْسَنْ يَكَامْ مُفُنْ

shi-na-zūa wani gari. Da ya kai gari da dare, sai
ya shiga chikin gari. Kōwa ya yi kwāna.
Shi-na-tafia chikin gari har ya kai gidan sarki.
Ya shiga har chikin gida, funtu, bābu rīga,
bābu wandō. Sai ya tāda sarki. Sarki
ya che, 'Daga ina?' Ya che, 'Daga gari kaza.' Sai sarki
ya che, 'Lāfia?' Yārō ya che, 'Da ni da ubana mu-ka-je
dāji yāwō halbi, ba mu sāmu kōmi, sai
kūsu guda daia, ya ba ni rikō, na manche shi
wani wuri. Da mu-ka-ji yunwa sai ya che, Kāwō kūsu,
mu gasa, mu chi. Sai na che, Nā yashe shi ban sani ba.
Sai ya yi fushi, ya dauki gātari, ya buge ni,
na sūma. Da mareche ya yi, sai na falka na tāshi,

(and) was going to a certain town. When he reached the town it was night; he entered into the town. Every one was asleep. He proceeded into the middle of the town until he reached the chief's house. He entered until he was right in the house, (he was) naked, without clothes, without trousers, and he met the chief. The chief said, 'From where?' (And) he replied, 'From such and such a village.' And the chief said, 'Is it well with you?' The boy said, 'Both I and my father went to the bush to walk and shoot. We did not find anything but one single rat, he gave (it) me to keep, I forgot it somewhere. When we became hungry, then he said, Bring the rat that we may roast it and eat. And I said, I have dropped it, I do not know where. Thereupon he became angry. He lifted his axe (and) struck me. I fainted. When evening came then I recovered (and) rose up,

شنادو :: ونغمي :: ديكن غمي :: د ديرن لسني ::

يشغ :: ثكن غمي :: كووا :: يايكوا نسن ::

شناقبي :: ثكن غمي :: قن بيكن :: غد نلسركم ::

يشغ :: قن ثكن غدا :: ڢنشو :: بدانڢ :: ريكني

بدانڢ :: وڢدو :: لسن يمتادن :: لسركم :: سركم ::

يبث :: دغد انكن :: يبث دغغمي :: كدا :: سن سركم ::

يبث :: لاقبن :: يدادو :: يبث دنم دابدانڢن :: مكجي

داج :: يدادو :: قلب :: بملسام :: كومن :: سن

كوسن غدادتن :: ميبادرن ڢو :: نمنبشن

ونوري :: دمكج :: يڢو :: لسن يبث :: كداو وكوس

مغسن :: مث :: لسن مبث :: قدايدا بشن :: منسيب

لسن يمن :: ڢشم بجعروك :: غد ابمي :: يبجنم

نسومن :: دصم مبث :: يمن لسن :: نبولك :: قنا ثين

na zō nan.' Sarki kūa ya je yāki, aka-kāma dansa aka yanke shi. Sarki ba shi da dā, namiji. Sai sarki ya che, 'Yanzu ba ka rufa mani asīri?' Yārō ya che, 'Rufin asīri kaman kāka? Sarki ya che, 'Ba ni da dā namiji, in gari ya wāye, in che kai dāna ne, da aka-kāma wurin yāki, ka gudānō, ka zō.' Yārō ya che, 'Wanan ai ba shi da wia.' Sarki ya shiga dāki, ya daukō bindiga, ya buga chikin dare. Sai [5] uwar gidansa ta fitō, ta che, 'Alfanda zāki bāda rāzana, bindigar me ka ke bugu da da darenga?' Sarki ya che, 'Wāne [6] yā zō.' Sai uwar gida ta rangada [7] gūda. Sai gari ya tāshi tsaye, ana-che, 'Menene ya fāru, gidan sarki ana-buga bindiga da dadarenga?' Aka-che dan sarki ya zō wanda aka-kāma

---

(and) came here.' Now the chief had gone to war, and his son had been captured and killed. The chief had no male child. And the chief said, 'Now will you not keep a secret for me?' The boy said, 'What kind of a secret?' The chief said, 'I have no male child, when dawn comes I shall say you are my son, who was caught at the war, and that you ran away and came back.' The boy said, 'That is surely not difficult.' (Then) the chief entered his room (and) took up his gun (and) fired it (it was) in the middle of the night. And 'the mother of the house' came out (and) said, 'King, lion who causes fear, what is the gun you are firing in the night?' The chief said, 'So-and-so has returned.' Thereupon the mother of the house raised the sound of joy, and the town rose up, (and) they were asking, 'What had happened at the chief's house, (seeing that) they are firing a gun at this time of night?' (And) they said that the chief's son had come, he who had been caught

تَخُوقَّنْ ؞ سَرْكِمْ ؞ كُوَّ ؞ يِ جِّنْ يِدَاكْ ؞ أَكِّكَامْ ؞ دْ قْسَرْ

أَكِيتْبْكُوشْ ؞ لَسْرْكِمْ ؞ بْدَاشْدْدَا ؞ تْمِجْ ؞ لَسْرْ لَسْرْكِمْ ؞

يِبْثْ ؞ يِمْنْخْ ؞ يِدَاكْرْ قَامْرْ ؞ أَلْسِيمْرْ ؞ يِدَاوْرَا أَبِيثْ رُقْمْ

أَلْسِيمْرْ ؞ يَكْمَنْ كْدَاكْ ؞ أَسْرْكِمْ ؞ يِبْثْ يِدُو ؞ دْ دّْسَا ؞ تْمِجْ

إِلْقْمْرْ ؞ يِدَاوْرَا أَيِشْ إِمْنْبْثْ كِينْ ؞ دْ أَمْدَا بْقِينْ ؞ دْ أَكِّكَا مْ ؞

أُوقْبَاكْ ؞ كُغْدَا أُمُو ؞ كْخْدُو ؞ يِدَارُو ؞ يِبْثْ وَقَّمْ

أَ بِدَاشْدْ رُيِدَا ؞ سَرْكِمْ ؞ يِمْتْشْغْ دَاكْ ؞ يِدّْ وُكُوَا ؞ بْنْدِغْ

يِبْغْ ؞ تْكْمْ دْبْرِنْ ؞ سْنْعُورْ ؞ غْدْ قْسَنْ ؞ تْقْبُتُو ؞ تَقْبْ

أَلْقْنْدْ ؞ دَاكْ ؞ يِدَادْرَاذْقْنْ ؞ بِنْدِ غْمْ بِنْ ؞ كْكْبْخْ

دْ ؞ دّْ دْ بَرْمَغْ ؞ أَسْرْكِمْ ؞ يِبْثْ وَانْقْنْ ؞ يِلْخْرْ ؞ لَسْنْ عُوَّرْغْدَا

تَمْ قْغْدْ ؞ غُودْ ؞ لَسْرْغْمْ ؞ يِتَّلَاشْ طِيبِنْ ؞ أَمْدَابْ ؞

مْبْنْبِنْ ؞ يِقَاوْ ؞ غْدْ قْسَرْكِمْ ؞ أَمْدَا أُبْغْ ؞ يِقْحْ غْمْ ؞ دْدْدْ

دْ ؞ دّْ دْ بَرْمَغْ ؞ أَكْبْ ؞ دْقْسْرْكِمْ ؞ يِبْخْدُو ؞ وَقْدْ أَكِّكَامْ

wurin yāki.' Aka che, 'Mādala, mādala.' Gari ya wāye,
yārō ya yi wanka, sarki ya gama masa
kāya, ya fitō. Fādanchi, wadansu su-na-chewa,
'Ba dansa ba ne.' Wadansu su-na-chewa, 'Dansa ne.' Ranan
sai sarākai su-ka-gama kai, su-ka-che, 'Ku bari
mu gani, izan dansa ne.' Su-ka-gama ma dīansu
kāya, su-ka-damra masu sirida bisa angarmu,
su-ka-hau, su-ka-che masu, 'Ku bi gidan sarki,
ku kirāyi dansa, ku che ku tafi kilīsa.' (sk)
Su-ka-che, 'In kun je, kun yi sukua, in kun zāme,
ku sabka, ku sāre dawākin, ku kōmō gida.'
Kōwa ya ba dansa kansakali, ya rātaya,
su ka je gidan sarki, su ka kira yārō. Ashe

---

at the war.' And they said, 'Indeed! indeed!' When it was dawn the boy bathed (and) the chief gave him (gifts) goods (and) he came forth. (Among) the councillors some said, 'It is not his son.' Others said, 'It is his son.' Now one day the head-men joined their heads together, (and) said, 'Wait, and we shall see if it is (really) his son.' Then they added goods (presents) to those their children already had, (and) they put the saddles on the war-horses for them. (And) they (the children) mounted, (and the fathers) said to them, 'Go to the chief's house and call his son, and say you are going to take horse exercise.' And they said, 'When you have gone and galloped and pulled up, you must dismount, (and) kill your horses, (and) come home.' (And) each one gave his son a sword (and) he slung it on his shoulder, (and) they came to the chief's house and called the boy. Now truly

ورفياك ∴ أكث مادّله ∴ مادّله ∴ غم ييوابى

يادرو ∴ ييقّ ∴ ونكس ∴ لسركم ∴ بغمن ∴ مسن

كديا ∴ يبغثو ∴ قادفثم ∴ ودفلس ∴ لسناثوا

بادفسبنس ∴ ودفلس ∴ لسناثوا ∴ دفسبنس ∴ رفّس

سنسراكث ∴ لسكغم كن ∴ لسكث ∴ كجم

مغنم ∴ إدن ∴ دفسبنس ∴ سكغمن ∴ مديفلس

كديا ∴ لسكدمر ∴ ملس ∴ لسردا ∴ يلس أنكم مد

لسحو ∴ لسكثمسن ∴ كبغدفسركه ∴

ككراس ∴ دفلس ∴ ككثكثقم ∴ كليبلس ∴ لسك

لسكث ∴ إوكنجث ∴ كفسّ ∴ لسكوا ∴ إركم دامى

كسبك ∴ كسدبرن ∴ دواكمن ∴ ككو موغدا

كووا ∴ يبمدفلس ∴ كنسفلم ∴ يراقيا ∴

لسكجن ∴ غدفسركم ∴ لسككم ∴ يادرو ∴ أنثس

makwarmachi yā ji, ya je, ya gaya ma sarki.
Sarki ya yi shiri ya aje ya che, 'Funtu ya yi
rawa, bale mai-rīga.' Sarki ya kirāyi yārō,
ya fada masa, ya che, 'In kun je, kōmi ka gani
sun yi, kai ma ka yi.' Yau yāra su-ka-zō, su-ka-kirāyi
dan sarki, su-ka-tafi. Da su-ka-je, su-ka-yi sukua,
sai su-ka-sabka, su-ka-sāre dawāki. Yau
dan sarki, shi ma ya yi suka, ya zāme,
ya sabka, ya sāre dōkinsa. Su-ka-kōmō gida.
Sai sarakai su-ka-che, 'Karia ne, gōbē
ku kōma, gari ya wāye su-ka-zō, su-ka-kira shi.'
Sarki ya sa dōgarai, su-ka-damra masa
sirdi bisa baban dōki, su-ka-tafi. Da su-ka-je

---

some tale-bearer has overheard, (and) he went and told the chief. The chief made similar preparation (horse, &c.) and put the things aside, (and) said, 'If the naked man can dance, much more can the man with the cloak.' The chief called the boy, (and) told him, (and) said, 'When you have gone, everything you see they have done, do you also do.' So the boys came, (and) called the son of the chief, (and) they set off. As they went they galloped; then they dismounted (and) killed their horses. So the son of the chief he too galloped, pulled up, dismounted, (and) killed his horse. They went home. And the head-men said, 'It is a lie, to-morrow you go back.' When it was dawn they came (and) called him. The chief caused (his) body-guard to fasten the saddle on a great horse for him. They went off; as they went

مكم مقم :: يماجم :: يجس :: يغيما قمسكم ::

سسكم :: يمسشم :: يماجس يمث :: قسوا يس

روا :: مبلس ميرمغس سسكم :: يكمراس يمارو

يمجدامس يمثا ركمجس كومم :: كغيم

سنس كيمس :: كس :: يمحيماوا :: سكدو :: سككراس

دمسسكم :: سكتيم :: د سكجس سكس سكوا ::

سس :: سك سبك :: سكسدارس دواكم :: يسو ::

دمسسكم :: شيمس يميسكم :: يدامس :: بد

يمسبك :: يمسدارس :: دوكمس سمكومومدا

سس سسدا كس سكث :: كمريما بمس غموبس

ككومم :: غمر يموبس سكدو :: سككراش

سسكم :: يمس دوغمر :: سكدمدامس بد

يسرد :: بسرسمس دوك :: سكتيم :: دسكجس

su-ka-yi sukūa. Sai su-ka-sasabka, [8] su-ka-sasāre dawākinsu. Dan sarki, shi kuma da ya yi suk(u)a, sai ya sāre dōkinsa, su-ka-kōmō gida.
Sai sarākai su-ka-bai dīansu bāyi, buduri māsu-chau, su-ka-che, 'Ku tafi da su chikin dāji, ku sasāre su.' Makwormachi ya je, ya kwormata ma sarki, sai sarki ya ba dansa [9] kuyangi bīū, ya che, 'Ku tafi, kōmi ka gani sun yi, kai ma ka yi.' Su-ka-tafi dāji, yan sarākai su-ka-sasāre kuyanginsu, dan sarki shi kuma ya sasāre nāsa, su-ka-kōmō gida. Sai su-ka-che dansa ne. Ana-nan,

---

they galloped. Then they dismounted, (and) killed their horses. The chief's son also, when he had galloped, then he killed his horse, (and) they returned home. Then the sub-chiefs gave their sons slaves, beautiful maidens, (and) said, 'Take them to the midst of the bush (and) slaughter them.' The tale-bearer (again) went and informed the chief, and the chief gave his son two female slaves, he said, 'Go, whatever you see they have done, do you do too.' They went to the bush. The sons of the head-men killed their female slaves (and) the chief's son also killed his, (and) they returned home. And they said, 'It is his son.' And so time went on,

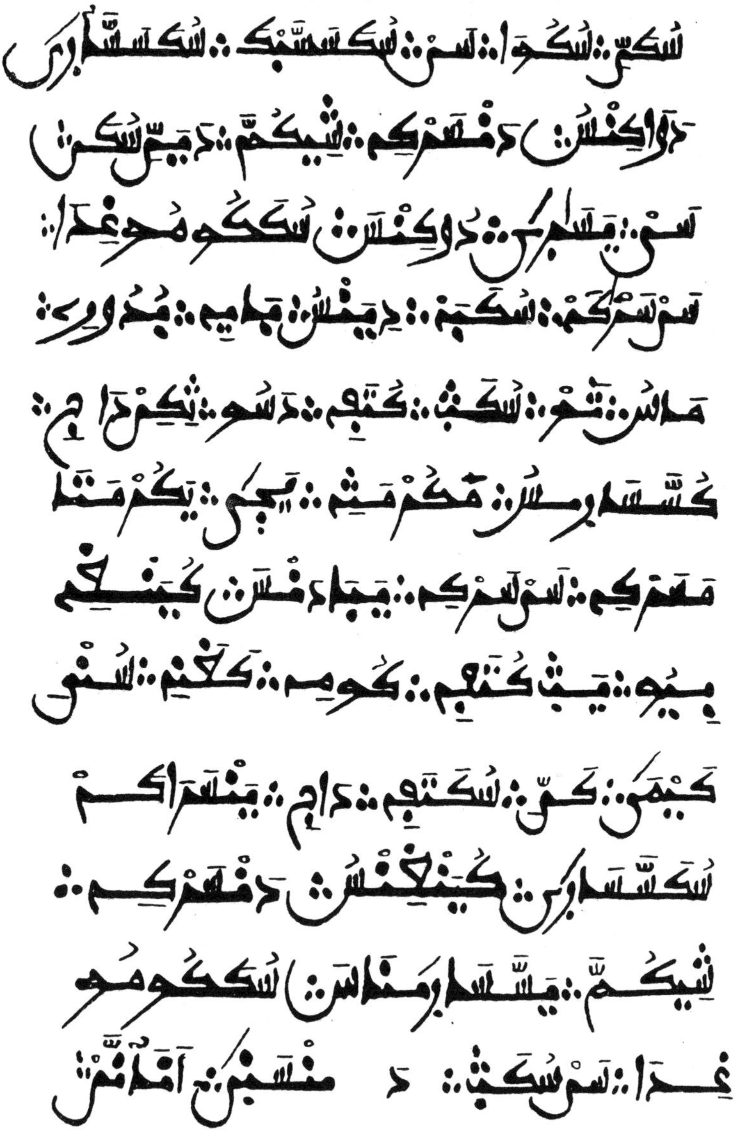

sai ranan uban yārō ya zō, shi-na-rātaye da kwori.
Ya iske fādanchi, ya chika, sai ya wuche har
gaban sarki, ya gaishe su. Yārō na zamne.
Sai ya che, 'Ba ka tāshi, mu je, mu yi ginan kūsanmu?'
Yārō shi na kurum. Sai sarki ya tāshi, ya shiga
gida, ya kirāye su, ya che, 'Mahalbi ka rufa mani
asīri, kōmi ka ke sō naa ba ka.' Mahalbi
ya kia. Sarki ya yi lālāshi, sarki ya che, 'Kōmi
na duniangа [10] naa baka dari dari.' Sai mahalbi
ya kia. Sarki ya che, 'Ku damra mani sirdi.'
Aka-damra sirdi, aka-damra ma yārō sirdi, sarki
ya ba yārō takōbi, ya rātaya. Su-ka-tafi

---

till one day the boy's father came; he was carrying his quiver slung. He met the councillors; he heard all he wished to know, (and) then passed on till (he came) before the chief. He greeted them; the boy was sitting (by his side); and he said, 'Are you not going to get up that we may go and dig for our rats?' The boy was silent. Then the chief rose up, (and) entered the house, (and) called them. He said, 'Hunter, keep the secret for me, and whatever you wish I will give you.' The hunter refused. The chief entreated him. The chief said, 'Everything in the world I will give you, one hundred of each.' But the hunter refused. The chief said, 'Saddle up for me.' They saddled, they saddled (a horse) for the boy. The chief gave the boy a sword, (and) slung it across his shoulder. They went off

لَسَرْ وَقَمْ ∴ اَمَسْ يَادُرو ∴ يَغْدُو ∴ لِشَنَا وَاتَبِينْ دَكُرِى

يَا اِسْكَنْ ∴ قَادَمْشِ ∴ يَا اِتَكَ ∴ لَسَرْ يَجُوبْ ∴ حَرْ

غَبَّرْ لَسَرْكِ ∴ يَغَيْبَشَسْ يَادُرو فَادَمْبَ

سَرْ يَبْ ∴ بَاكَنَّا اِلَّشْ مُجَمْ مُنَّ ∴ غَمُنْ كُوسَرْمْ

يَادُرو ∴ لِشَنَا كُرُمْ ∴ لَسَرْ لَسَرْكِ ∴ يَتَّالَشْ يَشَ

غِدَا ∴ يَمَكَرَابَسْ يَبْ مَعَلِّمْ ∴ كَرْقَامَرْ

اَسِيرِى ∴ كُومَ ∴ كَبْكُسُوا ∴ فَبَاكَ ∴ مَعَلِّمْ

يَكَنَّ سَرْكِ ∴ يَسَّلَالَشَ ∴ سَرْكِ يَبْ ∴ كُومَ

فَدُرُمَيْنَغْ ∴ فَابَاكَ ∴ عَرِدَرِى ∴ لَسَرْ مَعَلِّمْ ∴

يَفِّ ∴ لَسَرْكِ ∴ يَبْ كُدَمْرَامَرْ ∴ لِسَرْدِ ∴ اَكَدَمْرَ

لِسَرْدِ ∴ اَكَدَمْرَا ∴ مَيَادُرو ∴ لِسَرْدِ ∴ لَسَرْكِ ∴

يَبَ اَيَادُرُوا ∴ تَكُوبِ ∴ يَمَ اتَيَا ∴ سُكَتَبِ ∴

dāji. Sarki ya tsaya, ya che ma yārō, '[11] Au ka sāre ni, ka dauki kāyanga, ka ba ubanka, ku kōma gari, ku chi duniarku, au ka sāre ubanka, ni da kai mu kōma, mu zamna.' Yārō ya yi barkatai.

Tō in kai ne Batūre, chikinsu,
wa zaa ka sārewa chikinsu?
In ba ka san wanda zaa
ka sāre ba,
shi ke nan.
[12] Kungurus kan kū-
-su.

---

to the bush. The chief halted (and) said to the boy, 'Either you kill me, (and) take these goods (horse, &c.), (and) give to your father, (and) return to the town, (and) enter into your (kingship) world, or you kill your father, (and) you and I will go back and live (as before).' The boy was distracted, (not knowing what to do). Now if it were you, O white man, among them whom would you kill? If you do not know whom you would kill, there it is. Off with the rat's head.

دَاجِ ∴ لَسَرْكِمْ ∴ مِيطَنْ ∴ مِيشِ مَيَادُوُ ∴ أَوْكَسَدْرَمِيمْ

كَدْوْكَ ∴ كَدَيْفَخْ ∴ كَجَا ∴ أُمْنْكَ ∴ كُكُو مَ ∴

غَمِ ∴ كُشْدُوفِيمْكَ ∴ أَوْكَسَدْوَمُ ∴ أُبْنْكَ ∴

فِمِ دَكَنْ ∴ مَكُوم ∴ مُحَمَّدْ مَرْ ∴ يَادُرُ ∴ يِي مَرْكَشْ

ثُو ∴ إِرْكِيبَنْ جَشُوبَرْ ∴ ثِكَفْسْ

وَالله ذَا كَسَدْ وَمُوا الله ثِكَفْسْ

۞ إِرْبَكَسْفُو فَدْ ۞ دَمْ أُ

۞ كَسَدْوَبْ

۞ شِيكَنَّسْ

۞ فَنْغُرْسْ

۞ كَرْفُو

۞ سْ

No. 20.

Wanan tātsūnīar
dumā che da yārinya

Wani mutum ne, sūnansa Alabarma, atājiri. Shi-na da kurdi dayawa, bai sāmu haifua ba. Sai chikin sādakunsa, wata ana-che mata Watapansa, ita che [1] ta haifi dīa guda daia, mache, shi kūa Alabarma ba shi sō abinda ke taba yārinya nan. Ita kua yārinya sūnanta, Furaira. Yau ranan uwa tata ta gōya ta, su-ka-tafi dāji dōmin ta yi tōrōtso. Sai Furaira ta ga dan dūme guda daia, shi ke nan gare ta, bābu wani kuma. Sai ta che, 'Alabarma, tsumke mani dan dumē

This is a story about a pumpkin and a maiden. There was a certain man by name Alabarma, a rich man. He had much money, (but) he had not any children. But among his concubines was one called Watapansa, (and) she had given birth to one daughter; and he, Alabarma, did not wish anything to touch this little girl. Now the girl's name was Furaira. And one day her mother took her on her back and they went off to the bush in order that she might ease herself. And Furaira saw one young pumpkin, that was all she (the mother pumpkin) had; there was not another. And she, (the little girl) said, 'Alabarma (Watapansa?) pluck the baby pumpkin for me

وقمر تنا كوفيم

دما : فبهمه وقّ

وفتتنبو سوقنس أل : بمرم : أماجي

شنادكردي : دميو : ببيسام : مليقوا ب

سن تكر سادكولس رف : أما بثمت : وتقنس

إمث : تحيد : دميا غدادمن : محب : شيكو

ألبرم : بماشسو : أبنحكتب : ميارق

نرإتكو ميارن : سوفنت فريرا

يورفمن : عوأنت : تغوميات : سكتيبدا

دومرن : قمو : ثمورطو : سن فرمم : قمغ

غمدمبي : غدادرن : شيكفمن غمرمت : مجاب

وفكم : سن تبالبرم : طمبكمن دغمدمبن

in yi wāsa.' Sai Alabarma ta che, 'Haba Furaira
kāka dan dūme guda daia shi ke nan,
ga uwa(r)sa, ni ke tsumkēwa, in ba ki.' Sai Furaira
ta rika kūka, sai uwa tata Alabarma
ta che, 'Idan ki yi kūka ne, sai ki yi, ama
ba ni tsumke dan dumē guda dai in ba ki.'
Su-ka-zō gida, yārinya ta-na-kūka.
Ubanta ya tanbaya, uwa ta gaya masa
mafāri. Sai uban yārinya ya che, 'Kōma,
ki tsumke, ki ba ta.' Yau, ta kōma,
ta tsumke, ta ba ta. Ana-nan, sai ranan
dan dumē ya rika bin yārinya, shi-na-
-fadi, 'Nāma in chi Furaira, nāma in chi.'

---

to play (with).' But Alabarma (Watapansa?) said, 'Come now, Furaira, how is this? One solitary baby pumpkin is there. See, there is its mother, (which) I will pluck and give you.' But Furaira began to cry and her mother Alabarma (Watapansa?) said, 'If you are going to cry you must just cry, but I am not going to pluck the solitary baby pumpkin to give you.' They returned home, (and) the little girl continued weeping. Her father asked (the cause). Her mother told him from the beginning. And the little girl's father said, 'Go back, (and) pluck (it), and give to her.' So she returned, (and) plucked it, (and) gave her. Then that day the baby pumpkin commenced to follow the maiden. It kept saying, 'Meat I must eat, Furaira, meat I must eat.'

إِفْتِّ ∴ كَوَالسَّوْ ∴ لَسَنْ أَلّٓ مِرْم ∴ تَقْتَثْ جَبَسْ فُرَيْرَا ∴

كَدَاكَ ∴ دَ فْدُ مُبِيْ ∴ غُدَ ادَمَّرْ ∴ شِيكُنْشْ ∴

غُغُوسَّنْ ∴ نَكَبَطْهْكَ كُوَا ∴ إِفْبَاكَ ∴ لَسَنْ فُرَيْمْ

تَمْ رَكْ ∴ كُوكُمْ ∴ لَسَنْ غُوْ أَقَتْ أَلّٓ مِرْهُمْ ∴

تَنْثْ ∴ إِدّٓرْ كَبِّكُوكَدَا فْمُنْ ∴ لَعَسْنْ ∴ كِمّٓ ∴ أَمَّا

بَدَانُطَهْكُمْ ∴ دَ فْدُ مُبُوْ ∴ غُدَ أَدَمَّرْ ∴ إِفْبَاكَ

سُكُدُو ∴ غُدَا ∴ يَدُ وُفْمَّنْ ∴ مَتَنَا كُوكُمْ

أَمْبُنْتْ ∴ بِيَتْنَبِيَا ∴ غُوَاقَتْغَبِدَا قَمَّلْ

مَقَادَرِ ∴ لَسَنْ أُمَرْ يَادُوتِّنْ ∴ يَقِتْنَا كُوَمُمْ

كُطُهْكُمْ ∴ كُبَدَاقْ ∴ بِيُوْتَكُوْمَ ∴ مَ

نَطْهْكُمْ ∴ قَبَدَاقْ ∴ أَمَّا أُمُرْ ∴ لَسَنْ رَفْمُتْ

دَفْدُ مُكُنْ بِيَرْكَ ∴ بِيَتْنِيدُ وُفْنْ ∴ شِنَا

فَجَعْ ∴ فُلَامْ ∴ إِفْتِّ ∴ فُرَيْمْ ∴ فُدَامُنَا فُتْ

Sai aka-zō, aka-shaida masa, aka-che, 'Gā Furaira dan dumē na-bin ta, shi-na-che, wai nāma shi chi.' Alabarma ya che, 'Aje chikin akuyōyi.' Aka-kai shi chikin akuyōyi, ya chinye. Aka-kai shi ga wadansu, ya chinye, hakanan har ya chinye garken awāki dari uku da hamsin. Sai dumē ya kōmō, shi-na-fadi, 'Nāma in chi Fūraira, nāma in chi.' Aka-zō, aka-fada ma ubanta, sai ya che, 'Akai-shi garken tumāki.' Aka-kai shi, ya chainye garke dare bakwoi na tumāki, ya kōmō, shi-na-bin yārinya, shi-na-fadi, 'Nāma in chi Furaira, nāma in chi.' Sai aka-che, '[2] Yā chainye garken

---

And they came and bore witness to him saying, 'Look at Furaira, the baby pumpkin is following her (and) saying he must eat meat.' Alabarma said, 'Put it among the goats.' It (the pumpkin) was put among the goats. It ate them up. It was taken to some others. It ate them up. And so on till it had devoured three hundred and fifty flocks of goats. But the pumpkin returned and said, 'Meat I must eat, Furaira, meat I must eat.' They came and told her father and he said, 'Let it be taken to the sheep-fold.' It was taken, and ate up a flock of seven hundred sheep. It came back, (and) kept following the maiden, (and) saying, 'Meat I must eat, Furaira, meat I must eat.' And they said, 'It has eaten the flock of

تَسْ أَكَدُوْ ؞ أَكَشَيْمْ إِمَسَّنْ أَكَبْ ؞ غَمَا فُرْبِيَمْ ؞

دَفْدُ مِنْ فَامِغْتَ ؞ شَنَابُوبِيْنَامَ ؞ شَفَنَ

أَلَّبُمْرَمَ ؞ بِيَثْ أَجِنْ ثَكَمْ ؞ أَكِيُّوبِيمْ ؞ أَكَكِيْبِشْ

ثَكِمْ أَكِيُوبِيمْ ؞ بِيَتْشِيْنْ ؞ أَكَكِبْيِشْ ؞ غَمُودَفْلَسْ

يَتْشِيْنْ تَكَتْنَ ؞ حَمْ يَتْشِيْنْ غَمْبِكَمْ ؞ أَوَاكِمْ

كُرُبِي أُكَ ؞ دَخْلِسَنْ ؞ سَنْدُمِكَنْ ؞ يَكُو مُو ا

شَنَاقِحِ ؞ فَلَامَ ؞ إِنْشْ بُرْبِيمْ ؞ فَلَامَ ؞ إِفْشَ

أَكَدُوْ ؞ أَكَبْدَامَ ؞ أُبِغْتَ ؞ سَنْ يَبْ ؞ أَكِيْبِشْ

غَمْبِجَنْ فَمَلَكِمْ ؞ أَكَكِيْبِشْ يَثْنِبَرْ

غَمْ يِكَنْ دُرِبِي بَكَنْ ؞ فَتُمَرَكِمْ ؞ يَكُو مُوَا

شَنَبِنْبِيدُ وَفْمَرْ شَنَاقِدِ ؞ فَلَامَ إِفْشِ بُرْبِيمْ

فَلَمَ إِفْتِ ؞ سَنْ أَكَبْ ؞ يَلْشِنْبِنْ ؞ غَمْرِبِنْ

tumāki, [3] yā kōmō, shi-na-bin-ta.' Ubanta ya che, 'Akai shi garken shānu.' Aka-kai shi garken shānu, ya chainye garken shānu duka.
Ya kōmō, shi-na-bin yārinya, shi-na-fadi, 'Nāma in chi Furaira, nāma in chi.' Sai aka-zō, aka-gaya ma ubanta, sai shi kuma ya che, 'Akai-shi garken rākuma.' Aka-kai shi garken rākuma, sai ya chainye, ya kōmō, shi-na-bin yārinya, shi-na-fadi, 'Nāma in chi Furaira, nāma in chi.' Sai ya che, 'Akai-shi gidan bāyi?' Akai-shi gida-n bāyi, ya chainye-su, ya kōmō, shi-na-bin yārinya, shi-na-fadi, 'Nāma in chi Furaira, nāma in chi.'

---

sheep, (and) has come back and is following her (the maiden).' Her father said, 'Let it be taken to the cattle kraal.' It was taken to the cattle kraal. It ate up the whole kraal of cattle. It returned, (and) was following the maiden (and) saying, 'Meat I must eat, Furaira, meat I must eat.' And they came and told her father, and he again said, 'Let it be taken to the camel kraal.' It was taken to the camel kraal; but it ate them up, (and) returned. It was following the maiden (and) saying, 'Meat I must eat, Furaira, meat I must eat.' And they said, 'Let it be taken to the slaves' quarters.' It was taken to the slaves' quarters, it ate them up; it returned, (and) was following the maiden, (and) saying, 'Meat I must eat, Furaira, meat I must eat.'

ثملكم ∴ يلكومو ∴ شنا منت ∴ أمنت يب

أكيبش قمر بكر ∴ نسا قوا ∴ أككيبش نغمر بكر

نسا قوا ∴ يتشبين ∴ نغمر بكر ∴ نسا قوا ∴ دك

يكومو ∴ شنا بمر ∴ يد رقم ∴ نسا قد نت م

إقث ∴ فمر بير ∴ قدام إقش ∴ لسر أكذر ∴ ∴

أكغيدام ∴ أمنت ∴ لسر شيكم ∴ يبث ∴ أكيبش

نغمر بكر راقم ∴ أككيبش نغمر بكر راقم

لسر يتشبين يكومو ∴ شنا منيار قم ∴

شنا قد ∴ نقدام ∴ إقش فمر بير ∴ قدام إقش ∴

لسر يبث أكيبش نغد قبايم ∴ أككيبش نغمد

قبايم ∴ يتشبيس يكومو ∴ شنا ينيل رقم

نسا قد ∴ نقدام إقش ∴ فمر بير ∴ قدام إقش ∴

Ubanta ya che, 'Ku kai shi ruga.' Aka-kai shi ruga,
ya chainye mutānen ruga, ya kōmō, shi-na-fadi,
'Nāma in chi Furaira, nāma in chi.' Hakanan
har ya chainye mutāne duka, shānu, akuyōyi
tumāki, rākuma, dawāki, duka ya chainye,
hata kāji, zābi, agwagwa, tantabara,
duka, sauran mai-gida kadai. Sai ya bi yārinya,
sai ta gudu, ta bi ubanta, sai ubanta ya che,
'Bābu kōmi kuma sai ni kadai, idan ni
'zaa ka chi, dauke ni, ka chi.' Sai dan dumē ya dauke shi,
ya hadē. Sai ya bi yārinya, ta gudu, ta je
wurin rāgo lahia ubanta. Sai ya je, zaa shi kāma (ya)

Her father said, 'Take it to the cattle grazing ground.' They took it to the grazing ground (and) it devoured all the people on the ground, (and) came back, (and) said, 'Meat I must eat, Furaira, meat I must eat.' And so on, until it ate up all the people, cattle, goats, sheep, camels, horses, all it devoured, even the fowls, guinea-fowls, ducks, pigeons, everything (and) there remained only the master of the household. And it (the pumpkin) followed the maiden, and she ran, (and) went after her father, and her father said, 'There is nothing left but I myself. If it is I you would eat, take me, (and) eat me.' And the baby pumpkin took him up and swallowed him; then it followed the maid. She fled, and came to the paschal ram of her father's. And it came on, (and) was about to seize

أُبَنْتَ يَبْ ∴ كُكَيْشِ رُغَمَ ∴ أَكَكَيْشِ رُغَمَ

بَشْشِبِنْ مُتَابِنْ رُغَمَ ∴ يَكُومُو ∴ شِنَا بِجِ

قَدَمْ ∴ إِفْشِ بُجَرْبِيَرْ ∴ قَدَمْ إِفْشِ ∴ تَكَنْكِ

مَمْ بِشْشِبِنْ مُتَابِنْ ∴ دُكَ ∴ شَافُوا ∴ أَكُيُو بِيِ

تُمَاكِمْ ∴ وَافُمْ ∴ دَوَاكِمْ ∴ دُكَ ∴ يَافِنْيِسَ

تَشَّنْ كَدَاجِمْ ∴ تَوَيِمْ ∴ أَغُوَاغُمْ ∴ قُنْتَبَرَا ∴ =

دُكَ ∴ لَسُو رُفِنْيَغِدَا ∴ كُدِيِّ ∴ لَسَنْ يَبِمْ ∴ يَاوِفِسَ

سَنْ مَغُدُ ∴ تَبِ أُبَنْتَ ∴ لَسَنْ ∴ أُبَنْتَ يَبْ

بَأُبْ كُومِمْ ∴ كُمَّ ∴ لَسِيِنْ كَدِيِّ ∴ إِدَّنْ فِمْ

قَدَاكِشِ ∴ دَوْبِكِنِ ∴ كَكِشِ ∴ لَسَنْ دِفُدُ مِسَنْ ∴ بَدَّ كَنْشِ

وْ ∴ يَجِكَنْ لَسَنْ يَبِمْ ∴ يَاوِفِمَ ∴ مَكَدُ تَجِمْ

وُرُفِمْ اغُنُو ∴ شَحِمَ أُمَنْتَ ∴ سَنْ يَجَكُنْ ذَا أُشْكَا مَ يَا

yārinya, sai rāgon lahia ya zābura,
ya buga dan dumē da kafō. Sai ya pashe,
sai tumāki, da akuyōyi, da shānu, duka
su-ka-rika fitōwa. Shi ke nan. [5] Kunguru-
-s kan kūsu.

---

the maiden, but the paschal ram sprang forward, (and) struck the young pumpkin with his horn. And thereupon it split open, and sheep, and goats, and cattle, all kept coming forth. That is all. Off with the rat's head.

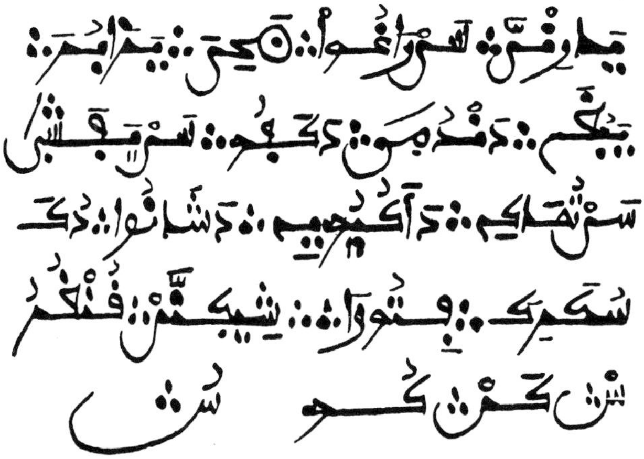

No. 21.

Wanan tātsunīar gāwō che
da yārinya.

Wani mutun ne, ana-che masa mālam Umaru mijin
[1] Lādi. Shi-na da [2] mātansa bīū, wanan, Mōwa, wanan,
Baura. Su duka su-na da yāyansu, mātā.
Wanan Mōwa nan, kulum, idan [3] tā yi shāra,
sai ta ba dīanta, ta kai gun gāwō, ta zubar.
Gāwō kūa shi-na da wani abu kamar chībi,
idan yārinyar nan ta kai shāra, sai ta taba,
ta che, 'Gāwō da chībi.' Kulum hakanan
ta ke yi. Ranan ta je, ta zuba shāra, sai ta taba.

This story is about a 'gawo'-tree and a maiden. There was a certain man, by name, Doctor Umaru, the husband of Ladi. He possessed two wives, one (called) Mowa, one (called) Baura. They both had children, girls. The one called Mowa, always, if she has swept, then she used to give (the sweepings) to her daughter, (and) she took them to where the gawo-tree was and threw (them) away. Now the gawo-tree had some growth on it that looked like a person's navel, and if this maiden took the sweepings (there) she used to touch (it) and say, 'The gawo-tree with the navel.' And it was always so she used to do. One day she went, (and) threw out the sweepings, (and) then touched (the mark).

وَمْ قَدْ طُوفِيَرْ ؞ غَدَارُوفْ

دَيَ وُفْسَ ؞

وَفِمْ مُتَنْبَنْ ؞ أَمَدْ بُهَسَنْ مَدَالَّمْ ؞ عُمَمْ ؞ بِجِمْ

اَلَّاحِ ؞ شِنَدَ دَمَاتُفْلَسَنْ بِيُوشْ وَفَّمْ مُووَّ ؞ وَقَّمْ

بُوْرَ ؞ سُودُكَ ؞ سُنَادِيَابُنْسَنْ مَاقَمْ ؞

وَقَّمْ ؞ مُووَقَّمْ ؞ كُلُّمْ ؞ إِدَّنْ ؞ قَدَاسِّ ؞ شَدَ رَا ؞

سَمْ تَنْبَادِ بَنْتَ ؞ تَكَمْ ؞ غُمْغَارُوِ ؞ تَذَبَرْ ؞

غَارُوِ ؞ كُوَّ ؞ شِنَدَ وِنَّابُ ؞ كَمَمْ ؞ ثِيبِ ؞

إِدَّنْ ؞ مِيَ رِفْيَبَرْ قَمَّنْ ؞ تَكَنْ ؞ شَدَ رَا ؞ سَمْ تَمْبَ ؞

تَبُّ ؞ غَارُوِ ؞ دَرِثِيبِ ؞ كُلُّمْ ؞ تَكَنَّا ؞ كَ

تَكَنَّ ؞ رَقَّمْ تَبَجِّمْ ؞ تَهْدُبْ ؞ شَدَ رَا ؞ سَمْ تَمْبَا ؞

Sai gāwō ya chire, ya bi ta, shi-na-fadi,
'Da sāfē, gāwō da chībi, da yama gāwō
da chībi.' Sai yārinya ta shēka, gāwō
ya bī ta. Ta je, ta iske māsu-shibka,
su-ka-che, 'Ke yārinya me ya fāru?' Ta che, 'Wani abu ne
ke bii na.' Su-ka-che, 'Zamna nan har shi zō.
Mu dauki abin shibka, mu bubugē shi, mu kashe.'
Aka-jima kadan sai gāwō ya zō, shi-na-
-fadi, 'Da sāfē gāwō da chībi, da yama gāwō
da chībi.' Sai māsu-shibka su-ka-che,
'Yārinya kāra gāba.' Sai yārinya
ta shēka, ta je, ta iske māsu-noma,
sai su-ka-che, 'Ke yārinya me ya fāru?'

But the gawo-tree pulled himself out (of the ground) (and) followed her, (and) was saying, 'Of a morning it 's, The gawo-tree with the navel; of an evening it 's, The gawo-tree with the navel.' Then the maiden ran away, (and) the gawo-tree followed her. She came (and) met some people sowing, (and) they said, 'You, maiden, what is the matter?' She said, 'Something is following me.' (And) they said, 'Sit down here till it comes. We will take the sowing implements, (and) beat him (and) kill (him).' They waited a little and then the gawo-tree came along. He was saying, 'In the morning it 's, The gawo-tree with the navel; in the evening it 's, The gawo-tree with the navel.' Thereupon the sowers said, 'Maiden, go further on.' And the maiden ran on. She came and met some people hoeing, and they said, 'Maiden, what is the matter?'

سن ∴ غداور ∴ يشبرلي ∴ ميبتا ∴ شنا قه ∴

د صا فن ∴ غداور ∴ د شيب ∴ د ميم غداور ∴

د شيب ∴ سن يد ومن ∴ تشبك ∴ غداور ∴

يبيا ∴ تجن ∴ ما سبكن ∴ ما ستيشبك ∴

سكب ∴ بكيد ومن ∴ ميبقار ∴ تب ∴ ومامبني

كبنن ∴ سكب ∴ د منا قمن صم شذ ور ∴

مدوك ∴ أمنشبك ∴ مبمغشن مكشبى

أكجم ∴ كدن ∴ سن غداور ∴ يدو ∴ شنا

قه ∴ د صا فن غداور د شيب د ميم غلور

د شيب ∴ سن ما ستيشبك ∴ سكب ∴

يد ومن ∴ كلوا ∴ غمبن ∴ سن يد ومن

تشبك ∴ تجن قد سبكن ∴ ما سنومن

سن ∴ سكب ∴ بكيد ومن ∴ ميبقاور ∴

Sai ta che, 'Wani abu ke bii na.' Su-ka-che, 'Tsaya nan
shi zō, kō hauyōmu ba mu dauki, mu [4] bubuge shi,
mu kashe?' Aka-jima, sai gāwō ya tafō,
shi-na-fadi, 'Da sāfē gāwō da chībi, da yama
gāwō da chībi, yau kī ga gāwō da chībi.'
Sai su-ka-che, 'Yārinya kāra gāba.' Sai ta kāra
gāba, ta je, ta iske māsu-fūda, su-na-
-fūda, sai su-ka-che, 'Ke yārinya me ya fārū?'
Ta che, 'Wani abu ke bii na.' Sai su-ka-che, 'Zamna
nan har shi zō.' Aka-jima, sai gāwō
ya tafō, shi-na-fadi, 'Da sāfē gāwō da
chībi, da yama gāwō da chībi, yau kī ga

And she said, 'Something is following me.' (And) they said, 'Stand here, let him come. Can we not then lift our hoes, (and) hit him, (and) kill (him)?' They waited a little while, then the gawo-tree came towards them; he was saying, 'In the morning it's, The gawo-tree with the navel; in the evening it's, The gawo-tree with the navel; to-day you see the gawo-tree with the navel.' And they said, 'Maiden, pass on.' So she passed on, and went and met some people ploughing. They were ploughing, and they said, 'You, maiden, what is the matter?' She replied, 'Something is following me.' And they said, 'Sit down here till he comes.' In a little while, then the gawo-tree came up; he was saying, 'In the morning it's, The gawo-tree with the navel; in the evening it's, The gawo-tree with the navel. To-day you see

تَسَمْ تَمْشْ ⁖ وَنَا أَبْ ⁖ بَكِمْنَمْ سُكَبْ ⁖ طَبَا قَمْ

شِذُو ⁖ كُوتَوبُوم ⁖ بَمُوكْرِكْ ⁖ مُبُغِشِ

مُكَشُبَنْ أَكِجَمْ ⁖ لَسَمْ غَدَاوُرْ ⁖ بِتَّقُوا ⁖ =

شِنَاقِدِ ⁖ دَصَافِيْ غَدَاوُدَ قِيبِ ⁖ دَمِيَمْ

غَدَاوُدَ قِيبِ ⁖ بَمُوكِيبُغْ ⁖ غَدَاوُدَ قِيبِ

لَسَمْ سُكَبْ ⁖ يَا رِقْمَ ⁖ كَدَارَغَبْ ⁖ لَسَمْ تَكَدَرْ

غَبْ ⁖ تَجْكَمْ قَدَا اِسْكَنْ ⁖ مَدَا سُجُودَا ⁖ لُسْنَدَ

قُودَا ⁖ لَسَمْ ⁖ سُكَبْ ⁖ بَكِيَارِقْمَ ⁖ جِيِقَدَارْ ⁖

تَمْبْ ⁖ وَقَا أَبْ ⁖ بَكِنْمَنْ لَسَمْ سُكَبْ ⁖ دَمِنَى

قَمْشْ تَمْ شِذُو ⁖ أَكِجَمْ ⁖ لَسَمْ غَدَاوُرْ ⁖

بِتَقُو ⁖ شِنَاقِدِ ⁖ دَصَافِيْ غَدَاوُدَ ⁖

شُتِبِ ⁖ دَمِيَمْ غَدَاوُرْ دَقِيبِ مِيوكِيبُغْ ⁖

gāwō da chībi.' Sai su-ka-che, 'Yārinya kāra gāba.' Sai yārinya ta shēka. Sai ta je ta iske kadangare, shi-na-sāka, shi-na-fadi, 'Kiryan, ba kiryan ba, zarta dāma, zarta hagu.' Sai ya che. 'Ke yārinya ina zaa ki, ki na gudu?' Ta che, 'Wani abu ke kōra na.' Ya che, 'Tsāya nan har shi zō.' Yārinya ta labe gun kadangare, shi-na-fadi, 'Kiryan, ba kiryan ba, zarta dāma, zarta hagu.' Har gāwō ya zō, shi-na-fadi, 'Da sāfē gāwō da chībi, da yama gāwō da chībi, yau kī ga gāwō da chībi.' Sai yārinya ta che, 'Ga shi chan zakūa.' Sai kadangare ya che, 'Bari shi zō, ama in yā zō, ina-raba ki da shi, ki-na-amre na?' Ta che, 'I.' Yau, sai gāwō ya zō.

---

the gawo-tree with the navel.' Thereupon they said, 'Maiden, pass on.' So the maiden ran on. Then she came (and) met a lizard; he was weaving and was saying, 'Kiryan, not kiryan, throw to the right, throw to the left (of the shuttle).' And he said, 'You, maiden, where are you going (that) you are running (so)?' She said, 'Something is pursuing me.' He said, 'Wait here till it comes.' The maiden nestled close up to the lizard, (who) was saying, 'Kiryan not kiryan, a cast to the right, a cast to the left,' until the gawo-tree came up. He was saying, 'In the morning it 's, The gawo-tree with the navel, in the evening it 's, The gawo-tree with the navel; to-day you see the gawo-tree with the navel.' And the maiden said, 'See, there he is coming.' And the lizard said, 'Let him come, but if he has come, (and) I save (lit. separate) you from him, are you going to marry me?' She said, 'Yes.' Now the gawo-tree came up.

غما ور ؞ دم قيب ؞ لسن ؞ سكث ؞ يما وقم ؞ كما وغب
لسن يما وقمن ؞ تشبك ؞ لسن تجم قما لبكم ؞ كد نغمبر
شنا لساك ؞ ؞ شنا فد ؞ كم ميمن ما كمبمن
دم قمدام ؞ دم قمغ ؞ لسن يمث ؞ كبيا رقمن ؞ =
إما ذاك ؞ كنا غمد ؞ قمث وما اب ؞ بكنكو وامى
يمث طيمن قمن ؞ قمن شغو ؞ يا رقمن ؞ تلبمن ؞ غمن
كد نغمبر ؞ شنا فد ؞ كم ميمن ما كمبمن ي
دمقمدام ؞ دم قمغ قمن غما ور ؞ بغو ؞ شنا فد
دصا قكى غما ورا دقيب ؞ دمم غما ور دقيب
يتوكبغ غما ور دقيب ؞ لسن يما وقمن ؞ قمث
غما شنم ؞ دكوا ؞ لسن كد نغمبر ؞ يمث
بم شغو ؞ آما ؞ إو يا ذو ؞ إن قم ما ك ؞ دشم
كنا امبمنا ؞ قمثا اي ؞ يمو قسن ؞ غما ور ؞ يغو

Ya che, 'Ina ajīana?' Kadangare ya che, 'Wani ajīa ka ba ni?' Gāwō ya che, 'Yārinya nan, da ke bāyanka.' Kadangare ya che, 'Wanan yā-rinya ta fi harfinka.' Sai gāwō ya che, 'Kadangare karanbani garēka.' Sai kadangare ya che, 'Ai namiji tonka ne, sai antaba, akan-san mai-yāji.' Sai gāwō ya yi fushi, ya kāma kadangare, ya hade, sai ya fitō ga idānun gāwō. Sai ya kuma kāma shi, ya hade, sai ya fitō ga kunuwansa. Sai ya kuma kāma shi, ya hade, sai ya fitō ga kirjinsa. Sai ya kuma kāma shi, ya hade, kadangare ya fitō

He said, 'Where is the thing I gave you to keep for me?' The lizard said, 'What did you give me?' The gawo-tree replied, 'The maiden who is behind you.' The lizard said, 'This (maid) is stronger than you.' And the gawo-tree said, 'Lizard, you are forward.' But the lizard replied, 'Ah! A man is like the little red peppers, not till you have touched (tasted) them do you know how hot they are.' Then the gawo-tree got angry. He seized hold of the lizard. He swallowed him, but he came out of the gawo-tree's eyes. Then he caught him again (and) swallowed him, but he came out at his ears. Then he caught him again and swallowed him, but he came out of his breast. Then he caught him again and swallowed him, but the lizard came out

يبث إلا، أجيا لا، كد فكم لس، ميث

ون أجيا، كجارن غاور، جبث، يادر فرنس

دجبا ينك، كد فكم ر، ميث، وفريا

ورفسن، قداف، كدر فنك، سن غاور

يبث كد فكم لمر، كد فجارن غجر يك، لسن

كد فغم ر، ميث، آ، فمج، فشكا ابس

لسن، أفتب، أكنسرن منى ياج، لسن

غاور نيسن فيشم، ميكام، كد فغم ر

يحج كر لسن، مبجتوا، غماء افغاور

لسن يكم، كدامادش، يحجر لسن يجتوا

غكنفوفلسن لسن يكم، كدامادشن، يحجرن

لسن يجتوا، غكم جنلسن، لسن يكم كدامادش

يجج مون لسن كد فغم رسن مجتو، م

ga chībīarsa. Sai gāwō ya fādi, ya mutu. Sai kadangare ya che, 'Tāshi in rake ki gida.' Sai ta tāshi. Su-ka-je gidansu, ya tsaya bākin kōfar gida, ita kūa ta shiga gida, ta yi zamanta. Aka-tanbaye-ta, 'Ina ki tafi?' Ta [5] kyale. Sai ubanta ya fitō, ya iske mutun [6] tsugunē kōfar gida. Sai ya che, 'Lāfia.' Ya che, 'Ni da yārinya nan mu-ka-zō, kāji kāji wada mu-ka-yi da ita.' Sai ubanta ya che, 'Ai ba ta fadi ba.' Sai ya shiga gida, ya gaia ma mātā. Sai aka-che, 'Kāka ki zō, ba ki fada ba?' Sai ta che, 'Ala shi kyāshe ni, in amri kadangare.' Sai ubanta ya kōma waje daia, ya kirāyi Baura,

---

at his navel. And the gawo-tree fell down and died. And the lizard said, 'Rise up, and I shall accompany you home.' So she rose up. They went to their (her) home. He (the lizard) stood at the entrance to the door of the house, but she entered into the house and went about her affairs. They asked her, 'Where did you go to?' She did not make any answer. Then her father came out, (and) met a man sitting at the door of the house. And he said, 'Greetings. Are you well?' He replied, 'I and the maiden have come, and so on, and so, and so, and so (relating all that happened), we did with her.' And her father said, 'Oh, she did not talk about (it).' And he entered the house, (and) told the women. Then they said, 'How is it you came and did not say anything about it?' And she said, 'May Allah save me from marrying a lizard.' Then her father went aside, (and) called Baura,

غيشيبر يسن . تسن غداو ر . . بقادي . . يمث . . يب

تسن يكد فغبر ني . يمث تداشن إور يكك . . غدا

تسن قتاشن تسكجي . . غدقسن يجلو وداقر

كو فجر غدا . . إنكو . . فقشغ . . غدا . . تمي

ذ ممتت أكتنبيت . . إمداك [redacted] تقى . . تكجلين . . تسن

أمنت . . يجتوا . . يبط إسكر . . مثر لطغنبى

كو فجر غدا . . تسن يمث لاقم . . يمث مم د

يبر فمر . . مكذو . . تكدامر . . ورد . .

مكن . . دم إمتا . . تسن . . أمنت يمث . . أي بتنجدي ب

تسن يمشغ . . غدا . . يغيام . . ملاقمى . . تسى

أكث . . تكدا كك [redacted] ور . . يكفجداي . . تسى

قث . . ألشكيدابشر . . إوامر . . كعر مغبرى

تسن أمنت . . يكوم . . وجد من يكر ابو مووز

ya che, 'Ba ki ba ni dīarki in yi keauta da ita?' Sai ta che, 'Haba [7] mālam, ina da dīa? Ai kai ke da abinka, kirāye ta, ka yi magāna da ita.' [8] Sai mālam ya kirāyi yārinya, ya che, 'Ina-sō in dauke ki, in yi keauta, [9] nā gaia ma uwarki, ta che in kirāye ki, in gaia maki.' Ta che, '[10] Ashā mālam, ai ba uwana ke da ni ba, kai kai ke da ni, kō kare, kō nāman dāji, ka dauke ni, ka ba shi, shi ke nan.' Sai ubanta ya che, 'Ala shi yi maki albarka.' Sai ya je, ya gaia ma kadangare. [11] Ashē dan sarki ne. Sai ya je gida, ya gaia ma ubansa, sai ubansa ya che, 'Mādala.' Ya bāda bāwa gōma, (k) kuyanga gōma, sānia gōma, kōmi duka gōma gōma, aka-kai ma ubanta. Kāna aka-bāda zanūa, aka-je aka-damra amre, aka-kāwō amarīa.

(and) said, 'Will you not give me your daughter, to make a present of (to the lizard)?' And she said, 'As for that, O learned one, do I possess a daughter? No, you are a master of your own property. Call her (and) speak with her.' Then the Doctor called the maiden, and said, 'I wish to take you away and make a present of you. I have told your mother, (and) she said I must call you (and) tell you.' She replied, 'O learned father, no, it is not my mother who possesses me, it is you, you possess me. Be it a dog or a wild beast, take me and give to him. That is all I have to say.' And her father said, 'May Allah bless you.' Then he came and told the lizard, in reality he was a chief's son. Then he went home (and) told his father, and his father said, 'Indeed!' And he gave him ten slaves, ten female slaves, ten cattle, and everything imaginable, ten of each, and took them to her (his future wife's) father's. Then he gave her clothes, (and) they came and were married, (and) he took away his bride.

تَبَّثْ ءَاسَمْ ∴ دَرَاقَ ∴ مْ تَمُوكِيبِّيرْ ∴ كِ دِيمْ وُ رَابَكِ بَدْ يِبَثْ

∴ كِنْبَاءَ بَدْ كِيمْءَا ∴ نَيِّدِ ءَدَّقَ ∴ مْلَّاءَمَ ∴ نَكْبَحَ

[redacted] ءَرَكِيبْ ∴ مَلَّاءَمْ سَنْ ∴ قَءَرِ دْ نَمَخَّمَ كِرِّكْ ∴ نَبِيءَرَكِ

مْقُوكَّنِّي ءَ ∴ كَمُكِوْدُ قَ ءَ ∴ وسَءَاقَ ءَ بَبِيْ ∴ نَمُقْرِدَيْ

كِمَءَانْقِ ءَ ∴ كِيبَرَكْءَ ءَ ∴ ثَّمُ ∴ كِوُّوقُمَ يِيغَمْ دَقْ

كِنْ ∴ بِيِفِيدَمَكْ ∴ دَقَءَا وُغَعَدْبَ ءَ ∴ مّلَّاءَمْ ءَاشَدْ ∴ ثَّمْ

نِكَّبُوْدَكْ ∴ جِءَادْنْقَدْ ءَاقُوكْ نْ رَبَحُكْ ∴ مِّقْدَكْبْ

كِمِّيِشْ ءَ ∴ لَّءَا ثَّبِيْ ∴ تَنْمُرْءَاسَ نْقَمْكِبِيِشْ ثَنَلِءَابْكَ

قِرْ ءَمّ نِلْشَبْءَا ∴ نْرَبَمْقَغَنْ كِمَءَ يِغَبْ ∴ نِحَبِيمْسَ ∴ كَنْرَبْءَ

∴ سَنْبَمُءَ ∴ مَءَايِغَبْ ∴ ءَادْغَ نْجِبِيمْسَ نْبِنْبِيكْرْسَ

كَدْ ∴ مَوُغْ ∴ وْءَابَدْ ءَايِيِ ∴ ةَلَّدَاءَمْ ثْبِيِ نْسَقْمُءَ ∴ نْسَ

كْدُّ ∴ مِوُكْ ∴ مَوُغْ ءَابِيِقْءَاسَ ∴ مَوُغْ ∴ نْخْنْيَّكُ

مَءَابِكْءَ ∴ وْءَدَكْ ∴ تَنْبُءَ ∴ مِيكَكْءَ ∴ مَوُغْ ∴ مَوُغْ

∴ ءَابْرْمَءَ ∴ وُءَادَكَكْءَ رْبْمَءَ ∴ مَرْدَكْءَ ∴ نْجِكْءَ ∴ وُنْقَطَ

Akwai wani bāwa ubansu, sūnansa Albarka, kuturū ne,
sai ya je gidansu, ya che shi-na-sō(n) wachan, da aka-ba kada-
-ngare, ta kia. Sai uwanta ta che, 'Me ta ke yi da kuturū?'
Sai dīarta ta che, '[12] Ina-sonsa, dan sarki ne.' Sai su-ka-che
anba shi. Su-ka-damra masu amre, har aka-kai ta gida-
-n miji, gōna, ba su ga kōwa ba, har ranan kadangare
da aka-ba shi maata, dīar Baura, sai ya che, [13] yaa je gewaiya
gōna. Ya hau dōki da kade [14] ana-gūda, su-ka-je,
ya che, 'Albarka na gida?' Sai ya fitō, ya gane shi, sai
ya kōma da gudu gida, ya che, 'Kāwō ma dan ubangijina, rua.'
Sai [15] maatar ta che, 'Ubangijinka?' Ya che, 'I,' 'Ashe kai bāwa ne?'
Ya che, 'I.' Ita kūa ta-na-daka. Sai ta aje tabarīa,
ta-na da chiki, sai ta shiga dāji. Mafārin shiga dāji
ke nan. [16] Kungurus kan kūsu.

Now their (the lizard's) father had a certain slave, by name Albarka, a leper, and he went to their house, and said he was in love with that one, whom they had given to the lizard (and who) had refused him. But her mother said to her, 'What will you do with a leper?' But her daughter said, 'I love him, he is the son of a chief, (in disguise).' So they said she was to be given to him. They were married (and all the ceremonies performed) even up to taking her to her husband's home; it was in the fields. And (the pair) did not see any one, till one day the lizard, who had been given the daughter of Baura for a wife, said he was going for a walk round the farms. He mounted his horse amid clapping and sounds of joy. They came (and) he said, 'Is Albarka at home?' Then he (Albarka) came out (and) saw him, then he ran back in haste to the house (and) said, 'Bring out water for my master's son.' But the wife said, 'Your master?' He replied, 'Yes.' 'You are indeed a slave?' He said, 'Yes.' Now she was pounding, then she put down the pestle. She was with child. Then she entered the bush. That was the first person who went to the bush (became mad). That is all. Off with the rat's head.

أكمن : ونبداو : أبشس : لسو مثس : البرك : . كثرونبس

سن يحس : غدفلس يبث : شنا لسوا : وثمر دأكبا : كد

نغمبرن : قفي : سن عموامد : قبث منتفس : دكثرو :

سن دي برق : قنبث : إفدا سنس : د فلسر كيمن : لسر سكبث

أقبدا لشن لسكدمر : مسر أمبرن : حمر أككيبث : غمد

نمج : غومن : مسر غكوواب : حمر ومر كدم غمبرس

دأكبدا لشن مأمن : د ميم مبورد : سن يثث : بيا جس ثمومس

غمونمن : يحوددوك : د كدكد : أقاغود : لسكحس

يبث البرك : قدا غدا : هن مجنوا : يغجشن لسن

بكوم دغد : غدا : يبث كداو هد قدا مسنغجبنا رو :

سن مامر : قبثن : أبن غجنك : بيثأي : أبشن كبياراقس

ميث أي : إتكو : قدادك : سن نابحس : قبر يداه

قنادا ثك : سن قلشغ : دابر : مجا وفشغا دا بر :

بكمقرن فنغمرس : كمكوس